ESSENTIAL PHARMACEUTICAL ANALYSIS

AS PER PCI 1ST B. PHARMACY SYLLABUS

SANTHOSH ILLENDULA, DR.
MADIREDDY MAMATA, PADURI AMANI

Made with ❤ on the Notion Press Platform
www.notionpress.com

Contents

Preface

Pharmaceutical analysis is a crucial aspect of the pharmaceutical sciences, serving as the backbone for ensuring the quality, safety, and efficacy of pharmaceutical products. As educators and professionals in the field, we have observed the challenges faced by students in accessing comprehensive and reliable reference materials that align with the Pharmacy Council of India's (PCI) syllabus for the first year of B. Pharmacy.

This book, Essential Pharmaceutical Analysis: As per PCI 1st B. Pharmacy Syllabus, is designed to fill this gap. Our primary goal is to provide students with a single, cohesive resource that covers all essential topics in depth. By doing so, we aim to eliminate the need for additional textbooks and articles, thereby simplifying the learning process.

Key Features of This Book:

Comprehensive Coverage: Each chapter meticulously addresses the entire PCI syllabus for first-year B. Pharmacy students, ensuring that no essential topic is overlooked.

In-depth Explanation: We delve deep into each subject, offering detailed explanations, practical examples, and relevant case studies to enhance understanding and retention.

Clear and Accessible Language: The content is written in simple Indian English, making complex concepts more digestible without compromising academic rigor.

Structured Format: The book is organized into clearly defined chapters and sections, with headings and subheadings formatted for easy navigation. Key terms and important concepts are highlighted for quick reference.

We extend our heartfelt gratitude to our colleagues, students, and families for their continuous support and encouragement. We hope that this book becomes an indispensable resource for students, helping them to not only excel academically but also to develop a profound appreciation for the importance of pharmaceutical analysis in the broader context of healthcare and medicine.

We welcome feedback and suggestions from our readers to help us improve future editions of this book.

Santhosh Illendula, M. Pharm (Ph.D)
Dr. Madireddy Mamata, M. Pharm, Ph.D.
Paduri Amani, M. Pharm (Ph.D)

Essential Pharmaceutical Analysis: As Per Pci 1st B. Pharmacy Syllabus

SANTHOSH ILLENDULA

ASSOCIATE PROFESSOR

DEPARTMENT OF PHARMACEUTICAL ANALYSIS

NALANDA COLLEGE OF PHARMACY

CHARLAPALLY, NALGONDA, TELANGANA, INDIA- 508001

Dr. MADIREDDY MAMATA

HOD & ASSOCIATE PROFESSOR

DEPARTMENT OF PHARMACEUTICAL ANALYSIS

TRINITY COLLEGE OF PHARMACEUTICAL SCIENCES

PEDDAPALLI, BANDARIKUNTA, 505172, TELANGANA

PADURI AMANI

ASSISTANT PROFESSOR

DEPARTMENT OF PHARMACEUTICAL ANALYSIS

BRILLIANT GROUP OF TECHNICAL INSTITUTIONS

ABDULLAPUR, RANGAREDDY, 500085, TELANGANA

Published by Notion Press

Notion Press, Inc.

800, West EI Camino Real #180,

California USA 94040

Notion Press Media Pvt Ltd,

#7, Red Cross Road,

Egmore, Chennai, Tamil Nadu 600008

Email ID: publish@notionpress.com

Phone Number: +91 44 46315631

ONE

INTRODUCTION TO PHARMACEUTICAL ANALYSIS

1.1 DEFINITION AND SCOPE

1.1.1 IMPORTANCE IN PHARMACEUTICAL SCIENCES

Pharmaceutical sciences encompass a broad range of scientific disciplines critical to the discovery, development, production, and regulation of drugs and medications. The importance of pharmaceutical analysis within this field cannot be overstated. This sub-discipline is pivotal in ensuring the safety, efficacy, and quality of pharmaceutical products, which directly impacts patient health outcomes and public health at large.

Pharmaceutical analysis involves the application of various techniques and methodologies to identify, quantify, and characterize the components of pharmaceutical substances. It plays a crucial role in all stages of drug development, from the initial discovery phase to the final product release and beyond. One of the primary goals of pharmaceutical analysis is to ensure that the medications produced meet the stringent regulatory standards set by health authorities such as the Food and Drug Administration (FDA), European Medicines Agency (EMA), and other global regulatory bodies.

In the early stages of drug development, pharmaceutical analysis is essential for the identification and quantification of potential drug candidates. Analytical techniques such as high-performance liquid chromatography (HPLC), gas chromatography (GC), mass spectrometry

(MS), and nuclear magnetic resonance (NMR) spectroscopy are employed to determine the chemical structure and purity of new compounds. These techniques provide critical data that helps researchers understand the pharmacokinetics and pharmacodynamics of the drug, including absorption, distribution, metabolism, and excretion (ADME) properties.

Once a potential drug candidate has been identified, pharmaceutical analysis continues to play a vital role in the formulation and manufacturing processes. The development of a stable and effective drug formulation requires a deep understanding of the physicochemical properties of the active pharmaceutical ingredient (API) and excipients. Analytical methods are used to assess the compatibility of different components, optimize the formulation, and ensure that the final product maintains its potency and stability throughout its shelf life.

Quality control (QC) and quality assurance (QA) are integral parts of the pharmaceutical manufacturing process, and pharmaceutical analysis is at the heart of these activities. Rigorous testing is conducted at various stages of production to ensure that the drug product meets the predefined specifications for identity, strength, purity, and quality. This involves both in-process testing and final product testing. Techniques such as titration, spectroscopy, and chromatographic methods are routinely used to monitor critical quality attributes and detect any deviations from the established standards.

Moreover, pharmaceutical analysis is crucial for the validation of manufacturing processes and cleaning procedures. Process validation involves demonstrating that the production process consistently produces a product that meets all quality criteria. This requires comprehensive analytical testing to confirm that all variables in the process are controlled and that the final product is free from contaminants and impurities. Cleaning validation ensures that residuals from previous production batches are adequately removed to prevent cross-contamination. Analytical methods are used to detect and quantify any residues, ensuring compliance with acceptable limits.

In addition to its role in quality control, pharmaceutical analysis is essential for regulatory compliance. Regulatory agencies require extensive documentation and analytical data to approve new drugs and manufacturing processes. This includes detailed information on the methods used for the analysis, validation data, and results of stability studies. Stability testing is particularly important, as it determines the shelf life of a drug product and ensures that it remains safe and effective throughout its intended use period. Analytical techniques are employed to study the degradation products and identify the factors that affect the stability of the drug.

The importance of pharmaceutical analysis extends to post-market surveillance as well. Even after a drug has been approved and released to the market, continuous monitoring is necessary to ensure its safety and efficacy. Adverse drug reactions and quality issues can arise, and pharmaceutical analysis helps in investigating these incidents. For instance, if a batch of a drug is found to be contaminated or sub-potent, analytical methods are used to trace the source of the problem and take corrective actions.

Pharmaceutical analysis also plays a critical role in the development and production of generic drugs. When the patent of a branded drug expires, generic manufacturers can produce and market bioequivalent versions of the drug. Pharmaceutical analysis is used to demonstrate that the generic product is identical in terms of active ingredients, dosage form, strength, route of administration, and performance characteristics to the original branded product. This involves rigorous testing and comparison using analytical methods to ensure that the generic product meets all regulatory requirements.

In the context of personalized medicine, pharmaceutical analysis is becoming increasingly important. Personalized medicine aims to tailor medical treatment to individual patients based on their genetic makeup and other factors. Analytical techniques are used to identify biomarkers and genetic variations that influence drug response. This information is used to develop targeted therapies and optimize drug dosing, thereby improving treatment outcomes and minimizing adverse effects.

Furthermore, pharmaceutical analysis is integral to the development of advanced drug delivery systems. These systems, such as controlled-release formulations, transdermal patches, and nanoparticles, require precise control over the release and delivery of the drug to the target site. Analytical methods are employed to characterize the release profiles, stability, and efficacy of these advanced formulations, ensuring that they deliver the therapeutic benefits as intended.

The environmental impact of pharmaceutical production and disposal is another area where pharmaceutical analysis plays a crucial role. Analytical techniques are used to monitor the presence of pharmaceutical residues in the environment, assess their impact on ecosystems, and develop strategies for their mitigation. This includes the analysis of wastewater from manufacturing plants, monitoring of pharmaceutical contaminants in water bodies, and studying the biodegradability of pharmaceutical compounds.

In conclusion, pharmaceutical analysis is a cornerstone of the pharmaceutical sciences, underpinning the entire lifecycle of drug development, production, and regulation. Its importance lies in ensuring that pharmaceutical products are safe, effective, and of high quality, thereby protecting patient health and supporting public health initiatives. The field continues to evolve with advancements in analytical technologies, driving innovation in drug development and enabling the production of better and safer medications. Through rigorous testing, validation, and regulatory compliance, pharmaceutical analysis helps build trust in the pharmaceutical industry and ensures that patients receive the best possible care.

1.1.2 ROLE IN QUALITY CONTROL AND DRUG DEVELOPMENT

The role of pharmaceutical analysis in quality control and drug development is foundational, as it ensures that all pharmaceutical products meet the necessary standards for safety, efficacy, and quality before they reach the market and continue to meet these standards throughout their lifecycle. This comprehensive process involves multiple stages, each relying heavily on analytical methods to verify the integrity and performance of the drug.

Quality Control

1. Raw Material Testing:

- Before any drug product is manufactured, the raw materials used must be tested for identity, purity, and quality. Analytical techniques such as high-performance liquid chromatography (HPLC), gas chromatography (GC), and mass spectrometry (MS) are commonly employed to ensure that the raw materials meet the required specifications. This step is crucial to prevent any impurities or contaminants from being carried forward into the final product.

2. In-Process Testing:

- During the manufacturing process, various in-process tests are conducted to monitor the production environment and the intermediate products. These tests ensure that the manufacturing process remains within predefined control limits and that any deviations are promptly addressed. Analytical methods such as pH measurement, viscosity testing, and particle size analysis are used to monitor these parameters.

3. Finished Product Testing:

- The final product undergoes rigorous testing to ensure it meets all quality specifications. This includes tests for potency, purity, dissolution, and stability. Techniques such as HPLC, UV-visible spectroscopy, and dissolution testing are used to assess these attributes. The results from these tests are compared against the product specifications to ensure consistency and compliance.

4. Stability Testing:

- Stability testing is a critical aspect of quality control, as it determines the shelf life and storage conditions for the drug product. Analytical methods are used to monitor the stability of the drug over time, under various environmental conditions (temperature, humidity, light). This testing helps to identify potential degradation products and ensures that the drug remains safe and effective throughout its intended shelf life.

5. Batch Release Testing:

- Before a batch of drug product is released to the market, it must pass a series of tests to confirm that it meets all quality standards. This includes testing for uniformity, content, and microbial contamination. Only batches that meet all the criteria are released for distribution, ensuring that each batch of product is of consistent quality.

Drug Development
1. Drug Discovery:

- In the initial stages of drug development, pharmaceutical analysis plays a key role in the identification and optimization of new drug candidates.

High-throughput screening and combinatorial chemistry generate large numbers of compounds, which are then analyzed for their potential therapeutic effects. Analytical methods are used to determine the chemical structure, purity, and biological activity of these compounds.

2. Preclinical Development:

- Once a promising drug candidate has been identified, it undergoes preclinical testing to assess its safety and efficacy in animal models. Analytical techniques are used to study the pharmacokinetics (absorption, distribution, metabolism, excretion) and pharmacodynamics (mechanism of action) of the drug. These studies provide critical data that supports the design of clinical trials.

3. Formulation Development:

- The formulation of the drug product is developed to ensure that it delivers the active ingredient effectively to the target site in the body. Analytical methods are used to optimize the formulation, ensuring that the drug is stable, bioavailable, and patient-friendly. This includes testing for excipient compatibility, dissolution rates, and stability.

4. Clinical Development:

- During clinical trials, pharmaceutical analysis is essential for monitoring the drug's performance and ensuring patient safety. Blood and urine samples from clinical trial participants are analyzed to determine drug levels and metabolites. This data helps to optimize dosing regimens and assess the drug's safety profile. Analytical methods also ensure that the drug supplied to clinical trial sites is of consistent quality.

5. Regulatory Submission:

- For a new drug to be approved by regulatory agencies such as the FDA or EMA, extensive analytical data must be provided. This includes information on the drug's chemical composition, manufacturing process, stability, and quality control measures. Pharmaceutical analysis ensures that all data submitted is accurate, reliable, and meets regulatory standards.

6. Post-Market Surveillance:

- After a drug has been approved and released to the market, ongoing monitoring is required to ensure its continued safety and efficacy. Pharmaceutical analysis helps to investigate any adverse drug reactions, quality issues, or product recalls. This involves re-analyzing samples of the drug product and conducting stability studies to ensure that it continues to meet quality standards over its shelf life.

7. Continuous Improvement:

- Pharmaceutical analysis also supports continuous improvement initiatives within the pharmaceutical industry. By analyzing process data and product performance, companies can identify areas for improvement in their manufacturing processes and quality control procedures. This helps to enhance product quality, reduce costs, and increase efficiency.

In conclusion, the role of pharmaceutical analysis in quality control and drug development is integral and multifaceted. It ensures that pharmaceutical products are safe, effective, and of high quality at every stage of their lifecycle, from raw material testing to post-market surveillance. Through rigorous testing, validation, and regulatory compliance, pharmaceutical analysis supports the development and production of innovative drugs that improve patient health and quality of life.

1.2 DIFFERENT TECHNIQUES OF ANALYSIS
1.2.1 OVERVIEW OF ANALYTICAL TECHNIQUES

Analytical techniques in pharmaceutical analysis are diverse and multifaceted, each serving specific purposes and applications in the identification, quantification, and characterization of pharmaceutical substances. These techniques are critical throughout the entire drug development process, from initial discovery through to quality control in manufacturing, ensuring the safety, efficacy, and quality of pharmaceutical products.

1. Spectroscopic Techniques:

- Spectroscopy involves the interaction of light with matter to produce an absorbance or emission spectrum. It includes several methods such as ultraviolet-visible (UV-Vis) spectroscopy, infrared (IR) spectroscopy, nuclear magnetic resonance (NMR) spectroscopy, and mass spectrometry (MS).
- **UV-Vis Spectroscopy:** Used to determine the concentration of a substance in solution by measuring the absorbance of UV or visible light. It's widely used for quantitative analysis of drugs.
- **IR Spectroscopy:** Measures the vibrations of molecules and is used to identify functional groups and molecular structures. It's essential for the characterization of raw materials and finished products.
- **NMR Spectroscopy:** Provides detailed information about the structure, dynamics, and environment of molecules. It's particularly useful for determining the structure of complex organic compounds.
- **Mass Spectrometry:** Determines the mass-to-charge ratio of ions, providing detailed molecular weight information and structural insights. It's crucial for identifying unknown compounds and confirming the identity of synthesized drugs.

2. Chromatographic Techniques:

- Chromatography separates components of a mixture based on their interactions with a stationary phase and a mobile phase. It includes techniques such as high-performance liquid chromatography (HPLC), gas chromatography (GC), thin-layer chromatography (TLC), and supercritical fluid chromatography (SFC).
- **HPLC:** Widely used for the separation, identification, and quantification of components in a mixture. It is highly efficient and versatile, suitable for a broad range of applications including the analysis of active pharmaceutical ingredients (APIs) and impurities.
- **GC:** Used for the separation and analysis of volatile and semi-volatile compounds. It is often used in the analysis of residual solvents and impurities in drug substances.
- **TLC:** A simple, quick, and inexpensive method used for preliminary analysis and identification of compounds. It is often used for purity checks and the identification of raw materials.

- **SFC:** Combines the advantages of gas and liquid chromatography, using supercritical fluids as the mobile phase. It is used for the separation of chiral compounds and non-volatile substances.

3. Electrochemical Techniques:

- These techniques involve the measurement of electrical properties such as voltage, current, and charge. Common methods include potentiometry, voltammetry, and conductometry.
- **Potentiometry:** Measures the potential difference between two electrodes to determine the concentration of an analyte. It is commonly used in pH measurements and ion-selective electrode analyses.
- **Voltammetry:** Measures the current as a function of applied potential to study redox properties of analytes. It is used for the detection and quantification of trace metals and organic compounds.
- **Conductometry:** Measures the electrical conductivity of a solution, which is related to the concentration of ionic species. It is used in titrations and purity assessments.

4. Thermal Analysis:

- Thermal analysis techniques study the changes in physical and chemical properties of substances as a function of temperature. These include differential scanning calorimetry (DSC), thermogravimetric analysis (TGA), and differential thermal analysis (DTA).
- **DSC:** Measures heat flow associated with phase transitions in materials. It is used to study the melting point, crystallinity, and thermal stability of pharmaceutical compounds.
- **TGA:** Measures the change in weight of a substance as it is heated, providing information on thermal stability and composition. It is used to analyze the content of volatile components and degradation patterns.
- **DTA:** Measures the temperature difference between a sample and a reference under identical conditions. It is used to identify exothermic and endothermic transitions, similar to DSC.

5. Spectrometric Techniques:

- Techniques such as atomic absorption spectroscopy (AAS) and inductively coupled plasma mass spectrometry (ICP-MS) are used to analyze elemental composition.
- **AAS:** Measures the absorption of light by free atoms, typically used for the quantitative analysis of metals in pharmaceuticals.
- **ICP-MS:** Combines a high-temperature plasma source with mass spectrometry for highly sensitive detection of trace elements and isotopes.

6. Microscopic Techniques:

- Microscopic techniques, including scanning electron microscopy (SEM) and transmission electron microscopy (TEM), provide detailed images of the surface and internal structure of materials at high magnification.
- **SEM:** Provides high-resolution images of the surface morphology of samples. It is used to study particle size, shape, and surface characteristics of drug formulations.
- **TEM:** Provides detailed images of the internal structure of samples. It is used to study the fine structure of crystalline materials and nanoparticles in drug delivery systems.

7. Immunoassays:

- Immunoassays are biochemical tests that use the binding of an antibody to its antigen to measure the presence and concentration of analytes. Techniques include enzyme-linked immunosorbent assay (ELISA) and radioimmunoassay (RIA).
- **ELISA:** Uses an enzyme-linked antigen or antibody to produce a measurable signal, usually colorimetric. It is used for the detection of proteins, hormones, and drugs in biological samples.
- **RIA:** Uses radioactively labeled antigens or antibodies to detect and quantify substances. It is highly sensitive and used in clinical and research settings for hormone and drug level measurement.

8. Molecular Techniques:

- Techniques such as polymerase chain reaction (PCR) and gel electrophoresis are used to analyze nucleic acids.

- **PCR:** Amplifies specific DNA sequences, making it possible to detect and quantify genetic material. It is used in the development and quality control of biopharmaceuticals and genetic testing.
- **Gel Electrophoresis:** Separates nucleic acids or proteins based on their size and charge. It is used for the analysis of DNA, RNA, and protein purity and integrity.

Each of these analytical techniques offers unique advantages and is chosen based on the specific requirements of the analysis. The appropriate selection and application of these techniques ensure the reliability and accuracy of the analytical results, which are critical for the development, approval, and manufacture of safe and effective pharmaceutical products. By leveraging these techniques, pharmaceutical scientists can ensure that drugs are produced to the highest standards, safeguarding public health and advancing medical science.

1.2 DIFFERENT TECHNIQUES OF ANALYSIS

1.2.2 COMPARISON AND APPLICATIONS

The various analytical techniques used in pharmaceutical analysis each have their own strengths, weaknesses, and specific applications. Understanding the differences between these techniques and their appropriate applications is crucial for selecting the best method for a given analysis.

1. Spectroscopic Techniques:

1.1 UV-Visible Spectroscopy:

- **Strengths:** Simple, rapid, and cost-effective. It provides quantitative data on concentration.
- **Weaknesses:** Limited to compounds that absorb UV or visible light.
- **Applications:** Quantification of drugs in formulations, quality control, and determination of impurities.

1.2 Infrared (IR) Spectroscopy:

- **Strengths:** Provides detailed information on molecular structure and functional groups. Non-destructive.
- **Weaknesses:** Requires pure samples and can be affected by water content.

- **Applications:** Identification of raw materials, determination of polymorphs, and study of molecular interactions.

1.3 Nuclear Magnetic Resonance (NMR) Spectroscopy:

- **Strengths:** Highly informative, providing detailed structural and dynamic information about molecules.
- **Weaknesses:** Expensive, requires large sample amounts and sophisticated interpretation.
- **Applications:** Structure elucidation, stereochemistry, and analysis of complex mixtures.

1.4 Mass Spectrometry (MS):

- **Strengths:** Extremely sensitive and precise, providing molecular weight and structural information.
- **Weaknesses:** Requires expensive equipment and complex data analysis.
- **Applications:** Identification and quantification of compounds, metabolite profiling, and impurity analysis.

2. Chromatographic Techniques:
2.1 High-Performance Liquid Chromatography (HPLC):

- **Strengths:** Versatile, high resolution, and capable of separating a wide range of compounds.
- **Weaknesses:** Requires expensive equipment and consumables.
- **Applications:** Purity testing, stability studies, and quantification of active pharmaceutical ingredients (APIs) and impurities.

2.2 Gas Chromatography (GC):

- **Strengths:** Excellent for volatile and semi-volatile compounds. High resolution and sensitivity.
- **Weaknesses:** Limited to compounds that can be vaporized without decomposition.
- **Applications:** Residual solvent analysis, determination of volatile impurities, and flavor and fragrance analysis.

2.3 Thin-Layer Chromatography (TLC):

- **Strengths:** Simple, quick, and inexpensive. Suitable for qualitative analysis.
- **Weaknesses:** Lower resolution and sensitivity compared to HPLC and GC.
- **Applications:** Preliminary screening, identification of raw materials, and monitoring reaction progress.

2.4 Supercritical Fluid Chromatography (SFC):

- **Strengths:** Combines advantages of both gas and liquid chromatography. Environmentally friendly.
- **Weaknesses:** Requires specialized equipment and expertise.
- **Applications:** Separation of chiral compounds, analysis of thermally labile substances, and pharmaceutical purity testing.

3. Electrochemical Techniques:
3.1 Potentiometry:

- **Strengths:** Simple, rapid, and cost-effective. Suitable for field analysis.
- **Weaknesses:** Limited to ionic species and requires calibration.
- **Applications:** pH measurements, determination of ion concentrations, and quality control of pharmaceuticals.

3.2 Voltammetry:

- **Strengths:** Sensitive and versatile, capable of analyzing trace levels of analytes.
- **Weaknesses:** Requires specialized electrodes and can be affected by matrix effects.
- **Applications:** Detection of heavy metals, analysis of electroactive pharmaceuticals, and environmental monitoring.

3.3 Conductometry:

- **Strengths:** Simple and rapid, suitable for monitoring ionic content.
- **Weaknesses:** Limited to solutions with significant ionic strength and cannot provide specific information on individual ions.

- **Applications:** Titrations, determination of total ionic content, and monitoring of cleaning processes.

4. Thermal Analysis:
4.1 Differential Scanning Calorimetry (DSC):

- **Strengths:** Provides detailed thermal profiles and information on phase transitions.
- **Weaknesses:** Requires careful sample preparation and can be affected by sample impurities.
- **Applications:** Stability studies, characterization of polymorphs, and compatibility testing.

4.2 Thermogravimetric Analysis (TGA):

- **Strengths:** Provides precise information on weight changes with temperature.
- **Weaknesses:** Limited to compounds that undergo weight changes upon heating.
- **Applications:** Analysis of thermal stability, determination of moisture content, and study of decomposition kinetics.

4.3 Differential Thermal Analysis (DTA):

- **Strengths:** Provides complementary data to DSC, useful for identifying exothermic and endothermic transitions.
- **Weaknesses:** Less sensitive than DSC and requires careful calibration.
- **Applications:** Analysis of thermal events, characterization of materials, and study of phase transitions.

5. Spectrometric Techniques:
5.1 Atomic Absorption Spectroscopy (AAS):

- **Strengths:** Highly sensitive for metal ion analysis.
- **Weaknesses:** Limited to metals and requires a separate calibration for each element.
- **Applications:** Trace metal analysis, quality control of raw materials, and environmental monitoring.

5.2 Inductively Coupled Plasma Mass Spectrometry (ICP-MS):

- **Strengths:** Extremely sensitive and capable of multi-element analysis.
- **Weaknesses:** Expensive and requires extensive sample preparation.
- **Applications:** Trace element analysis, contamination studies, and quality control in pharmaceuticals.

6. Microscopic Techniques:
6.1 Scanning Electron Microscopy (SEM):

- **Strengths:** Provides high-resolution images of sample surfaces.
- **Weaknesses:** Requires conductive samples and can be expensive.
- **Applications:** Analysis of particle size and shape, surface morphology studies, and quality control of solid dosage forms.

6.2 Transmission Electron Microscopy (TEM):

- **Strengths:** Provides detailed internal structure images at the atomic level.
- **Weaknesses:** Requires very thin samples and is technically demanding.
- **Applications:** Analysis of nanoparticles, structural characterization of materials, and investigation of drug delivery systems.

7. Immunoassays:
7.1 Enzyme-Linked Immunosorbent Assay (ELISA):

- **Strengths:** Highly specific and sensitive, suitable for detecting low concentrations of analytes.
- **Weaknesses:** Requires specific antibodies and can be expensive.
- **Applications:** Detection of proteins, hormones, and drugs in biological samples, and quality control of biopharmaceuticals.

7.2 Radioimmunoassay (RIA):

- **Strengths:** Extremely sensitive and specific.
- **Weaknesses:** Uses radioactive materials, requiring special handling and disposal.

- **Applications:** Hormone level measurement, drug monitoring, and clinical diagnostics.

8. Molecular Techniques:
8.1 Polymerase Chain Reaction (PCR):

- **Strengths:** Highly sensitive and specific, capable of amplifying small amounts of DNA.
- **Weaknesses:** Requires careful control to avoid contamination.
- **Applications:** Genetic testing, biopharmaceutical development, and forensic analysis.

8.2 Gel Electrophoresis:

- **Strengths:** Simple and effective for separating nucleic acids and proteins.
- **Weaknesses:** Limited to qualitative analysis and requires staining.
- **Applications:** DNA fingerprinting, protein analysis, and quality control of biological products.

By understanding the strengths, weaknesses, and specific applications of each analytical technique, pharmaceutical scientists can select the most appropriate methods for their needs. This ensures accurate, reliable, and efficient analysis, supporting the development and production of high-quality pharmaceutical products. Each technique's application must be carefully matched to the specific requirements of the analysis to achieve the best results, ultimately safeguarding public health and advancing pharmaceutical science.

1.3 METHODS OF EXPRESSING CONCENTRATION
1.3.1 MOLARITY, NORMALITY, AND OTHER CONCENTRATION UNITS

In pharmaceutical analysis, expressing the concentration of solutions accurately is crucial for the consistency and reliability of analytical results. The concentration of a solution can be expressed in several units, each with specific applications and significance. The most commonly used units include molarity, normality, and other related concentration units.

Molarity (M):

- Molarity is defined as the number of moles of solute per liter of solution. It is one of the most commonly used concentration units in chemistry and pharmaceutical sciences because it directly relates to the amount of substance in a given volume of solution.
- **Formula:** Molarity (M) = moles of solute / liters of solution
- **Applications:** Molarity is used in various chemical calculations, including stoichiometry, chemical kinetics, and equilibrium studies. It is particularly useful in titration procedures and when preparing standard solutions for analytical experiments.

Normality (N):

- Normality is defined as the number of equivalents of solute per liter of solution. An equivalent is the amount of substance that reacts with or supplies one mole of hydrogen ions (H+) in an acid-base reaction or one mole of electrons in a redox reaction.
- **Formula:** Normality (N) = equivalents of solute / liters of solution
- **Applications:** Normality is commonly used in acid-base titrations and redox reactions where the reacting species are involved in equivalent proportions. It simplifies the calculations in these types of reactions by directly relating the concentration to the reaction stoichiometry.

Molality (m):

- Molality is defined as the number of moles of solute per kilogram of solvent. Unlike molarity, molality is independent of temperature and pressure because it is based on the mass of the solvent rather than the volume of the solution.
- **Formula:** Molality (m) = moles of solute / kilograms of solvent
- **Applications:** Molality is used in colligative property calculations, such as boiling point elevation and freezing point depression, where the properties depend on the number of solute particles rather than their volume.

Percentage Concentrations:

- **Weight/Weight Percent (w/w%):** This is the mass of solute divided by the mass of the solution, multiplied by 100.

- **Formula:** w/w% = (mass of solute / mass of solution) × 100
- **Applications:** Used in formulations where the mass of components is more critical than their volume, such as in ointments and creams.

- **Weight/Volume Percent (w/v%):** This is the mass of solute divided by the volume of solution, multiplied by 100.

  - **Formula:** w/v% = (mass of solute / volume of solution) × 100
  - **Applications:** Commonly used in pharmaceutical preparations like syrups and solutions where the volume of the final product is fixed.

- **Volume/Volume Percent (v/v%):** This is the volume of solute divided by the volume of solution, multiplied by 100.

  - **Formula:** v/v% = (volume of solute / volume of solution) × 100
  - **Applications:** Used in liquid-liquid solutions, such as alcohol solutions and tinctures.

Parts per Million (ppm) and Parts per Billion (ppb):

- **Parts per Million (ppm):** This is the number of parts of solute per million parts of solution. It is equivalent to milligrams of solute per liter of solution (mg/L) for dilute aqueous solutions.

  - **Formula:** ppm = (mass of solute / mass of solution) × 10^6
  - **Applications:** Used for very dilute solutions, such as trace analysis of contaminants and pollutants in water and air.

- **Parts per Billion (ppb):** This is the number of parts of solute per billion parts of solution. It is equivalent to micrograms of solute per liter of solution (μg/L) for dilute aqueous solutions.

  - **Formula:** ppb = (mass of solute / mass of solution) × 10^9
  - **Applications:** Used for ultra-trace analysis, such as detecting heavy metals and organic pollutants in environmental samples.

Mole Fraction (χ):

- Mole fraction is the ratio of the number of moles of one component to the total number of moles of all components in the solution.
- **Formula:** χ = moles of solute / total moles of all components
- **Applications:** Used in thermodynamic calculations, such as Raoult's law for vapor pressure and in the study of gas mixtures.

Milliequivalents per Liter (mEq/L):

- This unit is used to express the concentration of ions in solution. One milliequivalent is one-thousandth of an equivalent.
- **Formula:** mEq/L = (millimoles of solute × valence) / volume of solution in liters
- **Applications:** Commonly used in clinical chemistry for reporting electrolyte concentrations in biological fluids, such as blood and urine.

1.3.2 CALCULATIONS AND CONVERSIONS

Accurate calculations and conversions between different concentration units are essential in pharmaceutical analysis to ensure consistency and reliability of results. The following are the key calculations and conversions used in the field:

1. Molarity Calculations:

- To calculate the molarity of a solution, divide the number of moles of solute by the volume of the solution in liters.
- **Example:** Calculate the molarity of a solution containing 5 moles of $NaCl$ in 2 liters of water.

  - **Solution:** Molarity (M) = 5 moles / 2 liters = 2.5 M

2. Normality Calculations:

- To calculate the normality, divide the number of equivalents of solute by the volume of the solution in liters.
- **Example:** Calculate the normality of a solution containing 2 equivalents of H_2SO_4 in 1 liter of water.

  - **Solution:** Normality (N) = 2 equivalents / 1 liter = 2 N

3. Molality Calculations:

- To calculate the molality, divide the number of moles of solute by the mass of the solvent in kilograms.
- **Example:** Calculate the molality of a solution containing 3 moles of glucose in 1.5 kilograms of water.

  - **Solution:** Molality (m) = 3 moles / 1.5 kilograms = 2 m

4. Percentage Concentration Calculations:

- **Weight/Weight Percent (w/w%):**

  - **Example:** Calculate the w/w% of a solution containing 10 grams of solute in 90 grams of solvent.

    - **Solution:** w/w% = (10 / (10 + 90)) × 100 = 10%

- **Weight/Volume Percent (w/v%):**

  - **Example:** Calculate the w/v% of a solution containing 5 grams of solute in 100 milliliters of solution.

    - **Solution:** w/v% = (5 / 100) × 100 = 5%

- **Volume/Volume Percent (v/v%):**

  - **Example:** Calculate the v/v% of a solution containing 30 milliliters of ethanol in 70 milliliters of water.

    - **Solution:** v/v% = (30 / (30 + 70)) × 100 = 30%

5. Parts per Million (ppm) and Parts per Billion (ppb) Calculations:

- **ppm:**

  - **Example:** Calculate the ppm of a solution containing 0.002 grams of solute in 1 liter of solution.

- **Solution:** ppm = (0.002 / 1) × 10^6 = 2000 ppm

- **ppb:**

  - **Example:** Calculate the ppb of a solution containing 0.0005 grams of solute in 1 liter of solution.

    - **Solution:** ppb = (0.0005 / 1) × 10^9 = 500,000 ppb

6. Mole Fraction Calculations:

- To calculate the mole fraction, divide the number of moles of one component by the total number of moles of all components.
- **Example:** Calculate the mole fraction of NaCl in a solution containing 2 moles of NaCl and 8 moles of water.

  - **Solution:** $\chi(NaCl)$ = 2 / (2 + 8) = 0.2

7. Milliequivalents per Liter (mEq/L) Calculations:

- To calculate milliequivalents per liter, multiply the millimoles of solute by the valence and divide by the volume of the solution in liters.
- **Example:** Calculate the mEq/L of a solution containing 50 millimoles of Ca^{2+} in 1 liter of solution.

  - **Solution:** mEq/L = (50 × 2) / 1 = 100 mEq/L

By mastering these calculations and conversions, pharmaceutical scientists ensure the accurate preparation of solutions and the precise expression of concentrations, which are fundamental to successful analytical procedures and the reliable production of pharmaceutical products.

1.4 PRIMARY AND SECONDARY STANDARDS
1.4.1 DEFINITIONS AND EXAMPLES

In pharmaceutical analysis, the accuracy and reliability of quantitative measurements depend heavily on the use of well-defined standards. These standards are classified into two main types: primary standards and secondary standards.

Primary Standards:

- **Definition:** A primary standard is a highly pure chemical substance that can be used to directly prepare a solution of known concentration. It must meet several criteria to ensure its reliability: high purity, stability under storage conditions, non-hygroscopic nature, known stoichiometry, and a high molar mass to minimize weighing errors.
- **Examples:**

  - **Potassium Hydrogen Phthalate (KHP):** Commonly used as a primary standard for acid-base titrations due to its high purity and stability. It reacts with strong bases like sodium hydroxide (NaOH) in a 1:1 molar ratio.
  - **Sodium Carbonate (Na2CO3):** Frequently used as a primary standard in acid-base titrations. It is stable, non-hygroscopic, and has a well-defined stoichiometry with acids.
  - **Silver Nitrate (AgNO3):** Used as a primary standard in precipitation titrations. Its high purity and stability make it suitable for titrating halides.
  - **Oxalic Acid (C2H2O4·2H2O):** Employed as a primary standard in redox titrations, particularly for standardizing potassium permanganate solutions.
  - **Potassium Dichromate (K2Cr2O7):** Utilized as a primary standard in redox titrations due to its stability and well-defined stoichiometry.

Secondary Standards:

- **Definition:** A secondary standard is a substance whose purity has been established by comparison with a primary standard. Secondary standards are used in routine analysis after being standardized against a primary standard.
- **Examples:**

  - **Sodium Hydroxide (NaOH):** Commonly used as a secondary standard in acid-base titrations. It is hygroscopic and absorbs carbon dioxide from the air, which affects its concentration. Therefore, it must be standardized frequently against a primary standard like KHP.

- **Hydrochloric Acid (HCl):** Widely used in titrations but must be standardized against a primary standard such as sodium carbonate due to its volatile nature.
- **Potassium Permanganate (KMnO4):** Used in redox titrations but must be standardized against a primary standard like oxalic acid because it can decompose over time.
- **Sulfuric Acid (H2SO4):** Utilized in various titrations and standardized against primary standards like sodium carbonate to ensure accuracy.
- **Iodine (I2):** Employed in iodometric titrations and standardized against primary standards such as sodium thiosulfate or arsenic trioxide.

1.4.2 IMPORTANCE IN STANDARDIZATION

Standardization is a critical process in pharmaceutical analysis, ensuring that analytical measurements are accurate, precise, and reliable. The use of primary and secondary standards plays a pivotal role in this process.

Ensuring Accuracy and Precision:

- **Primary Standards:** Due to their high purity and stability, primary standards provide a benchmark for accuracy. They are used to prepare solutions of known concentration, which serve as reference points for calibrating analytical instruments and methods.
- **Secondary Standards:** Secondary standards, once standardized against primary standards, are used for routine analysis. This process ensures that measurements remain accurate and precise over time, even with substances that may not be as stable or pure as primary standards.

Consistency in Analytical Results:

- The use of standardized solutions prepared from primary and secondary standards ensures consistency in analytical results. This is crucial for comparative studies, quality control, and regulatory compliance. Consistent results are essential for making informed decisions about the quality and safety of pharmaceutical products.

Regulatory Compliance:

- Regulatory agencies such as the FDA and EMA require rigorous standardization processes to ensure that pharmaceutical products meet predefined quality standards. Primary and secondary standards are integral to these processes, providing the necessary accuracy and reliability in quantitative analysis. Compliance with regulatory standards is essential for the approval and marketability of pharmaceutical products.

Quality Control:

- In the pharmaceutical industry, maintaining high-quality standards is paramount. Standardization using primary and secondary standards is a fundamental aspect of quality control, ensuring that raw materials, intermediates, and finished products meet the required specifications. This helps in identifying and eliminating sources of error, maintaining product quality, and safeguarding patient health.

Method Validation:

- Analytical methods used in pharmaceutical analysis must be validated to ensure their reliability and accuracy. Standardization with primary and secondary standards is a critical component of method validation, providing the necessary benchmarks to assess method performance. This includes evaluating parameters such as accuracy, precision, linearity, and robustness.

Cost-Effectiveness:

- While primary standards are essential for accuracy, they are often more expensive and less convenient for routine use. Secondary standards, once standardized, provide a cost-effective alternative for routine analysis. This approach balances the need for accuracy with practical considerations, ensuring that high-quality analytical results are obtained without incurring unnecessary costs.

Traceability and Documentation:

- The use of primary and secondary standards ensures traceability in analytical measurements. Accurate records of standardization processes, including the preparation and standardization of solutions, are essential for audit trails and regulatory inspections. This traceability supports transparency and accountability in pharmaceutical analysis.

In conclusion, the use of primary and secondary standards is fundamental to the accuracy, precision, and reliability of pharmaceutical analysis. These standards ensure consistent analytical results, support regulatory compliance, and maintain high-quality standards in the pharmaceutical industry. By adhering to rigorous standardization processes, pharmaceutical scientists can ensure the safety, efficacy, and quality of pharmaceutical products, ultimately protecting patient health and advancing medical science.

TWO

PREPARATION AND STANDARDIZATION OF SOLUTIONS

2.1 PREPARATION OF SOLUTIONS

2.1.2 NORMAL SOLUTIONS

Introduction to Normal Solutions

Normal solutions are fundamental in the field of **analytical chemistry**, playing a crucial role in various **titrimetric** and **volumetric analyses**. A normal solution is defined by its concentration in terms of equivalent weights per liter of solution. Specifically, one normal (1N) solution contains one equivalent of the solute dissolved in one liter of solution. The concept of normality is particularly useful when dealing with reactions where ions or molecules react in a definite stoichiometric ratio.

Definition and Calculation of Normality

Normality (N) is a measure of concentration equivalent to molarity, but it accounts for the reactive capacity of a molecule. Normality is calculated using the equation:

Normality (N)=Number of equivalents of solute / Volume of solution in liters

To find the number of equivalents, one must consider the solute's role in the chemical reaction. For acids and bases, the equivalents are determined by the number of hydrogen ions (H^+) or hydroxide ions (OH^-) they can donate or accept. For salts, the equivalents are based on the total positive or negative charge the ions can contribute.

For example, in the case of sulfuric acid (H_2SO_4), which can donate two hydrogen ions per molecule, one mole of H_2SO_4 provides two equivalents. Thus, a 1M solution of H_2SO_4 is 2N.

Preparation of Normal Solutions

The preparation of normal solutions requires precise measurements and calculations to ensure accuracy. The steps involve:

1. **Calculating the Required Quantity of Solute**: Determine the equivalent weight of the solute, which is the molecular weight divided by the number of reactive units (ions or functional groups). For instance, for H_2SO_4 (molecular weight = 98 g/mol), the equivalent weight is 98/2 = 49 g/equiv.
2. **Weighing the Solute**: Use a balance to weigh the precise amount of solute required. For a 1N H_2SO_4 solution, you would weigh 49 grams of H_2SO_4.
3. **Dissolving the Solute**: Add the solute to a volumetric flask and dissolve it in a small volume of distilled water.
4. **Diluting to the Mark**: After the solute is completely dissolved, dilute the solution with distilled water to the final desired volume (1 liter for a 1N solution).

Examples of Normal Solutions

Hydrochloric Acid (HCl)

Hydrochloric acid is a common laboratory reagent. Its preparation involves:

- Equivalent weight of HCl = 36.46 g/equiv (since it can donate one H^+ ion).
- To prepare a 1N solution, dissolve 36.46 g of HCl in enough water to make 1 liter.

Sodium Hydroxide (NaOH)

Sodium hydroxide is a strong base used in various titrations:

- Equivalent weight of NaOH = 40 g/equiv (since it can accept one H^+ ion).
- For a 1N NaOH solution, dissolve 40 g of NaOH in 1 liter of water.

Practical Applications and Importance

Normal solutions are integral in **standardizing solutions** and **calibrating instruments**. In **acid-base titrations**, normal solutions help determine the unknown concentration of analytes by reacting with a known concentration of titrant. Similarly, in **redox titrations**, normality is crucial for reactions involving electron transfer, such as the titration of Fe^{2+} with $KMnO_4$, where the normality of the titrant determines the endpoint.

Minute Details in Preparation

Temperature Considerations

Temperature can affect the volume of the solution, and thus the concentration. It is essential to prepare and standardize normal solutions at a consistent temperature, typically at 25°C.

Use of Volumetric Flasks

Volumetric flasks are calibrated to contain a precise volume at a specific temperature. Using these flasks ensures accuracy in the final concentration of the normal solution.

Standardization of Normal Solutions

After preparation, normal solutions must be standardized to confirm their concentration. This involves titrating the prepared solution against a primary standard, a substance with known high purity and stability. For example, to standardize NaOH, titrate it against a primary standard like potassium hydrogen phthalate (KHP).

Step-by-Step Procedure for Standardizing NaOH

1. **Weighing the Primary Standard**: Accurately weigh a known amount of KHP.
2. **Dissolving the Standard**: Dissolve the KHP in distilled water in a volumetric flask.
3. **Titration**: Titrate the NaOH solution with the KHP solution using phenolphthalein as an indicator. The endpoint is reached when a persistent pink color is observed.
4. **Calculating Normality**: Use the volume of NaOH solution used to reach the endpoint to calculate its normality.

Normality of NaOH=Weight of KHP / Equivalent weight of KHP×Volume of NaOH solution

Errors and Precautions

Errors in preparation and standardization can arise from improper weighing, incomplete dissolution, or inaccurate titration. To minimize these errors:

- Ensure precise measurements using calibrated equipment.
- Thoroughly dissolve solutes to avoid concentration discrepancies.
- Perform titrations slowly and observe the endpoint carefully.

2.1 PREPARATION OF SOLUTIONS
2.1.3 STEP-BY-STEP PROCEDURES

The preparation of solutions in **analytical chemistry** requires precise and systematic methods to ensure accuracy and reliability. This section provides detailed step-by-step procedures for preparing solutions, which are essential for various **laboratory analyses.**

General Steps for Preparing Solutions

1. **Selecting the Solvent**: Typically, distilled or deionized water is used. Ensure the solvent is pure and free from contaminants.
2. **Calculating the Amount of Solute**: Use the formula: Mass of Solute (g)=Molarity (M)×Molecular Weight (g/mol)×Volume (L)
3. **Weighing the Solute**: Use an analytical balance to measure the precise amount of solute.
4. **Dissolving the Solute**: Add the solute to a small volume of solvent in a beaker or flask and stir until fully dissolved.
5. **Transferring to a Volumetric Flask**: Pour the solution into a volumetric flask and rinse the container with the solvent to ensure all solute is transferred.
6. **Diluting to the Mark**: Add solvent up to the calibration mark on the flask. Ensure the meniscus is at the mark when viewed at eye level.
7. **Mixing the Solution**: Invert the flask multiple times or use a magnetic stirrer to ensure homogeneous mixing.

Example Procedures
Preparation of 1M Sodium Chloride (NaCl) Solution

1. **Calculate the Solute**: For 1 liter of 1M NaCl solution, the molecular weight of NaCl is 58.44 g/mol.

2. **Weigh the Solute**: Measure 58.44 grams of NaCl using an analytical balance.
3. **Dissolve the Solute**: Add the NaCl to a small volume of distilled water and stir until dissolved.
4. **Transfer and Dilute**: Pour the solution into a 1-liter volumetric flask and dilute to the mark with distilled water.
5. **Mix**: Invert the flask several times to ensure uniformity.

Preparation of 0.5N Sulfuric Acid (H_2SO_4) Solution

1. **Calculate the Solute**: The equivalent weight of H_2SO_4 is 49 g/equiv. For 1 liter of 0.5N solution: Mass of $H_2SO_4 = 0.5\ N \times 49\ \text{g/equiv} \times 1\ L = 24.5\ g$
2. **Weigh the Solute**: Measure 24.5 grams of H_2SO_4.
3. **Dissolve and Transfer**: Carefully add the H_2SO_4 to a small volume of water, then transfer to a 1-liter volumetric flask.
4. **Dilute and Mix**: Add distilled water to the mark and invert the flask to mix.

2.2 STANDARDIZATION TECHNIQUES

Standardization ensures the accuracy of **solution concentrations**. This involves titrating the solution against a primary standard with a known concentration. The following sections describe the standardization techniques for various common reagents.

2.2.1 OXALIC ACID

Oxalic Acid is often used as a primary standard due to its high purity and stability.

Standardization of Sodium Hydroxide (NaOH) with Oxalic Acid

1. **Prepare the Oxalic Acid Solution**: Weigh an accurate amount of oxalic acid ($H_2C_2O_4 \cdot 2H_2O$) and dissolve in distilled water to make a known concentration, typically 0.05M.
2. **Weigh and Dissolve**: Calculate the required mass of oxalic acid. For a 0.05M solution: Mass $= 0.05\ M \times 126.07\ \text{g/mol} \times 1\ L = 6.3035\ g$
3. **Dissolve and Transfer**: Dissolve the weighed oxalic acid in a small volume of water, then transfer to a volumetric flask and dilute to the mark.
4. **Titration**: Pipette a known volume of the oxalic acid solution into a conical flask. Add a few drops of phenolphthalein indicator.

5. **Titrate with NaOH**: Slowly titrate with NaOH until the solution turns pink, indicating the endpoint.
6. **Calculate Normality**: Use the titration data to calculate the normality of NaOH. N_{NaOH}=Volume of oxalic acid (L)×Normality of oxalic acid / Volume of NaOH (L)

2.2.2 SODIUM HYDROXIDE

Sodium Hydroxide solutions are standardized using primary standards like potassium hydrogen phthalate (KHP) or oxalic acid.

Standardization with KHP

1. **Prepare the KHP Solution**: Weigh an accurate amount of KHP and dissolve in distilled water.
2. **Weigh and Dissolve**: For a 0.1N solution: Mass=0.1 N×204.22 g/equiv×1 L=20.422 g
3. **Titration**: Pipette a known volume of KHP solution into a conical flask. Add phenolphthalein indicator.
4. **Titrate with NaOH**: Slowly add NaOH until the solution turns pink.
5. **Calculate Normality**: N_{NaOH}=Weight of KHP (g) / Equivalent weight of KHP (g/equiv)×Volume of NaOH (L)

2.2.3 HYDROCHLORIC ACID

Hydrochloric Acid is standardized using sodium carbonate (Na_2CO_3) as a primary standard.

Standardization with Sodium Carbonate

1. **Prepare the Sodium Carbonate Solution**: Weigh an accurate amount of Na_2CO_3 and dissolve in distilled water.
2. **Weigh and Dissolve**: For a 0.1N solution: Mass=0.1 N×106 g/mol×1 L=10.6 g
3. **Titration**: Pipette a known volume of Na_2CO_3 solution into a conical flask. Add methyl orange indicator.
4. **Titrate with HCl**: Slowly add HCl until the solution changes from yellow to pink.
5. **Calculate Normality**: N_{HCl}=Volume of Na_2CO_3 (L)×Normality of Na_2CO_3Volume of HCl (L)

2.2.4 SODIUM THIOSULPHATE

Sodium Thiosulphate is standardized using potassium dichromate ($K_2Cr_2O_7$) or iodine.

Standardization with Iodine

1. **Prepare the Iodine Solution**: Weigh and dissolve a known amount of iodine in a potassium iodide solution.
2. **Weigh and Dissolve**: For a 0.1N solution: Mass=$0.1\,N \times 253.81$ g/mol$\times 1$ L=25.381 g
3. **Titration**: Pipette a known volume of iodine solution into a conical flask. Add starch indicator.
4. **Titrate with $Na_2S_2O_3$**: Slowly add sodium thiosulphate until the solution changes from blue to colorless.
5. **Calculate Normality**: $N_{Na_2S_2O_3}=$Volume of iodine (L)$\times$Normality of iodine Volume of $Na_2S_2O_3$ (L)

2.2 STANDARDIZATION TECHNIQUES
2.2.5 SULPHURIC ACID

Sulphuric acid (H_2SO_4) is a strong acid commonly used in titrations and must be accurately standardized for precise analytical work. One method of standardization involves using a primary standard such as sodium carbonate (Na_2CO_3).

Standardization with Sodium Carbonate

1. **Prepare the Sodium Carbonate Solution**: Accurately weigh a known amount of anhydrous sodium carbonate and dissolve it in distilled water to prepare a standard solution. For a 0.1N solution, the calculation is: Mass=$0.1\,N \times 53$ g/mol$\times 1$ L=5.3 g
2. **Weigh and Dissolve**: Weigh 5.3 grams of anhydrous sodium carbonate, dissolve it in a small amount of distilled water, and transfer it to a 1-liter volumetric flask. Dilute to the mark with distilled water.
3. **Titration**: Pipette a known volume (e.g., 25 mL) of the sodium carbonate solution into a conical flask. Add a few drops of methyl orange indicator.
4. **Titrate with H_2SO_4**: Slowly add the sulphuric acid solution from a burette until the solution changes color from yellow to red, indicating the endpoint.
5. **Calculate Normality**: Use the titration data to calculate the normality of the sulphuric acid solution: $N_{H_2SO_4}=$Volume of Na_2CO_3 (L)$\times$Normality of Na_2CO_3 / Volume of H_2SO_4 (L)

2.2.6 POTASSIUM PERMANGANATE

Potassium permanganate (KMnO₄) is a powerful oxidizing agent used in redox titrations. It is often standardized using a primary standard such as sodium oxalate ($Na_2C_2O_4$) or oxalic acid ($H_2C_2O_4 \cdot 2H_2O$).

Standardization with Sodium Oxalate

1. **Prepare the Sodium Oxalate Solution**: Accurately weigh a known amount of sodium oxalate and dissolve it in distilled water. For a 0.05M solution, the calculation is: Mass=0.05 M×134 g/mol×1 L=6.7 g
2. **Weigh and Dissolve**: Weigh 6.7 grams of sodium oxalate, dissolve it in a small amount of distilled water, and transfer it to a 1-liter volumetric flask. Dilute to the mark with distilled water.
3. **Titration**: Pipette a known volume (e.g., 25 mL) of the sodium oxalate solution into a conical flask. Add dilute sulfuric acid to acidify the solution.
4. **Titrate with KMnO₄**: Slowly add the potassium permanganate solution from a burette while heating the conical flask to around 60°C until a faint pink color persists for 30 seconds, indicating the endpoint.
5. **Calculate Normality**: Use the titration data to calculate the normality of the potassium permanganate solution: NKMnO₄=Volume of $Na_2C_2O_4$ (L)×Normality of $Na_2C_2O_4$Volume of KMnO₄ (L)

2.2.7 CERIC AMMONIUM SULPHATE

Ceric ammonium sulphate [(NH₄)₄Ce(SO₄)₄·2H₂O] is used as a standard oxidizing agent in titrations, particularly in **redox titrations**. It can be standardized using a primary standard like arsenic trioxide (As_2O_3).

Standardization with Arsenic Trioxide

1. **Prepare the Arsenic Trioxide Solution**: Accurately weigh a known amount of arsenic trioxide and dissolve it in an alkaline medium. For a 0.1N solution, the calculation is: Mass=0.1 N×197.84 g/mol×1 L=19.784 g
2. **Weigh and Dissolve**: Weigh 19.784 grams of arsenic trioxide and dissolve it in a solution of sodium hydroxide to form sodium arsenite.
3. **Neutralize and Dilute**: Carefully neutralize the solution with dilute sulfuric acid, then transfer it to a 1-liter volumetric flask and dilute to the mark with distilled water.
4. **Titration**: Pipette a known volume (e.g., 25 mL) of the arsenic trioxide solution into a conical flask. Add a few drops of ferroin indicator.

5. **Titrate with Ceric Ammonium Sulphate**: Slowly add the ceric ammonium sulphate solution from a burette until the solution changes from red to light green, indicating the endpoint.

6. **Calculate Normality**: Use the titration data to calculate the normality of the ceric ammonium sulphate solution: $NCe(SO_4)_2 = $ Volume of As_2O_3 (L) × Normality of As_2O_3 / Volume of $Ce(SO_4)_2$ (L)

THREE

ERRORS IN PHARMACEUTICAL ANALYSIS

3.1 SOURCES OF ERRORS

In pharmaceutical analysis, achieving precise and accurate results is crucial for ensuring the safety, efficacy, and quality of pharmaceutical products. However, various sources of errors can affect the outcomes of analytical measurements. Understanding these sources and their impact on the analysis is essential for minimizing errors and improving the reliability of results. Errors in pharmaceutical analysis can be broadly classified into two categories: **systematic errors** and **random errors.**

3.1.1 SYSTEMATIC ERRORS

Systematic errors, also known as determinate errors, are consistent and reproducible inaccuracies that occur due to identifiable causes. These errors lead to a bias in the measurement, causing the results to consistently deviate from the true value in the same direction. Systematic errors can significantly affect the accuracy of analytical results and are often more challenging to detect and correct compared to random errors.

Causes of Systematic Errors:

1. **Instrumental Errors:**

- **Calibration Errors:** Incorrect calibration of analytical instruments, such as balances, spectrophotometers, and chromatographs, can lead to systematic errors. For example, if a balance is not properly calibrated, it may consistently overestimate or underestimate the weight of the samples.
- **Drift:** Over time, some instruments may exhibit a gradual change in their response, known as drift. This can occur due to factors such as temperature fluctuations, aging of electronic components, or mechanical wear and tear. Drift can cause a consistent deviation in the measurements.
- **Non-linearity:** Many analytical instruments have a linear response range, within which the instrument's output is directly proportional to the concentration of the analyte. If measurements are taken outside this linear range, non-linearity can introduce systematic errors.

2. **Reagent Errors:**

- **Impurities:** Impurities in reagents can lead to systematic errors by introducing additional substances that interfere with the analysis. For instance, impure solvents used in chromatography can produce extra peaks, complicating the interpretation of results.
- **Degradation:** Reagents that degrade over time or when exposed to certain conditions (such as light or air) can lead to systematic errors. Degraded reagents may not react as expected, leading to inaccurate results.

3. **Methodological Errors:**

- **Improper Sample Preparation:** Errors in sample preparation, such as incorrect weighing, incomplete dissolution, or improper mixing, can lead to systematic deviations. For example, incomplete dissolution of a sample can result in lower-than-expected analyte concentrations.
- **Incorrect Method Selection:** Choosing an inappropriate analytical method for the given sample or analyte can introduce systematic errors. Each method has its own limitations and specificities, and using the wrong method can yield biased results.

4. **Environmental Errors:**

   - **Temperature and Humidity:** Environmental conditions, such as temperature and humidity, can affect the performance of analytical instruments and the stability of samples and reagents. For example, variations in temperature can cause changes in the density of liquids, affecting volumetric measurements.
   - **Vibration and Air Currents:** External factors like vibrations from nearby equipment or air currents in the laboratory can impact sensitive measurements, particularly those involving balances or optical instruments.

5. **Personal Errors:**

   - **Bias and Subjectivity:** Human errors, such as bias and subjectivity in observations or measurements, can lead to systematic deviations. For example, an analyst may consistently read the meniscus of a liquid in a volumetric flask incorrectly, leading to systematic volumetric errors.
   - **Skill and Technique:** The skill and technique of the analyst can also contribute to systematic errors. Inconsistent handling of samples or reagents, incorrect pipetting, or improper use of instruments can introduce bias into the results.

Detection and Correction of Systematic Errors:

1. **Calibration and Maintenance:**

   - Regular calibration and maintenance of analytical instruments are essential to detect and correct systematic errors. Calibration should be performed using standard reference materials and should be documented meticulously. Routine maintenance can help identify and rectify issues that may cause drift or non-linearity.

2. **Use of Standard Reference Materials:**

   - Standard reference materials (SRMs) with known properties and concentrations can be used to validate analytical methods and detect systematic errors. Comparing the results obtained with SRMs to the expected values helps identify any consistent deviations.

3. **Method Validation:**

   - Method validation involves assessing the accuracy, precision, specificity, linearity, and robustness of an analytical method. Validation ensures that the method is suitable for its intended purpose and helps identify potential sources of systematic errors.

4. **Quality Control Procedures:**

   - Implementing stringent quality control procedures, such as using control samples and running blank determinations, can help detect systematic errors. Control charts and statistical tools can be used to monitor the consistency of analytical results over time.

5. **Training and Standard Operating Procedures:**

   - Providing comprehensive training to analysts and adhering to standard operating procedures (SOPs) can minimize personal errors. SOPs ensure that all steps of the analytical process are performed consistently and correctly.

3.1.2 RANDOM ERRORS

Random errors, also known as indeterminate errors, are unpredictable variations that occur during the measurement process. Unlike systematic errors, random errors do not have a consistent direction or magnitude and are caused by random fluctuations in experimental conditions. These errors affect the precision of analytical results and are typically characterized by a normal distribution around the true value.

Causes of Random Errors:

1. **Instrumental Fluctuations:**

   - **Electronic Noise:** Analytical instruments, especially those with electronic components, are subject to electronic noise, which can cause random fluctuations in measurements. For example, spectrophotometers may exhibit baseline noise, affecting absorbance readings.

- **Mechanical Variability:** Mechanical components of instruments, such as moving parts in chromatographs or balances, can introduce random errors due to slight variations in their operation.

2. Environmental Variability:

- **Temperature and Humidity Changes:** Small, random changes in temperature and humidity can affect the performance of instruments and the stability of samples and reagents. These fluctuations can lead to minor variations in measurements.
- **Air Currents and Vibrations:** Random air currents and vibrations in the laboratory can impact sensitive measurements, particularly those involving balances or optical instruments.

3. Sample and Reagent Variability:

- **Inhomogeneity:** Inhomogeneous samples or reagents can introduce random errors if the aliquots taken for analysis do not represent the overall composition accurately. For example, solid samples with varying particle sizes may not be uniformly distributed.
- **Random Contamination:** Occasional, unpredictable contamination of samples or reagents can introduce random errors. For instance, dust particles or trace impurities in reagents can cause fluctuations in measurements.

4. Personal Variability:

- **Human Factors:** Human factors, such as slight variations in the technique or timing of measurements, can introduce random errors. For example, differences in how an analyst reads a meniscus or performs a titration can result in minor variations in the results.

Detection and Minimization of Random Errors:

1. Replicate Measurements:

- Performing multiple replicate measurements of the same sample can help identify and quantify random errors. The standard deviation or variance of the replicate measurements provides an estimate of the precision of the method.

2. **Statistical Analysis:**

- Statistical tools, such as confidence intervals and hypothesis testing, can be used to assess the significance of random errors and determine their impact on the overall uncertainty of the measurement.

3. **Quality Control Samples:**

- Including quality control samples in each analytical batch helps monitor the precision of the method and detect random errors. Control charts can be used to track the performance of the method over time.

4. **Standard Operating Procedures:**

- Adhering to well-defined SOPs ensures that all steps of the analytical process are performed consistently, minimizing the impact of random errors due to human variability.

5. **Environmental Controls:**

- Implementing environmental controls, such as maintaining constant temperature and humidity and minimizing vibrations and air currents, can reduce the impact of environmental variability on measurements.

6. **Instrument Maintenance:**

- Regular maintenance and calibration of analytical instruments help minimize random errors caused by mechanical or electronic fluctuations. Ensuring that instruments are in good working condition reduces the likelihood of random variations in measurements.

Examples of Systematic and Random Errors:
Systematic Errors:

- **Example 1:** If an analytical balance is not properly calibrated, it may consistently overestimate the weight of samples by 0.1 grams. This calibration error leads to a systematic deviation in all weight measurements.
- **Example 2:** Using a reagent with a known impurity can introduce a consistent bias in the results. For instance, if a solvent used in chromatography contains an impurity that co-elutes with the analyte, it will cause systematic errors in the quantification of the analyte.

Random Errors:

- **Example 1:** During a titration, slight variations in the addition of the titrant or the timing of endpoint detection can lead to random fluctuations in the titration volume. These random errors affect the precision of the titration results.
- **Example 2:** Temperature fluctuations in the laboratory can cause random variations in the measurements obtained from a spectrophotometer. Even small changes in temperature can affect the absorbance readings, introducing random errors.

Understanding the sources of systematic and random errors is essential for improving the accuracy and precision of analytical measurements in pharmaceutical analysis. Systematic errors, which cause consistent deviations from the true value, can be detected and corrected through calibration, validation, and quality control procedures. Random errors, which cause unpredictable variations, can be minimized through replicate measurements, statistical analysis, and environmental controls. By addressing both types of errors, pharmaceutical analysts can ensure that their results are reliable and reproducible, ultimately supporting the development and quality control of safe and effective pharmaceutical products.

3.1 SOURCES OF ERRORS

In pharmaceutical analysis, achieving accurate and reliable results is essential for ensuring the quality, safety, and efficacy of pharmaceutical products. Various sources of errors can affect the outcomes of analytical measurements. Understanding these sources and their impact on analysis is crucial for minimizing errors and improving the reliability of results. Errors in pharmaceutical analysis can be broadly classified into three categories: **systematic errors, random errors,** and **common sources in laboratory settings**.

3.1.3 COMMON SOURCES IN LABORATORY SETTINGS

Laboratory settings present several common sources of errors that can affect the accuracy and precision of analytical measurements. These sources can be related to the environment, equipment, reagents, and human factors. Identifying and addressing these sources of errors is crucial for ensuring the reliability of analytical results.

Environmental Factors:

- **Temperature Variations:** Fluctuations in temperature can affect the stability of samples and reagents, as well as the performance of analytical instruments. For example, temperature changes can cause volumetric glassware to expand or contract, leading to inaccuracies in volume measurements.
- **Humidity:** High humidity can affect the weight of hygroscopic substances, such as certain chemicals and reagents, leading to errors in weighing. It can also impact the performance of sensitive instruments like balances and spectrophotometers.
- **Air Currents:** Drafts and air currents in the laboratory can cause instability in measurements taken with sensitive equipment, such as analytical balances. This can lead to fluctuations in readings and affect the precision of the results.
- **Vibrations:** Vibrations from nearby equipment or external sources can interfere with measurements taken with sensitive instruments, such as balances and chromatographs. This can lead to random variations in the data.

Equipment-Related Factors:

- **Calibration:** Improper calibration of analytical instruments, such as balances, spectrophotometers, and chromatographs, can lead to systematic errors. Regular calibration using standard reference materials is essential for maintaining the accuracy of the instruments.

- **Maintenance:** Poor maintenance of equipment can result in malfunctions and inaccuracies. For example, clogged or dirty detectors in chromatographs can affect the sensitivity and specificity of the measurements.
- **Aging Instruments:** Over time, the performance of analytical instruments can degrade due to wear and tear. This can lead to drift and other systematic errors that affect the accuracy of the results.

Reagent-Related Factors:

- **Purity:** Impurities in reagents can introduce additional substances that interfere with the analysis, leading to systematic errors. It is important to use high-purity reagents and validate their quality before use.
- **Degradation:** Some reagents are prone to degradation over time or when exposed to certain conditions, such as light or air. Degraded reagents may not react as expected, leading to inaccurate results.
- **Contamination:** Accidental contamination of reagents can introduce foreign substances that affect the analysis. Careful handling and storage of reagents are essential to prevent contamination.

Sample-Related Factors:

- **Homogeneity:** Inhomogeneous samples can lead to inaccurate measurements if the aliquots taken for analysis do not represent the overall composition accurately. Proper sample preparation and mixing are essential to ensure homogeneity.
- **Stability:** The stability of samples can be affected by factors such as temperature, light, and humidity. Unstable samples may degrade or react, leading to inaccurate results. Proper storage and handling of samples are essential to maintain their stability.

Human Factors:

- **Technique:** Variations in the technique and skill of the analyst can introduce errors. For example, inconsistent pipetting, improper handling of samples, and incorrect use of instruments can lead to inaccuracies.

- **Bias:** Human bias and subjectivity in observations or measurements can lead to systematic deviations. For example, an analyst may consistently read the meniscus of a liquid in a volumetric flask incorrectly, leading to volumetric errors.
- **Training:** Insufficient training of laboratory personnel can result in improper execution of analytical procedures and increased likelihood of errors. Continuous training and adherence to standard operating procedures (SOPs) are essential to minimize human errors.

Quality Control and Quality Assurance:

- **Quality Control (QC):** QC measures, such as running control samples and performing routine checks, help detect and correct errors. QC procedures ensure that the analytical results are reliable and within acceptable limits.
- **Quality Assurance (QA):** QA encompasses all activities that ensure the quality of the analytical results, including method validation, instrument calibration, and adherence to SOPs. QA helps identify and address potential sources of errors.

3.2 TYPES OF ERRORS

Errors in pharmaceutical analysis can be broadly classified into two main types: **systematic errors** and **random errors**. Understanding these types of errors and their impact on analytical results is essential for minimizing their effects and ensuring the reliability of the measurements.

Systematic Errors:

- **Definition:** Systematic errors, also known as determinate errors, are consistent and reproducible inaccuracies that occur due to identifiable causes. These errors lead to a bias in the measurement, causing the results to consistently deviate from the true value in the same direction.
- **Causes:** Systematic errors can arise from various sources, including instrumental errors (e.g., incorrect calibration, drift, non-linearity), reagent errors (e.g., impurities, degradation), methodological errors (e.g., improper sample preparation, incorrect method selection), environmental errors (e.g., temperature and humidity fluctuations, vibrations), and human errors (e.g., bias, subjectivity, skill level).

- **Impact:** Systematic errors affect the accuracy of the analytical results, causing a consistent deviation from the true value. They can be detected and corrected through calibration, validation, and quality control procedures.

Random Errors:

- **Definition:** Random errors, also known as indeterminate errors, are unpredictable variations that occur during the measurement process. Unlike systematic errors, random errors do not have a consistent direction or magnitude and are caused by random fluctuations in experimental conditions.
- **Causes:** Random errors can arise from various sources, including instrumental fluctuations (e.g., electronic noise, mechanical variability), environmental variability (e.g., temperature and humidity changes, air currents, vibrations), sample and reagent variability (e.g., inhomogeneity, random contamination), and human factors (e.g., slight variations in technique or timing).
- **Impact:** Random errors affect the precision of the analytical results, causing variations around the true value. They can be minimized through replicate measurements, statistical analysis, quality control samples, adherence to SOPs, and environmental controls.

Detection and Correction of Errors:
Systematic Errors:

1. **Calibration and Maintenance:**

    - Regular calibration and maintenance of analytical instruments are essential to detect and correct systematic errors. Calibration should be performed using standard reference materials and documented meticulously. Routine maintenance can help identify and rectify issues that may cause drift or non-linearity.

2. **Use of Standard Reference Materials:**

    - Standard reference materials (SRMs) with known properties and concentrations can be used to validate analytical methods and detect systematic errors. Comparing the results obtained with SRMs to the expected values helps identify any consistent deviations.

3. **Method Validation:**

   - Method validation involves assessing the accuracy, precision, specificity, linearity, and robustness of an analytical method. Validation ensures that the method is suitable for its intended purpose and helps identify potential sources of systematic errors.

4. **Quality Control Procedures:**

   - Implementing stringent quality control procedures, such as using control samples and running blank determinations, can help detect systematic errors. Control charts and statistical tools can be used to monitor the consistency of analytical results over time.

5. **Training and Standard Operating Procedures:**

   - Providing comprehensive training to analysts and adhering to SOPs can minimize personal errors. SOPs ensure that all steps of the analytical process are performed consistently and correctly.

Random Errors:

1. **Replicate Measurements:**

   - Performing multiple replicate measurements of the same sample can help identify and quantify random errors. The standard deviation or variance of the replicate measurements provides an estimate of the precision of the method.

2. **Statistical Analysis:**

   - Statistical tools, such as confidence intervals and hypothesis testing, can be used to assess the significance of random errors and determine their impact on the overall uncertainty of the measurement.

3. **Quality Control Samples:**

   - Including quality control samples in each analytical batch helps monitor the precision of the method and detect random errors. Control charts can be used to track the performance of the method over time.

4. **Standard Operating Procedures:**

   - Adhering to well-defined SOPs ensures that all steps of the analytical process are performed consistently, minimizing the impact of random errors due to human variability.

5. **Environmental Controls:**

   - Implementing environmental controls, such as maintaining constant temperature and humidity and minimizing vibrations and air currents, can reduce the impact of environmental variability on measurements.

6. **Instrument Maintenance:**

   - Regular maintenance and calibration of analytical instruments help minimize random errors caused by mechanical or electronic fluctuations. Ensuring that instruments are in good working condition reduces the likelihood of random variations in measurements.

Examples of Systematic and Random Errors:
Systematic Errors:

- **Example 1:** If an analytical balance is not properly calibrated, it may consistently overestimate the weight of samples by 0.1 grams. This calibration error leads to a systematic deviation in all weight measurements.
- **Example 2:** Using a reagent with a known impurity can introduce a consistent bias in the results. For instance, if a solvent used in chromatography contains an impurity that co-elutes with the analyte, it

will cause systematic errors in the quantification of the analyte.

Random Errors:

- **Example 1:** During a titration, slight variations in the addition of the titrant or the timing of endpoint detection can lead to random fluctuations in the titration volume. These random errors affect the precision of the titration results.

Example 2: Temperature fluctuations in the laboratory can cause random variations in the measurements obtained from a spectrophotometer. Even small changes in temperature can affect the absorbance readings, introducing random errors.

3.2 TYPES OF ERRORS

Errors in pharmaceutical analysis can be broadly categorized into two main types: **systematic errors** and **random errors**. Understanding these types of errors, their sources, and their impacts on analytical results is crucial for minimizing their effects and ensuring the reliability of the measurements.

3.2.1 SYSTEMATIC ERRORS

Systematic errors, also known as determinate errors, are reproducible inaccuracies that consistently occur in the same direction. These errors lead to a bias in the measurement, causing the results to deviate from the true value by a consistent amount. They can be identified and corrected once their source is known. Systematic errors can arise from several sources:

Instrumental Errors:

- **Calibration Errors:** Occur when analytical instruments are not properly calibrated. For example, if a balance consistently reads 0.1 grams higher than the true weight, all measurements taken with that balance will be systematically higher.
- **Drift:** Over time, instruments can exhibit a gradual change in their output, known as drift. This can occur due to aging components, temperature changes, or other environmental factors.
- **Non-linearity:** Many instruments have a linear response range, and measurements taken outside this range can lead to systematic deviations.

Reagent Errors:

- **Impurities:** Impurities in reagents can introduce systematic errors by adding unexpected substances that affect the analysis.
- **Degradation:** Reagents that degrade over time can cause systematic errors if their concentration or reactivity changes.

Methodological Errors:

- **Improper Sample Preparation:** Errors in sample preparation, such as incorrect weighing, incomplete dissolution, or improper mixing, can lead to systematic deviations.
- **Incorrect Method Selection:** Using an inappropriate analytical method for the sample or analyte can introduce systematic errors.

Environmental Errors:

- **Temperature and Humidity:** Variations in temperature and humidity can affect the performance of instruments and the stability of samples and reagents.
- **Vibration and Air Currents:** External factors like vibrations or air currents can impact sensitive measurements, particularly those involving balances or optical instruments.

Personal Errors:

- **Bias and Subjectivity:** Human bias and subjectivity in observations or measurements can lead to systematic deviations.
- **Skill and Technique:** Inconsistent handling of samples or reagents, incorrect pipetting, or improper use of instruments can introduce bias.

Detection and Correction of Systematic Errors:

- **Calibration and Maintenance:** Regular calibration and maintenance of analytical instruments are essential to detect and correct systematic errors. Calibration should be performed using standard reference materials and documented meticulously.

- **Use of Standard Reference Materials:** Standard reference materials (SRMs) with known properties and concentrations can be used to validate analytical methods and detect systematic errors.
- **Method Validation:** Method validation involves assessing the accuracy, precision, specificity, linearity, and robustness of an analytical method.
- **Quality Control Procedures:** Implementing stringent quality control procedures, such as using control samples and running blank determinations, can help detect systematic errors.
- **Training and Standard Operating Procedures:** Providing comprehensive training to analysts and adhering to SOPs can minimize personal errors.

3.2.2 RANDOM ERRORS

Random errors, also known as indeterminate errors, are unpredictable variations that occur during the measurement process. These errors do not have a consistent direction or magnitude and are caused by random fluctuations in experimental conditions. Unlike systematic errors, random errors affect the precision of analytical results, causing the results to vary around the true value.

Instrumental Fluctuations:

- **Electronic Noise:** Analytical instruments, especially those with electronic components, are subject to electronic noise, which can cause random fluctuations in measurements.
- **Mechanical Variability:** Mechanical components of instruments, such as moving parts in chromatographs or balances, can introduce random errors due to slight variations in their operation.

Environmental Variability:

- **Temperature and Humidity Changes:** Small, random changes in temperature and humidity can affect the performance of instruments and the stability of samples and reagents.
- **Air Currents and Vibrations:** Random air currents and vibrations in the laboratory can impact sensitive measurements, particularly those involving balances or optical instruments.

Sample and Reagent Variability:

- **Inhomogeneity:** Inhomogeneous samples or reagents can introduce random errors if the aliquots taken for analysis do not represent the overall composition accurately.
- **Random Contamination:** Occasional, unpredictable contamination of samples or reagents can introduce random errors.

Personal Variability:

- **Human Factors:** Human factors, such as slight variations in the technique or timing of measurements, can introduce random errors.

Detection and Minimization of Random Errors:

- **Replicate Measurements:** Performing multiple replicate measurements of the same sample can help identify and quantify random errors.
- **Statistical Analysis:** Statistical tools, such as confidence intervals and hypothesis testing, can be used to assess the significance of random errors and determine their impact on the overall uncertainty of the measurement.
- **Quality Control Samples:** Including quality control samples in each analytical batch helps monitor the precision of the method and detect random errors.
- **Standard Operating Procedures:** Adhering to well-defined SOPs ensures that all steps of the analytical process are performed consistently.
- **Environmental Controls:** Implementing environmental controls, such as maintaining constant temperature and humidity, can reduce the impact of environmental variability on measurements.
- **Instrument Maintenance:** Regular maintenance and calibration of analytical instruments help minimize random errors caused by mechanical or electronic fluctuations.

Examples of Random Errors:

- **Example 1:** During a titration, slight variations in the addition of the titrant or the timing of endpoint detection can lead to random fluctuations in the titration volume. These random errors affect the precision of the titration results.

- **Example 2:** Temperature fluctuations in the laboratory can cause random variations in the measurements obtained from a spectrophotometer. Even small changes in temperature can affect the absorbance readings, introducing random errors.

Understanding the sources of errors in pharmaceutical analysis and categorizing them into systematic and random errors is essential for improving the accuracy and precision of analytical measurements. Systematic errors, which cause consistent deviations from the true value, can be detected and corrected through calibration, validation, and quality control procedures. Random errors, which cause unpredictable variations, can be minimized through replicate measurements, statistical analysis, and environmental controls. By addressing both types of errors, pharmaceutical analysts can ensure that their results are reliable and reproducible, ultimately supporting the development and quality control of safe and effective pharmaceutical products.

3.2 TYPES OF ERRORS

In pharmaceutical analysis, errors are an inevitable part of the measurement process. Understanding and distinguishing between different types of errors, such as systematic and random errors, are crucial for achieving accurate and reliable results. Two fundamental concepts related to errors are **accuracy** and **precision**. These concepts help in assessing the quality of analytical measurements and in identifying areas for improvement.

3.2.1 ACCURACY

Accuracy refers to the closeness of a measured value to the true value or accepted reference value. It indicates the extent to which an analytical measurement represents the actual quantity being measured. High accuracy means that the measured values are close to the true value, while low accuracy indicates a significant deviation from the true value. Accuracy is influenced by systematic errors, which can cause consistent bias in the measurements.

Factors Affecting Accuracy:

1. **Instrument Calibration:**

- **Calibration Errors:** Inaccurate calibration of analytical instruments, such as balances, spectrophotometers, and chromatographs, can lead to systematic errors that affect accuracy. Regular calibration using standard reference materials is essential for maintaining accuracy.
- **Drift:** Over time, instruments can exhibit drift, where their response gradually changes due to factors such as aging components or environmental conditions. Drift can cause measurements to consistently deviate from the true value.

2. **Reagent Purity:**

- **Impurities:** Impurities in reagents can introduce additional substances that interfere with the analysis, leading to inaccurate results. Using high-purity reagents and validating their quality before use is crucial for ensuring accuracy.
- **Degradation:** Reagents that degrade over time or when exposed to certain conditions (e.g., light, air) can lead to inaccurate measurements. Proper storage and handling of reagents help maintain their stability and purity.

3. **Sample Preparation:**

- **Improper Sample Preparation:** Errors in sample preparation, such as incorrect weighing, incomplete dissolution, or improper mixing, can lead to inaccurate results. Ensuring thorough and consistent sample preparation is vital for achieving accurate measurements.
- **Homogeneity:** Inhomogeneous samples can lead to inaccurate measurements if the aliquots taken for analysis do not represent the overall composition accurately. Proper sample preparation and mixing ensure homogeneity.

4. **Method Selection:**

- **Incorrect Method Selection:** Choosing an inappropriate analytical method for the given sample or analyte can introduce systematic errors and affect accuracy. Each method has its own limitations and specificities, and using the wrong method can yield biased results.

5. **Environmental Conditions:**

   - **Temperature and Humidity:** Environmental conditions, such as temperature and humidity, can affect the performance of analytical instruments and the stability of samples and reagents. Maintaining controlled environmental conditions in the laboratory is essential for ensuring accuracy.

6. **Human Factors:**

   - **Bias and Subjectivity:** Human bias and subjectivity in observations or measurements can lead to systematic deviations from the true value. Training analysts to minimize bias and ensuring adherence to standard operating procedures (SOPs) are essential for achieving accurate results.

Assessing Accuracy:

1. **Use of Standard Reference Materials (SRMs):**

   - SRMs with known properties and concentrations are used to validate analytical methods and assess accuracy. Comparing the results obtained with SRMs to the expected values helps identify any deviations and assess the accuracy of the method.

2. **Recovery Studies:**

   - Recovery studies involve spiking a known amount of analyte into the sample and measuring the amount recovered. The recovery percentage indicates the accuracy of the analytical method. A high recovery percentage (close to 100%) indicates high accuracy.

3. **Method Validation:**

   - Method validation involves assessing various parameters, including accuracy, precision, specificity, linearity, and robustness, to ensure that the method is suitable for its intended purpose. Validation provides confidence in the accuracy of the method.

Improving Accuracy:

1. **Regular Calibration and Maintenance:**

   - Regular calibration and maintenance of analytical instruments are essential for maintaining accuracy. Calibration should be performed using standard reference materials and documented meticulously. Routine maintenance helps identify and rectify issues that may affect accuracy.

2. **Quality Control Procedures:**

   - Implementing stringent quality control procedures, such as using control samples and running blank determinations, helps monitor and improve accuracy. Control charts and statistical tools can be used to track the performance of the method over time.

3. **Training and SOPs:**

   - Providing comprehensive training to analysts and adhering to SOPs ensures consistent and accurate execution of analytical procedures. SOPs standardize the steps involved in the analysis, reducing the likelihood of errors.

3.2.2 PRECISION

Precision refers to the closeness of repeated measurements of the same sample under the same conditions. It indicates the reproducibility and consistency of the analytical method. High precision means that the measurements are closely grouped together, while low precision indicates significant variability among the measurements. Precision is influenced by random errors, which cause unpredictable variations in the measurements.

Types of Precision:

1. **Repeatability:**

   - **Definition:** Repeatability refers to the precision of measurements taken by the same analyst, using the same equipment, and under the same conditions within a short time interval.

- ○ **Importance:** High repeatability indicates that the analytical method produces consistent results when performed by the same analyst under identical conditions.

2. **Intermediate Precision:**

- ○ **Definition:** Intermediate precision, also known as intra-laboratory precision, refers to the precision of measurements taken by different analysts, using different equipment, or on different days within the same laboratory.
- ○ **Importance:** High intermediate precision indicates that the analytical method produces consistent results under varying conditions within the same laboratory.

3. **Reproducibility:**

- ○ **Definition:** Reproducibility refers to the precision of measurements taken by different laboratories, using different equipment, and performed by different analysts.
- ○ **Importance:** High reproducibility indicates that the analytical method produces consistent results across different laboratories, enhancing the reliability and robustness of the method.

Factors Affecting Precision:

1. **Instrumental Fluctuations:**

- ○ **Electronic Noise:** Analytical instruments, especially those with electronic components, are subject to electronic noise, which can cause random fluctuations in measurements.
- ○ **Mechanical Variability:** Mechanical components of instruments, such as moving parts in chromatographs or balances, can introduce random errors due to slight variations in their operation.

2. **Environmental Variability:**

- ○ **Temperature and Humidity Changes:** Small, random changes in temperature and humidity can affect the performance of instruments and the stability of samples and reagents.

- **Air Currents and Vibrations:** Random air currents and vibrations in the laboratory can impact sensitive measurements, particularly those involving balances or optical instruments.

3. **Sample and Reagent Variability:**

- **Inhomogeneity:** Inhomogeneous samples or reagents can introduce random errors if the aliquots taken for analysis do not represent the overall composition accurately.
- **Random Contamination:** Occasional, unpredictable contamination of samples or reagents can introduce random errors.

4. **Human Factors:**

- **Human Factors:** Human factors, such as slight variations in the technique or timing of measurements, can introduce random errors. Training analysts to minimize variability and ensuring adherence to SOPs are essential for achieving high precision.

Assessing Precision:

1. **Replicate Measurements:**

- Performing multiple replicate measurements of the same sample helps identify and quantify random errors. The standard deviation or variance of the replicate measurements provides an estimate of the precision of the method.

2. **Statistical Analysis:**

- Statistical tools, such as confidence intervals and hypothesis testing, can be used to assess the significance of random errors and determine their impact on the overall uncertainty of the measurement. The coefficient of variation (CV) is often used to express precision as a percentage of the mean value.

3. **Quality Control Samples:**

- Including quality control samples in each analytical batch helps monitor the precision of the method. Control charts can be used to track the performance of the method over time and detect any variations.

Improving Precision:

1. **Instrument Calibration and Maintenance:**

   - Regular calibration and maintenance of analytical instruments help minimize random errors caused by mechanical or electronic fluctuations. Ensuring that instruments are in good working condition reduces the likelihood of random variations in measurements.

2. **Environmental Controls:**

   - Implementing environmental controls, such as maintaining constant temperature and humidity and minimizing vibrations and air currents, can reduce the impact of environmental variability on measurements.

3. **Standard Operating Procedures:**

   - Adhering to well-defined SOPs ensures that all steps of the analytical process are performed consistently, minimizing the impact of random errors due to human variability.

4. **Training and Proficiency Testing:**

   - Providing comprehensive training to analysts and conducting regular proficiency testing helps ensure consistent and precise execution of analytical procedures. Proficiency testing involves comparing the results obtained by different analysts or laboratories to assess the precision and accuracy of the method.

5. **Quality Control Procedures:**

○ Implementing stringent quality control procedures, such as using control samples and running blank determinations, helps monitor and improve precision. Control charts and statistical tools can be used to track the performance of the method over time.

Examples of Precision:
Repeatability:

- **Example:** An analyst performs ten replicate measurements of the same sample using the same HPLC system under identical conditions. The results are closely grouped together, indicating high repeatability.

Intermediate Precision:

- **Example:** Two analysts perform measurements of the same sample using different HPLC systems and on different days within the same laboratory. The results are consistent, indicating high intermediate precision.

Reproducibility:

- **Example:** Several laboratories participate in an inter-laboratory study to measure the concentration of a specific analyte in a sample. The results from all laboratories are consistent, indicating high reproducibility.

3.3 METHODS TO MINIMIZE ERRORS

In pharmaceutical analysis, minimizing errors is essential to achieve accurate and reliable results. Various strategies and techniques can be employed to reduce both systematic and random errors, thereby improving the quality of analytical measurements.

1. Calibration and Maintenance of Instruments:

- **Regular Calibration:** Ensure that all analytical instruments, such as balances, spectrophotometers, and chromatographs, are calibrated regularly using standard reference materials. Calibration helps correct any deviations and ensures that the instruments provide accurate readings.

- **Routine Maintenance:** Perform routine maintenance on all instruments to prevent drift and mechanical wear. Regular checks and servicing can identify and rectify issues that may cause systematic errors.

2. Use of Standard Reference Materials (SRMs):

- **Validation of Methods:** Use SRMs with known properties and concentrations to validate analytical methods. SRMs provide a benchmark for accuracy and help identify any systematic errors.
- **Quality Control:** Incorporate SRMs into quality control procedures to monitor the performance of analytical methods over time. Comparing results with SRMs helps ensure consistent accuracy.

3. Method Validation:

- **Accuracy and Precision:** Validate analytical methods by assessing their accuracy, precision, specificity, linearity, and robustness. Validation ensures that the methods are suitable for their intended purpose and helps identify potential sources of error.
- **Recovery Studies:** Conduct recovery studies to evaluate the accuracy of the method. Spiking known amounts of analyte into the sample and measuring the recovery percentage provides insight into the method's accuracy.

4. Quality Control Procedures:

- **Control Samples:** Use control samples in each analytical batch to monitor the precision and accuracy of the method. Control charts can be used to track the performance of the method over time.
- **Blank Determinations:** Perform blank determinations to identify any contamination or interference in the reagents or instruments. Blank measurements help isolate and correct sources of error.

5. Environmental Controls:

- **Temperature and Humidity:** Maintain constant temperature and humidity in the laboratory to ensure the stability of samples, reagents, and instruments. Environmental fluctuations can affect the performance of analytical methods.

- **Minimize Vibrations and Air Currents:** Implement measures to reduce vibrations and air currents in the laboratory, which can impact sensitive measurements. Stabilizing the environment helps improve the precision of analytical results.

6. Proper Sample Preparation:

- **Homogeneous Samples:** Ensure that samples are homogeneous and well-mixed before analysis. Inhomogeneous samples can lead to inaccurate measurements.
- **Accurate Weighing and Dissolution:** Use precise weighing techniques and ensure complete dissolution of samples to avoid systematic errors in sample preparation.

7. Training and Standard Operating Procedures (SOPs):

- **Comprehensive Training:** Provide comprehensive training to analysts to minimize human errors. Well-trained analysts are less likely to introduce variability in measurements.
- **Adherence to SOPs:** Develop and adhere to SOPs for all analytical procedures. SOPs standardize the steps involved in the analysis, reducing the likelihood of errors.

8. Statistical Analysis:

- **Replicate Measurements:** Perform multiple replicate measurements of the same sample to identify and quantify random errors. Statistical analysis of replicates provides an estimate of the precision of the method.
- **Confidence Intervals:** Use confidence intervals and hypothesis testing to assess the significance of errors and determine their impact on the overall uncertainty of the measurement.

9. Instrument-Specific Techniques:

- **Blank Corrections:** For instruments such as spectrophotometers and chromatographs, perform blank corrections to account for any baseline noise or interference. Subtracting the blank measurement from the sample measurement improves accuracy.

- **Internal Standards:** Use internal standards in chromatographic methods to account for variability in sample injection and detector response. Internal standards help normalize the results and improve precision.

10. Continuous Improvement:

- **Regular Reviews:** Regularly review and update analytical methods and procedures to incorporate new technologies and best practices. Continuous improvement helps maintain high standards of accuracy and precision.
- **Feedback Mechanisms:** Implement feedback mechanisms to identify and address sources of errors. Encouraging analysts to report issues and suggest improvements fosters a culture of quality.

3.4 SIGNIFICANT FIGURES

Significant figures (or significant digits) are the digits in a number that contribute to its precision. They include all the certain digits in a measurement plus one uncertain digit. Proper use of significant figures is crucial in pharmaceutical analysis to convey the precision of measurements and calculations accurately.

Rules for Determining Significant Figures:

1. **Non-Zero Digits:** All non-zero digits are considered significant.

   - Example: In the number 123.45, all five digits are significant.

2. **Leading Zeros:** Leading zeros (zeros before the first non-zero digit) are not significant.

   - Example: In the number 0.00123, only the digits 1, 2, and 3 are significant.

3. **Captive Zeros:** Zeros between non-zero digits are significant.

○ Example: In the number 1002.03, all six digits are significant.

4. **Trailing Zeros:** Trailing zeros (zeros at the end of a number) are significant if they are to the right of a decimal point.

   ○ Example: In the number 123.4500, all seven digits are significant.
   ○ If trailing zeros are to the left of a decimal point, they may or may not be significant depending on whether they indicate precision.
   ○ Example: In the number 1200, the significance of the trailing zeros depends on the context or notation used (e.g., 1.2×10^3 indicates two significant figures).

Significant Figures in Calculations:

1. **Addition and Subtraction:**

   ○ In addition and subtraction, the result should have the same number of decimal places as the measurement with the fewest decimal places.
   ○ Example: 12.345 (three decimal places) + 0.1 (one decimal place) = 12.445, which should be rounded to 12.4 (one decimal place).

2. **Multiplication and Division:**

   ○ In multiplication and division, the result should have the same number of significant figures as the measurement with the fewest significant figures.
   ○ Example: 12.3 (three significant figures) × 0.456 (three significant figures) = 5.6088, which should be rounded to 5.61 (three significant figures).

Rounding Rules:

1. **If the digit to be dropped is less than 5, the last retained digit remains unchanged.**

   ○ Example: Rounding 12.443 to three significant figures gives 12.4.

2. **If the digit to be dropped is 5 or greater, the last retained digit is increased by one.**

   - Example: Rounding 12.446 to three significant figures gives 12.5.

Importance of Significant Figures in Pharmaceutical Analysis:

1. **Precision and Accuracy:**

   - Proper use of significant figures reflects the precision of the measurements and the accuracy of the analytical method. It ensures that the reported results are not misleading in terms of their precision.

2. **Consistency in Reporting:**

   - Consistent use of significant figures in reporting results helps maintain uniformity and clarity in data presentation. It avoids confusion and misinterpretation of the precision of measurements.

3. **Calculation of Uncertainty:**

   - Significant figures are essential in the calculation and reporting of uncertainty in analytical measurements. They help convey the reliability and confidence in the reported values.

4. **Regulatory Compliance:**

   - Adherence to guidelines on significant figures is important for compliance with regulatory requirements. Regulatory agencies often specify the level of precision required in analytical reports.

Examples of Applying Significant Figures:

1. **Example 1: Addition**

   - Measurement 1: 12.345 g
   - Measurement 2: 0.1 g

- Sum: 12.445 g (rounded to 12.4 g to match the precision of 0.1 g)

2. **Example 2: Multiplication**

- Measurement 1: 6.78 mL (three significant figures)
- Measurement 2: 0.456 g/mL (three significant figures)
- Product: 3.09048 g (rounded to 3.09 g to match the three significant figures)

3.4 SIGNIFICANT FIGURES

Understanding and properly using significant figures in analytical measurements is crucial in pharmaceutical analysis. Significant figures help convey the precision of measurements and ensure the accuracy and reliability of reported results.

3.4.1 IMPORTANCE IN ANALYTICAL MEASUREMENTS
Significant Figures and Precision:

- **Precision Representation:** Significant figures represent the precision of a measurement. Each digit in a significant figure provides valuable information about the confidence in the measurement. For instance, a measurement of 23.45 g indicates more precision than 23.4 g.
- **Conveying Uncertainty:** The number of significant figures indicates the level of uncertainty in a measurement. A result with more significant figures has less uncertainty and greater precision. For example, 0.1234 has four significant figures, indicating higher precision than 0.123, which has three significant figures.

Consistency and Standardization:

- **Uniform Reporting:** Using significant figures consistently helps maintain uniformity in data presentation across different laboratories and reports. This standardization avoids confusion and ensures that the reported data is interpreted correctly by different stakeholders.
- **Compliance with Guidelines:** Regulatory agencies, such as the FDA and EMA, often specify guidelines on the level of precision required in analytical reports. Adhering to these guidelines by using appropriate

significant figures ensures compliance with regulatory standards.

Accuracy and Reliability:

- **Reflecting Method Precision:** The use of significant figures ensures that the reported data accurately reflects the precision of the analytical method used. Overstating the precision of a measurement by using too many significant figures can be misleading and result in incorrect conclusions.
- **Error Propagation:** In analytical calculations, the proper use of significant figures helps manage the propagation of errors. Using the correct number of significant figures ensures that the final result accurately represents the cumulative uncertainty of the measurements involved.

Calculation and Interpretation:

- **Mathematical Operations:** Significant figures play a crucial role in mathematical operations, such as addition, subtraction, multiplication, and division. The rules for significant figures guide how the precision of the result should be maintained, ensuring that the final value is not over- or understated.
- **Data Interpretation:** Properly using significant figures helps in the accurate interpretation of analytical data. It allows scientists and researchers to make informed decisions based on the precision and accuracy of the reported measurements.

Examples of Importance:

1. **Quality Control:**

   - In quality control processes, significant figures help ensure that the measured quantities of active pharmaceutical ingredients (APIs) meet the specified criteria. Accurate representation of precision is crucial for maintaining the quality and efficacy of pharmaceutical products.

2. **Regulatory Submissions:**

- When submitting data to regulatory authorities, the use of significant figures ensures that the reported measurements comply with regulatory standards. This is essential for the approval and marketability of pharmaceutical products.

3. **Research and Development:**

- In research and development, significant figures guide the precision of measurements in experiments and studies. Accurate representation of data precision is essential for drawing valid conclusions and advancing scientific knowledge.

3.4.2 RULES FOR DETERMINING SIGNIFICANT FIGURES
Non-Zero Digits:

- **Rule:** All non-zero digits are considered significant.
- **Example:** In the number 123.45, all five digits are significant.

Leading Zeros:

- **Rule:** Leading zeros (zeros before the first non-zero digit) are not significant.
- **Example:** In the number 0.00123, only the digits 1, 2, and 3 are significant.

Captive Zeros:

- **Rule:** Zeros between non-zero digits are significant.
- **Example:** In the number 1002.03, all six digits are significant.

Trailing Zeros:

- **Rule:** Trailing zeros (zeros at the end of a number) are significant if they are to the right of a decimal point.
- **Example:** In the number 123.4500, all seven digits are significant.
- **Context-Dependent:** If trailing zeros are to the left of a decimal point, they may or may not be significant depending on whether they indicate precision.

- **Example:** In the number 1200, the significance of the trailing zeros depends on the context or notation used (e.g., 1.2×10^3 indicates two significant figures).

Addition and Subtraction:

- **Rule:** In addition and subtraction, the result should have the same number of decimal places as the measurement with the fewest decimal places.
- **Example:** 12.345 (three decimal places) + 0.1 (one decimal place) = 12.445, which should be rounded to 12.4 (one decimal place).

Multiplication and Division:

- **Rule:** In multiplication and division, the result should have the same number of significant figures as the measurement with the fewest significant figures.
- **Example:** 12.3 (three significant figures) × 0.456 (three significant figures) = 5.6088, which should be rounded to 5.61 (three significant figures).

Rounding Rules:

1. **If the digit to be dropped is less than 5, the last retained digit remains unchanged.**

   - **Example:** Rounding 12.443 to three significant figures gives 12.4.

2. **If the digit to be dropped is 5 or greater, the last retained digit is increased by one.**

   - **Example:** Rounding 12.446 to three significant figures gives 12.5.

Examples of Applying Significant Figures:

1. **Addition Example:**

   - Measurement 1: 12.345 g
   - Measurement 2: 0.1 g

- ◦ Sum: 12.445 g (rounded to 12.4 g to match the precision of 0.1 g)

2. **Multiplication Example:**

- ◦ Measurement 1: 6.78 mL (three significant figures)
- ◦ Measurement 2: 0.456 g/mL (three significant figures)
- ◦ Product: 3.09048 g (rounded to 3.09 g to match the three significant figures)

By adhering to the rules of significant figures, analysts can ensure that their measurements and calculations accurately reflect the precision of the data. This practice supports the reliability and validity of analytical results, ultimately contributing to the quality and safety of pharmaceutical products.

FOUR

PHARMACOPOEIA AND IMPURITIES IN MEDICINAL AGENTS

4.1 PHARMACOPOEIA

4.1.1 ROLE AND IMPORTANCE

A **pharmacopoeia** is an official publication containing a list of medicinal drugs, their effects, directions for their use, and standards for their preparation and quality. It serves as an authoritative reference for the pharmaceutical industry, healthcare professionals, and regulatory authorities to ensure the safety, efficacy, and quality of medicines.

Role of Pharmacopoeia:

1. **Standardization of Medicines:**

   - Pharmacopoeias provide detailed descriptions and specifications for drugs and their formulations, including the required purity, strength, and quality. This standardization ensures that all medicines meet consistent and acceptable standards, regardless of the manufacturer or geographic location.

2. **Quality Control:**

- By setting forth methods for testing and validating the quality of drugs, pharmacopoeias play a crucial role in quality control. They provide procedures for the identification of impurities, validation of active ingredients, and assessment of stability, ensuring that drugs are safe and effective for patient use.

3. **Regulatory Compliance:**

- Pharmacopoeias are used by regulatory agencies as a benchmark for approving and monitoring pharmaceutical products. Compliance with pharmacopoeial standards is often a legal requirement for the production and sale of medicines, ensuring that pharmaceutical companies adhere to high-quality standards.

4. **Guidance for Manufacturers:**

- Pharmaceutical manufacturers use pharmacopoeias as a guide for the preparation, formulation, and testing of drugs. This ensures that their products are consistent with established standards, reducing the risk of variability and ensuring the safety and efficacy of their medications.

5. **Support for Healthcare Professionals:**

- Healthcare professionals rely on pharmacopoeias for accurate and up-to-date information on drug formulations, dosages, and administration methods. This helps them to prescribe and dispense medications safely and effectively, improving patient care.

Importance of Pharmacopoeia:

1. **Ensuring Drug Safety and Efficacy:**

- Pharmacopoeias play a vital role in ensuring that all medicinal products are safe for consumption and effective in treating the intended conditions. By setting rigorous standards for the quality and purity of drugs, pharmacopoeias help protect public health.

2. **Facilitating International Trade:**

   - International pharmacopoeias, such as the European Pharmacopoeia (EP), the United States Pharmacopeia (USP), and the Japanese Pharmacopoeia (JP), help harmonize standards across different countries. This facilitates international trade in pharmaceuticals by ensuring that products meet globally accepted standards.

3. **Promoting Innovation:**

   - By providing standardized methods and criteria for the development and testing of new drugs, pharmacopoeias encourage innovation in the pharmaceutical industry. Researchers and developers can rely on these standards to ensure that their new products are safe, effective, and of high quality.

4. **Improving Public Health:**

   - Pharmacopoeias contribute to improving public health by ensuring that only high-quality medicines are available to consumers. They provide a framework for the continuous improvement of pharmaceutical products, leading to better health outcomes and increased trust in the healthcare system.

5. **Educational Resource:**

   - Pharmacopoeias serve as valuable educational resources for students and professionals in the pharmaceutical sciences. They provide comprehensive information on drug formulations, testing methods, and quality standards, helping to train the next generation of pharmaceutical scientists and healthcare providers.

Examples of Major Pharmacopoeias:

1. **United States Pharmacopeia (USP):**

   - The USP sets standards for the quality, purity, strength, and consistency of drugs, food ingredients, and dietary supplements in the United States. It is a key reference for the pharmaceutical industry and healthcare professionals.

2. **European Pharmacopoeia (EP):**

   - The EP provides common quality standards for medicines and their components across Europe. It is a critical tool for ensuring the safety and efficacy of pharmaceuticals in the European Union and other countries that adopt its standards.

3. **Japanese Pharmacopoeia (JP):**

   - The JP establishes official standards for the description and quality of drugs in Japan. It ensures that medicines are safe, effective, and of high quality, supporting the healthcare system in Japan.

4. **British Pharmacopoeia (BP):**

   - The BP sets standards for the quality of medicines in the United Kingdom and is used globally as a reference for pharmaceutical quality standards. It ensures that drugs are safe and effective for use in the UK and other countries that follow its guidelines.

5. **Indian Pharmacopoeia (IP):**

   - The IP sets standards for drugs manufactured and marketed in India. It ensures that pharmaceutical products in India meet the required quality and safety standards, supporting the healthcare system in the country.

The role and importance of pharmacopoeias in pharmaceutical analysis cannot be overstated. They provide the foundation for the standardization, quality control, and regulatory compliance of medicinal products. By setting rigorous standards for the purity, strength, and quality of drugs, pharmacopoeias ensure that all pharmaceutical products are safe, effective, and of high quality. They facilitate international trade, promote innovation, improve public health, and serve as valuable educational resources. Adherence to pharmacopoeial standards is essential for the development, production, and distribution of safe and effective medicines, ultimately protecting public health and enhancing the quality of healthcare worldwide.

4.1.2 OVERVIEW OF MAJOR PHARMACOPOEIAS

Pharmacopoeias are essential references in the pharmaceutical industry, providing standardized information on drug quality, purity, strength, and consistency. Here is an overview of some major pharmacopoeias and their roles in the global pharmaceutical landscape:

1. United States Pharmacopeia (USP):

- **History and Authority:** The USP was first published in 1820 and is a non-profit organization. It sets standards for the quality, purity, strength, and consistency of drugs, dietary supplements, and food ingredients in the United States.
- **Key Features:**

  - Provides monographs for drugs and their formulations.
  - Includes general chapters on analytical methods and guidelines.
  - Sets standards for excipients and dietary supplements.

- **Global Influence:** The USP standards are widely recognized and used internationally, influencing drug quality regulations in many countries.

2. European Pharmacopoeia (EP):

- **History and Authority:** The EP was first published in 1969 by the Council of Europe. It aims to harmonize quality standards for medicines across Europe.
- **Key Features:**

  - Provides comprehensive monographs for drugs, excipients, and dosage forms.
  - Includes methods for the identification, purity testing, and quantification of substances.
  - Sets standards for biologicals, herbal drugs, and vaccines.

- **Global Influence:** The EP is recognized beyond Europe and is used as a reference in many other countries.

3. Japanese Pharmacopoeia (JP):

- **History and Authority:** The JP was first published in 1886 and is revised every five years by the Ministry of Health, Labour, and Welfare in Japan.
- **Key Features:**

  - Provides monographs for drugs and pharmaceutical products.
  - Includes general tests, reference standards, and guidelines for drug development.
  - Emphasizes the quality and safety of medicines in Japan.

- **Global Influence:** The JP standards are recognized and respected in various countries, particularly in Asia.

4. British Pharmacopoeia (BP):

- **History and Authority:** The BP was first published in 1864 and is issued by the British Pharmacopoeia Commission, under the authority of the Medicines and Healthcare products Regulatory Agency (MHRA) in the UK.
- **Key Features:**

  - Provides monographs for medicinal substances, formulated preparations, and dietary supplements.
  - Includes analytical methods and quality control procedures.
  - Sets standards for radiopharmaceuticals and biologicals.

- **Global Influence:** The BP is used in over 100 countries and serves as a critical reference for drug quality standards.

5. Indian Pharmacopoeia (IP):

- **History and Authority:** The IP was first published in 1955 and is compiled by the Indian Pharmacopoeia Commission under the Ministry of Health and Family Welfare.

- **Key Features:**

  - Provides monographs for drugs, pharmaceutical aids, and dosage forms.
  - Includes analytical methods and specifications for identity, purity, and strength.
  - Sets standards for herbal products and biologicals.

- **Global Influence:** The IP is primarily used in India but also serves as a reference in neighboring countries.

4.2 SOURCES OF IMPURITIES

Impurities in medicinal agents can arise from various sources during the manufacturing, storage, and handling processes. Identifying and controlling these impurities is essential for ensuring the safety and efficacy of pharmaceutical products.

1. Raw Materials:

- **Source:** Impurities can be introduced from raw materials used in drug synthesis. These can include residual solvents, reagents, catalysts, and starting materials.
- **Impact:** Impurities in raw materials can affect the purity and quality of the final product. For example, residual solvents can be toxic and must be controlled to acceptable levels.

2. Manufacturing Process:

- **Source:** The manufacturing process can introduce impurities through incomplete reactions, side reactions, degradation, and contamination.
- **Impact:** Process-related impurities can affect the drug's safety, efficacy, and stability. For instance, degradation products formed during synthesis can be harmful or reduce the drug's potency.

3. Storage Conditions:

- **Source:** Improper storage conditions, such as exposure to light, heat, moisture, or air, can lead to the degradation of the drug substance and the formation of impurities.
- **Impact:** Storage-related impurities can compromise the stability and shelf life of the product. For example, moisture can cause hydrolysis, leading to the formation of degradation products.

4. Packaging Materials:

- **Source:** Packaging materials, including containers, closures, and seals, can introduce impurities through leaching, migration, or interaction with the drug product.
- **Impact:** Packaging-related impurities can affect the drug's purity and safety. For instance, plasticizers from plastic containers can leach into the drug product.

5. Cross-Contamination:

- **Source:** Cross-contamination can occur during manufacturing, packaging, or handling due to inadequate cleaning procedures or equipment sharing between different products.
- **Impact:** Cross-contamination can lead to the presence of unintended substances in the drug product, posing safety risks to patients.

6. Environmental Contaminants:

- **Source:** Environmental contaminants, such as dust, microorganisms, and airborne particles, can be introduced during the manufacturing and packaging processes.
- **Impact:** Environmental impurities can affect the sterility and quality of the product. For example, microbial contamination can lead to infections and adverse reactions.

7. Degradation Products:

- **Source:** Degradation products can form during the shelf life of the drug due to chemical reactions, such as hydrolysis, oxidation, and photolysis.

- **Impact:** Degradation products can compromise the drug's efficacy and safety. Regulatory guidelines specify acceptable limits for degradation products in pharmaceutical products.

Control and Minimization of Impurities:

1. **Good Manufacturing Practices (GMP):**

   - Adhering to GMP ensures that the manufacturing process is controlled and consistent, minimizing the introduction of impurities. GMP guidelines cover all aspects of production, including raw material handling, process validation, and quality control.

2. **Proper Storage Conditions:**

   - Storing drug substances and products under appropriate conditions, such as controlled temperature and humidity, helps prevent degradation and the formation of impurities.

3. **Use of High-Purity Raw Materials:**

   - Using high-purity raw materials and reagents reduces the risk of introducing impurities during the manufacturing process. Raw materials should be tested and validated before use.

4. **Robust Analytical Methods:**

   - Employing robust analytical methods for detecting and quantifying impurities ensures that they are identified and controlled within acceptable limits. Methods should be validated for accuracy, precision, specificity, and sensitivity.

5. **Quality Control and Quality Assurance:**

   - Implementing stringent quality control and quality assurance procedures helps monitor and control impurities at every stage of production. Regular testing and validation ensure that impurities are within acceptable limits.

6. **Appropriate Packaging Materials:**

   - Selecting appropriate packaging materials that do not interact with the drug product helps minimize the risk of leaching and contamination. Packaging materials should be tested for compatibility with the drug product.

7. **Environmental Controls:**

   - Maintaining a clean and controlled manufacturing environment reduces the risk of environmental contamination. Proper air filtration, hygiene practices, and controlled access areas help maintain product quality.

4.2.1 RAW MATERIALS

Raw Materials:

In pharmaceutical manufacturing, raw materials serve as the foundation for the production of drug substances. These materials can include active pharmaceutical ingredients (APIs), excipients, solvents, and other chemicals. The quality of raw materials is paramount, as impurities present at this stage can compromise the safety, efficacy, and quality of the final product.

Sources of Impurities in Raw Materials:

1. **Natural Sources:**

   - **Mineral Impurities:** Raw materials derived from natural sources, such as minerals, can contain impurities like heavy metals (lead, mercury, arsenic) that can be harmful if not adequately controlled.
   - **Organic Contaminants:** Plant-based raw materials can introduce organic impurities, such as pesticides, herbicides, and mycotoxins, which can pose health risks.

2. **Synthetic Sources:**

   - **Reagents and Solvents:** Impurities can arise from the reagents and solvents used during the synthesis of APIs. For instance, residual solvents like benzene, toluene, and chloroform can remain in the final product if not properly removed.

- **Reaction By-products:** Side reactions during the synthesis process can lead to the formation of by-products, which may remain as impurities in the raw material.

3. **Handling and Storage:**

- **Cross-Contamination:** Inadequate handling and storage practices can lead to cross-contamination between different raw materials. This can occur due to shared equipment, improper labeling, or insufficient cleaning procedures.
- **Degradation:** Exposure to adverse environmental conditions, such as heat, light, and moisture, can cause the degradation of raw materials, leading to the formation of impurities.

Control and Minimization of Impurities in Raw Materials:

1. **Supplier Qualification:**

- Establish stringent criteria for selecting and qualifying suppliers of raw materials. This includes evaluating their quality control measures, production processes, and adherence to regulatory standards.

2. **Specification and Testing:**

- Define clear specifications for the quality and purity of raw materials. Conduct comprehensive testing to ensure that the raw materials meet these specifications before use in manufacturing.

3. **Proper Storage:**

- Implement proper storage conditions for raw materials to prevent degradation and contamination. This includes controlled temperature, humidity, and protection from light.

4. **Documentation and Traceability:**

- Maintain detailed documentation and traceability of raw materials, including batch numbers, supplier information, and testing results. This helps in tracking and managing potential sources of impurities.

4.2.2 MANUFACTURING PROCESS

Manufacturing Process:

The manufacturing process encompasses all the steps involved in transforming raw materials into finished pharmaceutical products. This includes synthesis, formulation, purification, and packaging. Impurities introduced during manufacturing can arise from various sources and can significantly impact the quality of the final product.

Sources of Impurities in the Manufacturing Process:

1. **Synthesis:**

   - **Reaction By-products:** Side reactions during the synthesis of APIs can produce by-products that remain as impurities in the final product.
   - **Residual Solvents:** Solvents used in the synthesis process may not be completely removed, leading to residual solvent impurities.
   - **Catalysts and Reagents:** Trace amounts of catalysts and reagents used in chemical reactions can remain as impurities if not adequately removed during purification.

2. **Formulation:**

   - **Excipients:** Excipients used in drug formulations can introduce impurities if they are not of high quality or if they interact with the active ingredients.
   - **Contamination:** During the mixing and formulation stages, contamination from equipment, environment, or personnel can introduce impurities.

3. **Purification:**

   - **Incomplete Purification:** Inefficient purification processes can result in the retention of impurities, such as unreacted starting materials, by-products, and degradation products.

- ○ **Leaching:** Impurities can leach from purification equipment and materials, such as filters and chromatography columns, into the product.

4. **Packaging:**

- ○ **Material Interaction:** Interaction between the drug product and packaging materials can lead to the introduction of impurities. For example, plasticizers from plastic containers can migrate into the drug product.
- ○ **Environmental Contamination:** During the packaging process, environmental contaminants such as dust and microorganisms can be introduced.

Control and Minimization of Impurities in the Manufacturing Process:

1. **Process Validation:**

- ○ Validate all manufacturing processes to ensure that they consistently produce products meeting quality specifications. This includes validating synthesis, purification, and formulation processes.

2. **Quality Control:**

- ○ Implement stringent quality control measures at each stage of the manufacturing process. Regularly test intermediates and final products to ensure they meet predefined purity standards.

3. **Good Manufacturing Practices (GMP):**

- ○ Adhere to GMP guidelines to minimize the risk of contamination and impurities. GMP encompasses all aspects of production, including equipment cleaning, personnel hygiene, and environmental controls.

4. **Use of High-Quality Excipients:**

- ○ Source high-quality excipients that meet stringent purity standards. Conduct thorough testing of excipients to ensure they do not introduce impurities into the final product.

5. **Proper Equipment Maintenance:**

- Regularly clean and maintain manufacturing equipment to prevent contamination. Implement standard operating procedures (SOPs) for equipment cleaning and maintenance.

4.2.3 STORAGE CONDITIONS

Storage Conditions:

The storage conditions of pharmaceutical products and raw materials play a critical role in maintaining their stability and quality. Improper storage can lead to the degradation of the product, resulting in the formation of impurities that can compromise its safety and efficacy.

Sources of Impurities Due to Storage Conditions:

1. **Temperature:**

- **Heat Degradation:** Exposure to high temperatures can accelerate chemical reactions that degrade the drug substance, leading to the formation of impurities.
- **Cold Storage:** Improper cold storage can cause crystallization or phase separation in liquid formulations, introducing impurities.

2. **Humidity:**

- **Moisture Absorption:** Hygroscopic substances can absorb moisture from the air, leading to hydrolysis and degradation. This is particularly important for drugs that are sensitive to moisture.
- **Microbial Growth:** High humidity can promote the growth of microorganisms in the product or packaging, leading to contamination and degradation.

3. **Light Exposure:**

- **Photodegradation:** Exposure to light, especially ultraviolet (UV) light, can cause photodegradation of the drug substance, resulting in the formation of impurities. This is common in drugs that are light-sensitive.

4. **Oxygen Exposure:**

   - **Oxidation:** Exposure to oxygen can cause the oxidation of sensitive drug substances, leading to the formation of oxidative degradation products.

5. **Container-Closure Systems:**

   - **Leaching:** Impurities can leach from the container-closure system into the drug product. For example, plasticizers from plastic containers or chemicals from rubber stoppers can migrate into the product.
   - **Adsorption:** Active ingredients or excipients can adsorb onto the surface of the container, reducing the drug's potency and leading to the presence of impurities.

Control and Minimization of Storage-Related Impurities:

1. **Controlled Storage Conditions:**

   - Store pharmaceutical products and raw materials under controlled conditions, including appropriate temperature, humidity, and light protection, as specified by the manufacturer.

2. **Use of Appropriate Packaging:**

   - Use packaging materials that protect the product from environmental factors such as light, moisture, and oxygen. For example, amber glass bottles protect light-sensitive drugs from photodegradation.

3. **Stability Testing:**

   - Conduct stability testing under various environmental conditions to determine the appropriate storage conditions for the product. Stability testing helps identify potential impurities that may form during storage.

4. **Monitoring and Documentation:**

   ◦ Monitor storage conditions regularly and maintain accurate records. This includes tracking temperature, humidity, and other environmental parameters in storage areas.

5. **First-In-First-Out (FIFO) System:**

   ◦ Implement a FIFO system to ensure that older stock is used first, reducing the risk of degradation over time.

6. **Preventive Measures:**

   ◦ Implement preventive measures, such as nitrogen flushing, to minimize oxygen exposure in containers. Use desiccants to control moisture levels in packaging.

4.3 LIMIT TESTS

4.3.1 PURPOSE AND PROCEDURES
Purpose of Limit Tests:

Limit tests are qualitative or semi-quantitative analytical procedures used to identify and control impurities within specified limits in pharmaceutical substances and products. The primary purpose of limit tests is to ensure that the levels of impurities do not exceed the acceptable threshold, thereby guaranteeing the safety and quality of the pharmaceutical product. These tests are critical for regulatory compliance and are often included in pharmacopoeial monographs.

Key Objectives of Limit Tests:

1. **Ensuring Safety:**

   ◦ Impurities in pharmaceutical products can be toxic or harmful to patients. Limit tests help in detecting and controlling such impurities to ensure the safety of the product.

2. **Maintaining Quality:**

   - High levels of impurities can affect the stability, efficacy, and overall quality of pharmaceutical products. Limit tests help maintain the product's quality by ensuring that impurities are within acceptable limits.

3. **Regulatory Compliance:**

   - Regulatory agencies, such as the FDA, EMA, and WHO, require pharmaceutical products to meet specific impurity limits. Compliance with these regulations is mandatory for the approval and marketing of pharmaceutical products.

4. **Quality Control:**

   - Limit tests are an essential part of the quality control process in pharmaceutical manufacturing. They help in monitoring and controlling the quality of raw materials, intermediates, and final products.

Procedures for Conducting Limit Tests:

1. **Preparation of Sample Solution:**

   - A specified amount of the pharmaceutical substance is dissolved or dispersed in a suitable solvent to prepare the sample solution. The solvent is chosen based on its ability to dissolve the substance and not interfere with the test.

2. **Preparation of Standard Solution:**

   - A standard solution containing a known concentration of the impurity is prepared. This solution is used as a reference to compare with the sample solution during the test.

3. **Addition of Reagents:**

- Specific reagents are added to both the sample and standard solutions to react with the impurity. The choice of reagents depends on the nature of the impurity and the test being performed.

4. **Development of Reaction:**

- The reaction is allowed to proceed for a specified period under controlled conditions (such as temperature, pH, and light). The reaction between the impurity and the reagent leads to the formation of a detectable product (e.g., color, precipitate).

5. **Comparison and Interpretation:**

- The sample solution is compared with the standard solution visually or using an instrument (e.g., spectrophotometer). If the intensity of the reaction product in the sample solution is less than or equal to that of the standard solution, the impurity is within the acceptable limit.

Common Limit Tests in Pharmaceutical Analysis:

1. **Limit Test for Chlorides:**

- **Purpose:** To detect and quantify chloride ions in pharmaceutical substances.
- **Procedure:** The sample solution is treated with a dilute solution of silver nitrate in the presence of dilute nitric acid. Chloride ions react with silver nitrate to form a white precipitate of silver chloride. The turbidity of the sample solution is compared with that of a standard solution containing a known concentration of chlorides.

2. **Limit Test for Sulphates:**

- **Purpose:** To detect and quantify sulfate ions in pharmaceutical substances.
- **Procedure:** The sample solution is treated with a solution of barium chloride in the presence of dilute hydrochloric acid. Sulfate ions react with barium chloride to form a white precipitate of barium sulfate.

The turbidity of the sample solution is compared with that of a standard solution containing a known concentration of sulfates.

3. **Limit Test for Iron:**

   - **Purpose:** To detect and quantify iron impurities in pharmaceutical substances.
   - **Procedure:** The sample solution is treated with a solution of thioglycolic acid in the presence of hydrochloric acid. Iron ions react with thioglycolic acid to form a purple-colored complex. The color intensity of the sample solution is compared with that of a standard solution containing a known concentration of iron.

4. **Limit Test for Heavy Metals:**

   - **Purpose:** To detect and quantify heavy metal impurities (such as lead, mercury, and cadmium) in pharmaceutical substances.
   - **Procedure:** The sample solution is treated with a reagent that reacts with heavy metals to form a colored complex or precipitate. The color intensity or turbidity of the sample solution is compared with that of a standard solution containing a known concentration of heavy metals.

5. **Limit Test for Arsenic:**

   - **Purpose:** To detect and quantify arsenic impurities in pharmaceutical substances.
   - **Procedure:** The sample solution is treated with a reagent that reacts with arsenic to form a colored complex. The color intensity of the sample solution is compared with that of a standard solution containing a known concentration of arsenic.

Factors Influencing Limit Tests:

1. **Reagent Quality:**

   - The quality and purity of reagents used in limit tests can significantly influence the accuracy and reliability of the results. High-purity reagents should be used to avoid introducing additional impurities.

2. **Environmental Conditions:**

   - Environmental factors, such as temperature, humidity, and light, can affect the reactions involved in limit tests. Conducting tests under controlled conditions ensures consistency and reliability of the results.

3. **Analyst Proficiency:**

   - The skill and proficiency of the analyst conducting the limit test can impact the accuracy of the results. Proper training and adherence to standard operating procedures (SOPs) are essential for obtaining reliable results.

4. **Equipment Calibration:**

   - Instruments used for detecting and measuring impurities (such as spectrophotometers) should be regularly calibrated and maintained to ensure accurate measurements.

Limit Test for Chlorides

The limit test for chlorides is a qualitative or semi-quantitative test used to detect and quantify chloride ions in pharmaceutical substances and products. Chlorides are common impurities that can originate from raw materials, manufacturing processes, or environmental contamination. The test ensures that the chloride content does not exceed the acceptable limits specified in pharmacopoeial monographs, thereby maintaining the safety and quality of pharmaceutical products.

Purpose of the Limit Test for Chlorides:

1. **Ensure Safety:**

   - Chlorides, if present in excessive amounts, can cause undesirable effects, such as irritation or corrosion, and can affect the stability of the pharmaceutical product. The limit test helps ensure that chloride levels remain within safe limits.

2. **Maintain Quality:**

   - High levels of chlorides can impact the quality and efficacy of pharmaceutical products. The limit test helps maintain product quality by controlling chloride impurities.

3. **Regulatory Compliance:**

   - Compliance with regulatory standards for chloride content is essential for the approval and marketing of pharmaceutical products. The limit test ensures adherence to these standards.

Procedure for Conducting the Limit Test for Chlorides:
$$Cl^{-}(aq)+AgNO_3(aq)\rightarrow AgCl(s)+NO_3^{-}(aq)$$

1. **Preparation of Sample Solution:**

   - Dissolve or dilute a specified amount of the pharmaceutical substance in a suitable solvent, typically distilled water, to prepare the sample solution.

2. **Preparation of Standard Solution:**

   - Prepare a standard solution containing a known concentration of chloride ions. This solution is used as a reference to compare with the sample solution during the test. The concentration of the standard solution is typically chosen to match the chloride limit specified in the pharmacopoeia.

3. **Addition of Reagents:**

   - Add a few drops of dilute nitric acid to both the sample and standard solutions. The nitric acid helps to ensure the complete precipitation of chlorides by neutralizing any alkaline impurities that may interfere with the reaction.

4. **Addition of Silver Nitrate Solution:**

   - Add a specific volume of silver nitrate solution to both the sample and standard solutions. Silver nitrate reacts with chloride ions to form a white precipitate of silver chloride (AgCl). The reaction is as follows:

5. **Development of Turbidity:**

   - Allow the reaction to proceed, and observe the development of turbidity due to the formation of silver chloride precipitate. The reaction is typically allowed to stand for a specified period to ensure complete precipitation.

6. **Comparison and Interpretation:**

   - Compare the turbidity of the sample solution with that of the standard solution. This comparison can be done visually or using an instrument, such as a nephelometer or spectrophotometer. If the turbidity of the sample solution is less than or equal to that of the standard solution, the chloride content is within the acceptable limit.

Example Calculation:

- Suppose the pharmacopoeial limit for chloride in a particular substance is 0.01%. Prepare a standard solution with a chloride concentration equivalent to 0.01%. If 1 gram of the substance is dissolved in 100 mL of water, the standard solution would contain 0.01 grams of chloride per 100 mL.

Factors Influencing the Limit Test for Chlorides:

1. **Reagent Quality:**

   - The purity and concentration of reagents, such as silver nitrate and nitric acid, can significantly influence the test results. High-purity reagents should be used to avoid introducing additional impurities.

2. **Environmental Conditions:**

- Conduct the test under controlled environmental conditions to minimize the effects of temperature, humidity, and light on the reaction. Consistent conditions help ensure reliable results.

3. **Sample Preparation:**

- Ensure that the sample is fully dissolved or dispersed in the solvent to obtain an accurate representation of the chloride content. Incomplete dissolution can lead to inaccurate results.

4. **Analyst Proficiency:**

- The skill and experience of the analyst conducting the test can impact the accuracy of the results. Proper training and adherence to standard operating procedures (SOPs) are essential for obtaining reliable results.

Applications of the Limit Test for Chlorides:

1. **Quality Control of Raw Materials:**

- The test is used to monitor the chloride content in raw materials, such as active pharmaceutical ingredients (APIs) and excipients, to ensure they meet quality specifications.

2. **Quality Control of Finished Products:**

- The test is applied to finished pharmaceutical products to verify that the chloride content is within the specified limits, ensuring the product's safety and efficacy.

3. **Regulatory Compliance:**

- The test helps pharmaceutical manufacturers comply with regulatory requirements for chloride content in their products, facilitating product approval and marketability.

Limit Test for Sulphates

The limit test for sulphates is a qualitative or semi-quantitative test used to detect and quantify sulfate ions in pharmaceutical substances and products. Sulphates can be common impurities resulting from raw materials, manufacturing processes, or environmental contamination. Ensuring that the sulfate levels do not exceed acceptable limits is crucial for maintaining the safety and quality of pharmaceutical products.

Purpose of the Limit Test for Sulphates:

1. **Ensure Safety:**

   - Excessive sulphates can cause adverse reactions or interfere with the therapeutic efficacy of pharmaceutical products. The limit test helps ensure that sulfate levels remain within safe limits.

2. **Maintain Quality:**

   - High levels of sulphates can impact the stability and overall quality of pharmaceutical products. The limit test helps maintain product quality by controlling sulfate impurities.

3. **Regulatory Compliance:**

   - Compliance with regulatory standards for sulfate content is essential for the approval and marketing of pharmaceutical products. The limit test ensures adherence to these standards.

Procedure for Conducting the Limit Test for Sulphates:

1. **Preparation of Sample Solution:**

   - Dissolve or dilute a specified amount of the pharmaceutical substance in a suitable solvent, typically distilled water, to prepare the sample solution.

2. **Preparation of Standard Solution:**

- Prepare a standard solution containing a known concentration of sulfate ions. This solution is used as a reference to compare with the sample solution during the test. The concentration of the standard solution is typically chosen to match the sulfate limit specified in the pharmacopoeia.

3. **Addition of Reagents:**

- Add a few drops of dilute hydrochloric acid to both the sample and standard solutions. The hydrochloric acid helps to maintain the pH of the solution and ensure complete precipitation of sulphates.

4. **Addition of Barium Chloride Solution:**

- Add a specific volume of barium chloride solution to both the sample and standard solutions. Barium chloride reacts with sulfate ions to form a white precipitate of barium sulfate (BaSO4). The reaction is as follows:
- $SO4^{2-} + BaCl_2 \rightarrow BaSO4{\downarrow} + 2Cl^{-}$

  - **Development of Turbidity:**

    - Allow the reaction to proceed, and observe the development of turbidity due to the formation of barium sulfate precipitate. The reaction is typically allowed to stand for a specified period to ensure complete precipitation.

5. **Comparison and Interpretation:**

- Compare the turbidity of the sample solution with that of the standard solution. This comparison can be done visually or using an instrument, such as a nephelometer or spectrophotometer. If the turbidity of the sample solution is less than or equal to that of the standard solution, the sulfate content is within the acceptable limit.

Example Calculation:

- Suppose the pharmacopoeial limit for sulfate in a particular substance is 0.02%. Prepare a standard solution with a sulfate concentration equivalent to 0.02%. If 1 gram of the substance is dissolved in 100 mL of water, the standard solution would contain 0.02 grams of sulfate per 100 mL.

Factors Influencing the Limit Test for Sulphates:

1. **Reagent Quality:**

   - The purity and concentration of reagents, such as barium chloride and hydrochloric acid, can significantly influence the test results. High-purity reagents should be used to avoid introducing additional impurities.

2. **Environmental Conditions:**

   - Conduct the test under controlled environmental conditions to minimize the effects of temperature, humidity, and light on the reaction. Consistent conditions help ensure reliable results.

3. **Sample Preparation:**

   - Ensure that the sample is fully dissolved or dispersed in the solvent to obtain an accurate representation of the sulfate content. Incomplete dissolution can lead to inaccurate results.

4. **Analyst Proficiency:**

   - The skill and experience of the analyst conducting the test can impact the accuracy of the results. Proper training and adherence to standard operating procedures (SOPs) are essential for obtaining reliable results.

Applications of the Limit Test for Sulphates:

1. **Quality Control of Raw Materials:**

- The test is used to monitor the sulfate content in raw materials, such as active pharmaceutical ingredients (APIs) and excipients, to ensure they meet quality specifications.

2. **Quality Control of Finished Products:**

- The test is applied to finished pharmaceutical products to verify that the sulfate content is within the specified limits, ensuring the product's safety and efficacy.

3. **Regulatory Compliance:**

- The test helps pharmaceutical manufacturers comply with regulatory requirements for sulfate content in their products, facilitating product approval and marketability.

Limit Test for Iron

The limit test for iron is a qualitative or semi-quantitative test used to detect and quantify iron impurities in pharmaceutical substances and products. Iron, as an impurity, can originate from raw materials, manufacturing processes, or environmental contamination. Controlling iron levels is crucial for ensuring the safety, quality, and efficacy of pharmaceutical products.

Purpose of the Limit Test for Iron:

1. **Ensure Safety:**

- Excessive iron can cause adverse reactions and may interfere with the therapeutic efficacy of pharmaceutical products. The limit test ensures that iron levels remain within safe limits.

2. **Maintain Quality:**

- High levels of iron can affect the stability and overall quality of pharmaceutical products. The limit test helps maintain product quality by controlling iron impurities.

3. **Regulatory Compliance:**

- Compliance with regulatory standards for iron content is essential for the approval and marketing of pharmaceutical products. The limit test ensures adherence to these standards.

Procedure for Conducting the Limit Test for Iron:

1. **Preparation of Sample Solution:**

- Dissolve or dilute a specified amount of the pharmaceutical substance in a suitable solvent, typically distilled water, to prepare the sample solution.

2. **Preparation of Standard Solution:**

- Prepare a standard solution containing a known concentration of iron ions. This solution is used as a reference to compare with the sample solution during the test. The concentration of the standard solution is typically chosen to match the iron limit specified in the pharmacopoeia.

3. **Addition of Reagents:**

- Add a few drops of hydrochloric acid to both the sample and standard solutions to acidify them. The acidification helps to release iron ions into the solution.

4. **Addition of Thioglycolic Acid or Ammonium Thiocyanate:**

- Add a specific volume of thioglycolic acid or ammonium thiocyanate solution to both the sample and standard solutions. These reagents react with iron ions to form a colored complex. Thioglycolic acid forms a purple complex with iron, while ammonium thiocyanate forms a red complex.

5. **Development of Color:**

- Allow the reaction to proceed, and observe the development of color due to the formation of the iron complex. The reaction is typically allowed to stand for a specified period to ensure complete color development.

6. **Comparison and Interpretation:**

- Compare the color intensity of the sample solution with that of the standard solution. This comparison can be done visually or using an instrument, such as a spectrophotometer. If the color intensity of the sample solution is less than or equal to that of the standard solution, the iron content is within the acceptable limit.

Example Calculation:

- Suppose the pharmacopoeial limit for iron in a particular substance is 10 ppm. Prepare a standard solution with an iron concentration equivalent to 10 ppm. If 1 gram of the substance is dissolved in 100 mL of water, the standard solution would contain 10 mg of iron per 100 mL.

Factors Influencing the Limit Test for Iron:

1. **Reagent Quality:**

- The purity and concentration of reagents, such as hydrochloric acid and thioglycolic acid or ammonium thiocyanate, can significantly influence the test results. High-purity reagents should be used to avoid introducing additional impurities.

2. **Environmental Conditions:**

- Conduct the test under controlled environmental conditions to minimize the effects of temperature, humidity, and light on the reaction. Consistent conditions help ensure reliable results.

3. **Sample Preparation:**

- Ensure that the sample is fully dissolved or dispersed in the solvent to obtain an accurate representation of the iron content. Incomplete dissolution can lead to inaccurate results.

4. **Analyst Proficiency:**

- The skill and experience of the analyst conducting the test can impact the accuracy of the results. Proper training and adherence to standard operating procedures (SOPs) are essential for obtaining reliable results.

Applications of the Limit Test for Iron:

1. **Quality Control of Raw Materials:**

- The test is used to monitor the iron content in raw materials, such as active pharmaceutical ingredients (APIs) and excipients, to ensure they meet quality specifications.

2. **Quality Control of Finished Products:**

- The test is applied to finished pharmaceutical products to verify that the iron content is within the specified limits, ensuring the product's safety and efficacy.

3. **Regulatory Compliance:**

- The test helps pharmaceutical manufacturers comply with regulatory requirements for iron content in their products, facilitating product approval and marketability.

Limit Test for Lead

The limit test for lead is a crucial analytical procedure used to detect and quantify lead impurities in pharmaceutical substances and products. Lead is a toxic heavy metal that can cause severe health issues if present in high concentrations. Ensuring that lead levels do not exceed acceptable limits is essential for maintaining the safety and quality of pharmaceutical products. **Purpose of the Limit Test for Lead:**

1. **Ensure Safety:**

   - Lead is highly toxic and can cause various health problems, including neurological damage, especially in children. The limit test ensures that lead levels remain within safe limits to protect patients.

2. **Maintain Quality:**

   - High levels of lead can compromise the quality of pharmaceutical products. The limit test helps maintain product quality by controlling lead impurities.

3. **Regulatory Compliance:**

   - Compliance with regulatory standards for lead content is essential for the approval and marketing of pharmaceutical products. The limit test ensures adherence to these standards.

Procedure for Conducting the Limit Test for Lead:

1. **Preparation of Sample Solution:**

   - Dissolve or dilute a specified amount of the pharmaceutical substance in a suitable solvent, typically distilled water, to prepare the sample solution. Ensure the solution is clear and free from particulate matter.

2. **Preparation of Standard Solution:**

   - Prepare a standard solution containing a known concentration of lead ions. This solution is used as a reference to compare with the sample solution during the test. The concentration of the standard solution is typically chosen to match the lead limit specified in the pharmacopoeia.

3. **Addition of Reagents:**

○ Add a few drops of nitric acid to both the sample and standard solutions to acidify them. Acidification helps to release lead ions into the solution and prevents interference from other metal ions.

4. **Addition of Ammonium Citrate and Potassium Cyanide:**

○ Add ammonium citrate solution to both solutions to complex with interfering metal ions, and then add potassium cyanide solution. These reagents help in selectively precipitating lead ions by forming a lead complex.

5. **Addition of Sodium Sulfide Solution:**

○ Add sodium sulfide solution to both the sample and standard solutions. Lead ions react with sodium sulfide to form a brownish-black precipitate of lead sulfide (PbS). The reaction is as follows:

- $Pb^{2+} + Na_2S \rightarrow PbS\downarrow + 2Na^{+}$

6. **Development of Color:**

○ Allow the reaction to proceed, and observe the development of color due to the formation of the lead sulfide precipitate. The reaction is typically allowed to stand for a specified period to ensure complete precipitation.

7. **Comparison and Interpretation:**

○ Compare the color intensity or turbidity of the sample solution with that of the standard solution. This comparison can be done visually or using an instrument, such as a spectrophotometer. If the color intensity or turbidity of the sample solution is less than or equal to that of the standard solution, the lead content is within the acceptable limit.

Example Calculation:

- Suppose the pharmacopoeial limit for lead in a particular substance is 10 ppm. Prepare a standard solution with a lead concentration equivalent to 10 ppm. If 1 gram of the substance is dissolved in 100 mL of water, the standard solution would contain 10 mg of lead per 100 mL.

Factors Influencing the Limit Test for Lead:

1. **Reagent Quality:**

   - The purity and concentration of reagents, such as nitric acid, ammonium citrate, potassium cyanide, and sodium sulfide, can significantly influence the test results. High-purity reagents should be used to avoid introducing additional impurities.

2. **Environmental Conditions:**

   - Conduct the test under controlled environmental conditions to minimize the effects of temperature, humidity, and light on the reaction. Consistent conditions help ensure reliable results.

3. **Sample Preparation:**

   - Ensure that the sample is fully dissolved or dispersed in the solvent to obtain an accurate representation of the lead content. Incomplete dissolution can lead to inaccurate results.

4. **Analyst Proficiency:**

   - The skill and experience of the analyst conducting the test can impact the accuracy of the results. Proper training and adherence to standard operating procedures (SOPs) are essential for obtaining reliable results.

Applications of the Limit Test for Lead:

1. **Quality Control of Raw Materials:**

- The test is used to monitor the lead content in raw materials, such as active pharmaceutical ingredients (APIs) and excipients, to ensure they meet quality specifications.

2. **Quality Control of Finished Products:**

- The test is applied to finished pharmaceutical products to verify that the lead content is within the specified limits, ensuring the product's safety and efficacy.

3. **Regulatory Compliance:**

- The test helps pharmaceutical manufacturers comply with regulatory requirements for lead content in their products, facilitating product approval and marketability.

The limit test for lead is a critical analytical procedure in pharmaceutical analysis, ensuring that lead impurities are within acceptable limits. By following standardized procedures and controlling influencing factors, pharmaceutical manufacturers can maintain the safety, quality, and compliance of their products. Proper implementation of the limit test for lead, along with rigorous quality control measures, is essential for the successful production of safe and effective pharmaceutical products.

8.3.5 Limit Test for Heavy Metals

The limit test for heavy metals is an essential analytical procedure used to detect and quantify heavy metal impurities in pharmaceutical substances and products. Heavy metals, such as lead, mercury, cadmium, and arsenic, are toxic and can pose serious health risks if present in significant amounts. Ensuring that heavy metal levels do not exceed acceptable limits is crucial for maintaining the safety and quality of pharmaceutical products.

Purpose of the Limit Test for Heavy Metals:

1. **Ensure Safety:**

- Heavy metals are highly toxic and can cause various health problems, including neurological damage, kidney failure, and cancer. The limit test ensures that heavy metal levels remain within safe limits to protect patients.

2. **Maintain Quality:**

   - High levels of heavy metals can compromise the quality and efficacy of pharmaceutical products. The limit test helps maintain product quality by controlling heavy metal impurities.

3. **Regulatory Compliance:**

   - Compliance with regulatory standards for heavy metal content is essential for the approval and marketing of pharmaceutical products. The limit test ensures adherence to these standards.

Procedure for Conducting the Limit Test for Heavy Metals:

1. **Preparation of Sample Solution:**

   - Dissolve or dilute a specified amount of the pharmaceutical substance in a suitable solvent, typically distilled water, to prepare the sample solution. Ensure the solution is clear and free from particulate matter.

2. **Preparation of Standard Solution:**

   - Prepare a standard solution containing a known concentration of heavy metals. This solution is used as a reference to compare with the sample solution during the test. The concentration of the standard solution is typically chosen to match the heavy metal limit specified in the pharmacopoeia.

3. **Addition of Reagents:**

   - Add a few drops of nitric acid to both the sample and standard solutions to acidify them. Acidification helps to release heavy metal ions into the solution and prevents interference from other metal ions.

4. **Addition of Thioacetamide or Hydrogen Sulfide:**

   - Add thioacetamide solution or pass hydrogen sulfide gas through both the sample and standard solutions. These reagents react with heavy metal ions to form colored or turbid sulfide complexes. The specific reaction depends on the heavy metal present.

5. **Development of Color or Turbidity:**

   - Allow the reaction to proceed, and observe the development of color or turbidity due to the formation of the heavy metal sulfide complexes. The reaction is typically allowed to stand for a specified period to ensure complete precipitation.

6. **Comparison and Interpretation:**

   - Compare the color intensity or turbidity of the sample solution with that of the standard solution. This comparison can be done visually or using an instrument, such as a spectrophotometer. If the color intensity or turbidity of the sample solution is less than or equal to that of the standard solution, the heavy metal content is within the acceptable limit.

Example Calculation:

- Suppose the pharmacopoeial limit for heavy metals in a particular substance is 20 ppm. Prepare a standard solution with a heavy metal concentration equivalent to 20 ppm. If 1 gram of the substance is dissolved in 100 mL of water, the standard solution would contain 20 mg of heavy metals per 100 mL.

Factors Influencing the Limit Test for Heavy Metals:

1. **Reagent Quality:**

   - The purity and concentration of reagents, such as nitric acid and thioacetamide or hydrogen sulfide, can significantly influence the test results. High-purity reagents should be used to avoid introducing additional impurities.

2. **Environmental Conditions:**

   - Conduct the test under controlled environmental conditions to minimize the effects of temperature, humidity, and light on the reaction. Consistent conditions help ensure reliable results.

3. **Sample Preparation:**

   - Ensure that the sample is fully dissolved or dispersed in the solvent to obtain an accurate representation of the heavy metal content. Incomplete dissolution can lead to inaccurate results.

4. **Analyst Proficiency:**

   - The skill and experience of the analyst conducting the test can impact the accuracy of the results. Proper training and adherence to standard operating procedures (SOPs) are essential for obtaining reliable results.

Applications of the Limit Test for Heavy Metals:

1. **Quality Control of Raw Materials:**

   - The test is used to monitor the heavy metal content in raw materials, such as active pharmaceutical ingredients (APIs) and excipients, to ensure they meet quality specifications.

2. **Quality Control of Finished Products:**

   - The test is applied to finished pharmaceutical products to verify that the heavy metal content is within the specified limits, ensuring the product's safety and efficacy.

3. **Regulatory Compliance:**

- The test helps pharmaceutical manufacturers comply with regulatory requirements for heavy metal content in their products, facilitating product approval and marketability.

The limit test for heavy metals is a critical analytical procedure in pharmaceutical analysis, ensuring that heavy metal impurities are within acceptable limits. By following standardized procedures and controlling influencing factors, pharmaceutical manufacturers can maintain the safety, quality, and compliance of their products. Proper implementation of the limit test for heavy metals, along with rigorous quality control measures, is essential for the successful production of safe and effective pharmaceutical products.

Limit Test for Arsenic

The limit test for arsenic is a crucial analytical procedure used to detect and quantify arsenic impurities in pharmaceutical substances and products. Arsenic is a toxic element that can pose severe health risks even at low concentrations. Ensuring that arsenic levels do not exceed acceptable limits is essential for maintaining the safety and quality of pharmaceutical products.

Purpose of the Limit Test for Arsenic:

1. **Ensure Safety:**

   - Arsenic is highly toxic and can cause various health problems, including skin lesions, cancer, cardiovascular disease, and neurological effects. The limit test ensures that arsenic levels remain within safe limits to protect patients.

2. **Maintain Quality:**

   - High levels of arsenic can compromise the quality and efficacy of pharmaceutical products. The limit test helps maintain product quality by controlling arsenic impurities.

3. **Regulatory Compliance:**

- Compliance with regulatory standards for arsenic content is essential for the approval and marketing of pharmaceutical products. The limit test ensures adherence to these standards.

Procedure for Conducting the Limit Test for Arsenic:

1. **Preparation of Sample Solution:**

   - Dissolve or dilute a specified amount of the pharmaceutical substance in a suitable solvent, typically distilled water, to prepare the sample solution. Ensure the solution is clear and free from particulate matter.

2. **Preparation of Standard Solution:**

   - Prepare a standard solution containing a known concentration of arsenic ions. This solution is used as a reference to compare with the sample solution during the test. The concentration of the standard solution is typically chosen to match the arsenic limit specified in the pharmacopoeia.

3. **Addition of Reagents:**

   - Add a few drops of hydrochloric acid to both the sample and standard solutions to acidify them. Acidification helps to release arsenic ions into the solution and prevents interference from other metal ions.

4. **Reduction of Arsenic:**

   - Add a reducing agent, such as stannous chloride, to both the sample and standard solutions. This reagent reduces arsenic to its trivalent state (arsenic(III)), which is more reactive with the detecting reagents.

5. **Generation of Arsine Gas:**

   - Pass hydrogen sulfide gas or add zinc granules and hydrochloric acid to the solutions to generate arsine gas (AsH3). Arsine gas is formed by the reaction of arsenic(III) with hydrogen. The reaction is as follows:
   - $As^{3+} + 3H_2 \rightarrow AsH_3$

6. **Absorption of Arsine Gas:**

   - Collect the arsine gas in a suitable absorbing solution containing silver diethyldithiocarbamate (Ag-DDTC) or mercuric chloride (HgCl2). These reagents react with arsine to form a colored complex.

7. **Development of Color:**

   - Allow the reaction to proceed, and observe the development of color due to the formation of the arsenic complex. The reaction is typically allowed to stand for a specified period to ensure complete color development.

8. **Comparison and Interpretation:**

   - Compare the color intensity of the sample solution with that of the standard solution. This comparison can be done visually or using an instrument, such as a spectrophotometer. If the color intensity of the sample solution is less than or equal to that of the standard solution, the arsenic content is within the acceptable limit.

Example Calculation:

- Suppose the pharmacopoeial limit for arsenic in a particular substance is 1 ppm. Prepare a standard solution with an arsenic concentration equivalent to 1 ppm. If 1 gram of the substance is dissolved in 100 mL of water, the standard solution would contain 1 mg of arsenic per 100 mL.

Factors Influencing the Limit Test for Arsenic:

1. **Reagent Quality:**

   - The purity and concentration of reagents, such as hydrochloric acid, stannous chloride, and silver diethyldithiocarbamate or mercuric chloride, can significantly influence the test results. High-purity reagents should be used to avoid introducing additional impurities.

2. **Environmental Conditions:**

- Conduct the test under controlled environmental conditions to minimize the effects of temperature, humidity, and light on the reaction. Consistent conditions help ensure reliable results.

3. **Sample Preparation:**

- Ensure that the sample is fully dissolved or dispersed in the solvent to obtain an accurate representation of the arsenic content. Incomplete dissolution can lead to inaccurate results.

4. **Analyst Proficiency:**

- The skill and experience of the analyst conducting the test can impact the accuracy of the results. Proper training and adherence to standard operating procedures (SOPs) are essential for obtaining reliable results.

Applications of the Limit Test for Arsenic:

1. **Quality Control of Raw Materials:**

- The test is used to monitor the arsenic content in raw materials, such as active pharmaceutical ingredients (APIs) and excipients, to ensure they meet quality specifications.

2. **Quality Control of Finished Products:**

- The test is applied to finished pharmaceutical products to verify that the arsenic content is within the specified limits, ensuring the product's safety and efficacy.

3. **Regulatory Compliance:**

- The test helps pharmaceutical manufacturers comply with regulatory requirements for arsenic content in their products, facilitating product approval and marketability.

The limit test for arsenic is a critical analytical procedure in pharmaceutical analysis, ensuring that arsenic impurities are within acceptable limits. By following standardized procedures and controlling influencing factors, pharmaceutical manufacturers can maintain the safety, quality, and compliance of their products. Proper implementation of the limit test for arsenic, along with rigorous quality control measures, is essential for the successful production of safe and effective pharmaceutical products.

FIVE

ACID-BASE TITRATION

Acid-base titration is a fundamental and versatile analytical technique employed to determine the concentration of an acid or a base in a given solution. This method is integral to various scientific disciplines, including **chemistry, biology, environmental science, and pharmaceutical analysis**. The process involves the gradual addition of a titrant, a solution of known concentration, to a sample solution until the chemical reaction between the acid and base reaches its endpoint. The endpoint is typically indicated by a noticeable change, such as a color shift in an indicator or a specific pH value measured using a pH meter.

Understanding the **theories of acid-base indicators** is crucial for accurate titration. These indicators are substances that change color at a specific pH level, providing a visual cue that the titration has reached its endpoint. The mechanism by which these indicators operate involves a structural change in the indicator molecules in response to the pH of the solution. Selecting the correct indicator is essential, as it must change color at the pH corresponding to the equivalence point of the titration. This selection ensures that the endpoint is accurately identified, allowing for precise calculations of the unknown concentration.

The classification of acid-base titrations is based on the strength of the acids and bases involved. **Strong acids and bases** completely dissociate in water, resulting in a sharp change in pH at the equivalence point. This makes the titration straightforward and the endpoint easily identifiable. In contrast, **weak acids and bases** only partially dissociate, leading to a more gradual pH change and requiring careful selection of indicators and more precise measurements. Understanding these differences is crucial for conducting accurate titrations and interpreting the results correctly.

Another important aspect of acid-base titration is the use of **neutralization curves**. These curves plot the pH of the solution as a function of the volume of titrant added, providing a visual representation of the titration process. Analyzing these curves helps in understanding the titration's progress and in identifying the equivalence point. This analysis is essential for accurately determining the concentration of the analyte.

Non-aqueous titration is a specialized form of acid-base titration used when the substances being analyzed are insoluble or unstable in water. This method employs non-aqueous solvents to dissolve the sample, allowing for the titration of compounds that would otherwise be challenging to analyze. Non-aqueous titrations are particularly important in pharmaceutical analysis, where many active pharmaceutical ingredients are either insoluble in water or require a different solvent for stability reasons. The principles and solvents used in non-aqueous titrations are carefully chosen to ensure accurate and reliable results.

5.1 THEORIES OF ACID-BASE INDICATORS

5.1.2 SELECTION CRITERIA FOR INDICATORS

Selecting the appropriate acid-base indicator for a titration or pH determination is crucial for obtaining accurate and reliable results. The selection is based on several factors, which include the pH range of the indicator, the type of titration, and the specific requirements of the analytical procedure. Here are the key criteria for selecting acid-base indicators:

1. pH Range of the Indicator:

- **Transition Range:** The indicator's transition range should match the pH range over which the titration's endpoint occurs. For a sharp and clear endpoint, the indicator's pH transition range should fall within the steep part of the titration curve.
- **Indicator pKa:** Select an indicator whose pKa is close to the pH of the expected endpoint. This ensures that the color change occurs near the equivalence point.

2. Type of Titration:

- **Strong Acid vs. Strong Base:** Indicators with a wide pH range are suitable for titrations involving strong acids and strong bases, as these titrations have a significant pH change at the equivalence point. Examples include phenolphthalein and bromothymol blue.

- **Weak Acid vs. Strong Base:** For titrations involving a weak acid and a strong base, choose an indicator that changes color at a higher pH. Phenolphthalein is often used because its transition range is appropriate for the higher pH at the equivalence point.
- **Strong Acid vs. Weak Base:** For titrations involving a strong acid and a weak base, select an indicator that changes color at a lower pH. Methyl orange is suitable because its transition range covers the lower pH of the equivalence point.
- **Weak Acid vs. Weak Base:** These titrations have very subtle pH changes at the equivalence point, making it challenging to choose an appropriate indicator. Often, potentiometric methods are preferred over indicators in such cases.

3. Desired Sensitivity and Precision:

- **Color Change Intensity:** The intensity and visibility of the color change should be distinct and easy to observe. Indicators that provide a sharp and clear color change at the endpoint are preferred for precise titrations.
- **Sensitivity to pH Changes:** The indicator should be sensitive to small pH changes near the equivalence point, ensuring an accurate determination of the endpoint.

4. Chemical Compatibility:

- **Reaction with Analytes:** Ensure that the indicator does not react with the analytes or other components in the solution, which could interfere with the titration results. The indicator should be inert in the context of the specific chemical reaction being monitored.
- **Solubility:** The indicator should be soluble in the titration medium. Incompatibility with the solvent can lead to incomplete color change and inaccurate results.

5. Environmental and Safety Considerations:

- **Toxicity:** Select indicators that are safe and non-toxic, especially when used in educational laboratories or when handling large volumes. Avoid indicators that pose significant health hazards.

- **Stability:** The indicator should be chemically stable under the conditions of the titration. Indicators that degrade or change color over time should be avoided.

Examples of Common Indicators and Their Uses:

1. **Phenolphthalein:**

   - **pH Range:** 8.3 to 10.0
   - **Color Change:** Colorless to pink
   - **Applications:** Suitable for titrations of strong acids with strong bases, and weak acids with strong bases.

2. **Methyl Orange:**

   - **pH Range:** 3.1 to 4.4
   - **Color Change:** Red to yellow
   - **Applications:** Ideal for titrations of strong acids with weak bases.

3. **Bromothymol Blue:**

   - **pH Range:** 6.0 to 7.6
   - **Color Change:** Yellow to blue
   - **Applications:** Suitable for titrations involving strong acids and strong bases, and for measuring near-neutral pH.

4. **Litmus:**

   - **pH Range:** 4.5 to 8.3
   - **Color Change:** Red to blue
   - **Applications:** General purpose indicator for a wide range of titrations, though less precise than other indicators.

The selection of an appropriate acid-base indicator is a critical step in ensuring the accuracy and reliability of titration results. By considering the pH range, type of titration, sensitivity, chemical compatibility, and safety of the indicator, analysts can achieve precise and accurate endpoint determination. Properly chosen indicators enhance the effectiveness of acid-base titrations, making them indispensable tools in pharmaceutical analysis.

5.2 CLASSIFICATION OF ACID-BASE TITRATIONS

Acid-base titrations are analytical techniques used to determine the concentration of an acid or base in a solution by reacting it with a base or acid of known concentration. The classification of acid-base titrations is based on the strength of the acid and base involved. The different types of acid-base titrations include:

1. Strong Acid vs. Strong Base Titrations:

- **Example:** Hydrochloric acid (HCl) titrated with sodium hydroxide (NaOH)
- **Characteristics:**

  - The titration curve exhibits a sharp and large pH change at the equivalence point.
  - The equivalence point typically occurs at a pH of 7.
  - Suitable indicators: Phenolphthalein, bromothymol blue.

2. Weak Acid vs. Strong Base Titrations:

- **Example:** Acetic acid (CH3COOH) titrated with sodium hydroxide (NaOH)
- **Characteristics:**

  - The pH change at the equivalence point is less pronounced compared to strong acid-strong base titrations.
  - The equivalence point occurs at a pH greater than 7 due to the formation of a weak conjugate base.
  - Suitable indicators: Phenolphthalein.

3. Strong Acid vs. Weak Base Titrations:

- **Example:** Hydrochloric acid (HCl) titrated with ammonia (NH3)
- **Characteristics:**

- ○ The pH change at the equivalence point is less pronounced compared to strong acid-strong base titrations.
- ○ The equivalence point occurs at a pH less than 7 due to the formation of a weak conjugate acid.
- ○ Suitable indicators: Methyl orange.

4. Weak Acid vs. Weak Base Titrations:

- **Example:** Acetic acid (CH_3COOH) titrated with ammonia (NH_3)
- **Characteristics:**

- ○ The pH change at the equivalence point is very gradual and not distinct.
- ○ The equivalence point pH depends on the relative strengths of the weak acid and weak base.
- ○ Suitable indicators: Potentiometric methods are often preferred due to the subtle pH change.

5. Polyprotic Acid Titrations:

- **Example:** Sulfuric acid (H_2SO_4) titrated with sodium hydroxide ($NaOH$)
- **Characteristics:**

- ○ Polyprotic acids can donate more than one proton, leading to multiple equivalence points.
- ○ Each equivalence point corresponds to the complete neutralization of one of the protons.
- ○ Suitable indicators: Different indicators for each equivalence point, or potentiometric methods.

Titration Curves and Equivalence Points:

1. **Titration Curve for Strong Acid vs. Strong Base:**

- ○ The curve shows a sharp, almost vertical rise in pH near the equivalence point, typically around pH 7.

2. **Titration Curve for Weak Acid vs. Strong Base:**

◦ The curve shows a gradual increase in pH, with a less pronounced inflection at the equivalence point, which is above pH 7.

3. **Titration Curve for Strong Acid vs. Weak Base:**

◦ The curve shows a gradual decrease in pH, with the equivalence point below pH 7.

4. **Titration Curve for Weak Acid vs. Weak Base:**

◦ The curve shows a very gradual change in pH, with no sharp inflection, making it difficult to determine the equivalence point visually.

Applications of Acid-Base Titrations:

1. **Pharmaceutical Analysis:**

◦ Determination of the concentration of active pharmaceutical ingredients (APIs) in formulations.
◦ Quality control of raw materials and finished products.

2. **Environmental Analysis:**

◦ Measurement of acidity or alkalinity of water and soil samples.

3. **Food Industry:**

◦ Analysis of acid content in food products, such as vinegar and fruit juices.

4. **Clinical Chemistry:**

◦ Determination of blood gas levels and urine pH in medical diagnostics.

5.2.1 STRONG ACIDS AND BASES

Definition: Strong acids and bases are substances that completely dissociate into their ions in aqueous solutions. This complete dissociation means that strong acids release all their hydrogen ions (H+) and strong bases release all their hydroxide ions (OH⁻) when dissolved in water.

Examples:

- **Strong Acids:** Hydrochloric acid (HCl), sulfuric acid (H2SO4), nitric acid (HNO3).
- **Strong Bases:** Sodium hydroxide (NaOH), potassium hydroxide (KOH), calcium hydroxide (Ca(OH)2).

Titration of Strong Acids with Strong Bases:

- **Reaction:** A typical titration involves a strong acid reacting with a strong base to form water and a salt. For example:

  - HCl+NaOH→NaCl+H2O

- **Titration Curve:**

  - The titration curve for a strong acid and a strong base shows a very sharp and steep rise in pH near the equivalence point. The equivalence point occurs around pH 7.0, where the number of moles of H+ equals the number of moles of OH-.
  - Initially, the pH changes gradually, but as it approaches the equivalence point, the pH increases rapidly.

- **Indicators:**

  - **Phenolphthalein:** Changes from colorless to pink at a pH range of 8.3 to 10.0.
  - **Bromothymol Blue:** Changes from yellow to blue at a pH range of 6.0 to 7.6.

Titration of Strong Bases with Strong Acids:

- **Reaction:** Similar to the titration of strong acids with strong bases, but the strong base is titrated with a strong acid. For example:

- ◦ NaOH+HCl→NaCl+H2O

- **Titration Curve:**

  - ◦ The titration curve is essentially the mirror image of the acid-base titration curve, with a steep decline in pH near the equivalence point.

- **Indicators:**

  - ◦ Similar indicators are used, such as phenolphthalein and bromothymol blue, to identify the equivalence point.

Applications:

1. **Pharmaceutical Analysis:**

   - ◦ Determining the concentration of acidic or basic pharmaceutical compounds.
   - ◦ Quality control of antacid formulations.

2. **Industrial Applications:**

   - ◦ Monitoring and controlling the pH of industrial processes involving acids and bases.
   - ◦ Wastewater treatment to neutralize acidic or basic waste streams.

3. **Environmental Monitoring:**

   - ◦ Measuring the acidity or alkalinity of water bodies to assess pollution levels.
   - ◦ Soil testing to determine the pH for agricultural purposes.

Procedure:

1. **Preparation:**

   - ◦ Prepare the strong acid or base solution with a known concentration.
   - ◦ Fill a burette with the titrant (strong acid or strong base).

2. Indicator Addition:

- Add a few drops of the appropriate indicator (e.g., phenolphthalein) to the analyte solution.

3. Titration:

- Slowly add the titrant from the burette to the analyte solution while continuously stirring.
- Monitor the pH change or observe the color change of the indicator.

4. Equivalence Point Detection:

- The equivalence point is detected when the indicator shows a permanent color change or the pH meter indicates a sharp change in pH.

5. Calculation:

- Calculate the concentration of the unknown solution using the volume of titrant added and the stoichiometry of the reaction.

Example Calculation:

- If 25.0 mL of 0.1 M HCl is titrated with 0.1 M NaOH, the volume of NaOH required to reach the equivalence point can be calculated as follows:

  - Moles of HCl = Volume (L) × Molarity (M) = 0.025 L × 0.1 M = 0.0025 moles
  - Moles of NaOH required = 0.0025 moles (since 1 mole of HCl reacts with 1 mole of NaOH)
  - Volume of NaOH required = Moles / Molarity = 0.0025 moles / 0.1 M = 0.025 L = 25.0 mL

Titrations involving strong acids and strong bases are fundamental analytical techniques in chemistry, providing precise and reliable measurements of the concentration of acidic or basic solutions. The sharp and distinct pH change at the equivalence point, coupled with suitable indicators, makes these titrations highly accurate and widely applicable in various fields, including pharmaceuticals, industry, and environmental science.

5.2.3 NEUTRALIZATION CURVES AND END-POINT DETECTION

Neutralization Curves:

Neutralization curves, also known as titration curves, graphically represent the pH change of a solution as a titrant is added during an acid-base titration. These curves are crucial for understanding the behavior of acids and bases during titration and for accurately detecting the endpoint.

Components of a Neutralization Curve:

1. **Initial pH:**

   - The starting pH of the analyte solution before any titrant is added.

2. **Buffer Region:**

   - The region where the pH changes gradually due to the buffering action of the weak acid or base and its conjugate salt.

3. **Equivalence Point:**

   - The point at which the number of moles of acid equals the number of moles of base. For strong acid-strong base titrations, this typically occurs at pH 7.

4. **Post-Equivalence Region:**

   - The region beyond the equivalence point where the pH changes more slowly again.

Types of Neutralization Curves:

1. **Strong Acid with Strong Base:**

   - **Example:** Titration of HCl with NaOH.
   - **Characteristics:**

- The curve starts at a low pH (acidic).
- A sharp rise in pH occurs near the equivalence point.
- The equivalence point is at pH 7.
- After the equivalence point, the pH rises gradually.

2. **Weak Acid with Strong Base:**

   - **Example:** Titration of acetic acid (CH3COOH) with NaOH.
   - **Characteristics:**

     - The curve starts at a higher pH compared to strong acids.
     - A buffer region is observed where the pH changes slowly.
     - The equivalence point is above pH 7 due to the formation of a weak conjugate base.
     - After the equivalence point, the pH rises sharply.

3. **Strong Acid with Weak Base:**

   - **Example:** Titration of HCl with ammonia (NH3).
   - **Characteristics:**

     - The curve starts at a low pH.
     - A gradual pH increase is observed as the weak base is added.
     - The equivalence point is below pH 7 due to the formation of a weak conjugate acid.
     - After the equivalence point, the pH increases more slowly.

4. **Weak Acid with Weak Base:**

   - **Example:** Titration of acetic acid with ammonia.
   - **Characteristics:**

     - The curve shows a very gradual pH change.
     - No sharp inflection point, making endpoint detection difficult.
     - The equivalence point is influenced by the relative strengths of the weak acid and weak base.

End-Point Detection:

End-point detection is the process of identifying the point in a titration where the reaction between the titrant and analyte is complete. This point is crucial for accurate titration results and can be detected using various methods.

Methods of End-Point Detection:

1. **Visual Indicators:**

   - **Mechanism:** Indicators are substances that change color at specific pH levels. The color change signals the endpoint of the titration.
   - **Examples:**

     - **Phenolphthalein:** Colorless in acidic solutions and pink in basic solutions. Used in strong acid-strong base and weak acid-strong base titrations.
     - **Methyl Orange:** Red in acidic solutions and yellow in basic solutions. Suitable for strong acid-weak base titrations.

2. **pH Meter:**

   - **Mechanism:** A pH meter measures the pH of the solution continuously throughout the titration. The equivalence point is detected by the sharp change in pH on the titration curve.
   - **Advantages:** Provides precise and accurate measurements, useful for titrations with no clear visual endpoint.

3. **Conductometric Titration:**

   - **Mechanism:** Measures the conductivity of the solution. The conductivity changes as ions react and form water and neutral salts, showing a distinct change at the equivalence point.
   - **Advantages:** Useful for titrations involving ions that significantly change the conductivity of the solution.

4. **Potentiometric Titration:**

   - **Mechanism:** Uses an electrode that measures the potential difference (voltage) in the solution. The equivalence point is identified by a sudden change in the electrode potential.

- **Advantages:** Suitable for titrations where pH meters or visual indicators are not effective.

5. **Spectrophotometric Titration:**

- **Mechanism:** Monitors the absorbance of light by the solution at specific wavelengths. The equivalence point is determined by a change in absorbance corresponding to the reaction progress.
- **Advantages:** Effective for colored solutions or reactions producing colored products.

Factors Affecting Endpoint Detection:

1. **Indicator Selection:**

- Choosing the correct indicator based on the expected pH at the equivalence point ensures a clear and accurate endpoint.

2. **Solution Concentration:**

- Highly concentrated solutions can cause rapid pH changes, making precise detection more challenging. Dilute solutions provide a more gradual change, aiding accurate detection.

3. **Titration Speed:**

- Adding the titrant too quickly can overshoot the endpoint. A slower, controlled addition ensures better accuracy.

4. **Temperature:**

- Temperature variations can affect the dissociation of acids and bases and the performance of indicators. Conduct titrations at a consistent temperature for reliable results.

Applications:

1. **Pharmaceutical Quality Control:**

   - Determining the concentration of active ingredients and excipients.
   - Ensuring the correct pH range for stability and efficacy.

2. **Environmental Analysis:**

   - Measuring the acidity or alkalinity of water samples to assess pollution levels.

3. **Food and Beverage Industry:**

   - Determining the acid content in products like vinegar, wine, and dairy.

4. **Clinical Laboratories:**

   - Analyzing blood and urine samples for diagnostic purposes.

Understanding neutralization curves and endpoint detection methods is essential for accurate and effective acid-base titrations. By selecting the appropriate method and carefully controlling experimental conditions, reliable and precise titration results can be achieved. These techniques are widely used in various fields, including pharmaceuticals, environmental science, food industry, and clinical diagnostics, highlighting their importance in analytical chemistry.

5.3 NON-AQUEOUS TITRATION

5.3.1 PRINCIPLES AND SOLVENTS USED

Principles of Non-Aqueous Titration:

Non-aqueous titration is a technique used to titrate substances that are either insoluble or only sparingly soluble in water or when the reaction in an aqueous medium is not sufficiently sharp to detect the endpoint accurately. The principles of non-aqueous titration revolve around the use of non-aqueous solvents to achieve better solubility, stability, and sharper endpoints for certain analytes.

Key Principles:

1. **Solvent Choice:**

   ○ Non-aqueous solvents are chosen based on their ability to dissolve both the analyte and the titrant effectively. The solvent should not react with the titrant or the analyte.

2. **Acid-Base Reactions:**

   ○ Non-aqueous titrations typically involve acid-base reactions, similar to aqueous titrations. However, the use of non-aqueous solvents can alter the strength and behavior of acids and bases, often leading to sharper endpoints.

3. **Endpoint Detection:**

   ○ The endpoint in non-aqueous titrations can be detected using indicators, potentiometric methods, or other instrumental techniques. The choice of detection method depends on the nature of the titration and the properties of the solvent.

Advantages of Non-Aqueous Titration:

1. **Improved Solubility:**

   ○ Many organic compounds, including pharmaceuticals, are more soluble in non-aqueous solvents than in water, enabling more accurate titrations.

2. **Sharper Endpoints:**

   ○ Non-aqueous solvents can provide sharper and more distinct endpoints, improving the precision and accuracy of the titration.

3. **Broader Applicability:**

   ○ Non-aqueous titration is applicable to a wide range of substances, including weak acids and bases, which may not be effectively titrated in aqueous media.

Common Solvents Used in Non-Aqueous Titration:

1. **Glacial Acetic Acid:**

   - **Properties:** Weakly acidic solvent, miscible with many organic compounds.
   - **Applications:** Used for titrations involving weak bases. It stabilizes the anions formed during the titration, providing sharp endpoints.
   - **Example:** Titration of ephedrine HCl.

2. **Acetic Anhydride:**

   - **Properties:** Strong dehydrating agent, reacts with water to form acetic acid.
   - **Applications:** Used to remove water from the system, enhancing the titration of certain compounds.

3. **Methanol:**

   - **Properties:** Polar solvent, miscible with water and many organic solvents.
   - **Applications:** Used for titrations involving both weak and strong acids and bases.
   - **Example:** Titration of sodium benzoate.

4. **Ethanol:**

   - **Properties:** Polar solvent, miscible with water and many organic solvents.
   - **Applications:** Commonly used for titrations involving organic acids and bases.

5. **Toluene:**

   - **Properties:** Non-polar solvent, immiscible with water.
   - **Applications:** Used as a solvent for non-polar organic compounds and in Karl Fischer titration for water determination.

6. **Chloroform:**

   - **Properties:** Non-polar solvent, immiscible with water.
   - **Applications:** Used for titrations involving non-polar compounds, providing a distinct endpoint due to its different solvent properties.

Types of Non-Aqueous Titrations:

1. **Acidimetry in Non-Aqueous Solvents:**

   - **Principle:** Involves the titration of weak bases with strong acids in non-aqueous solvents.
   - **Example:** Titration of amines using perchloric acid in glacial acetic acid.

2. **Alkalimetry in Non-Aqueous Solvents:**

   - **Principle:** Involves the titration of weak acids with strong bases in non-aqueous solvents.
   - **Example:** Titration of organic acids using sodium methoxide in methanol.

Indicators for Non-Aqueous Titration:

1. **Crystal Violet:**

   - **Color Change:** Yellow to violet.
   - **Application:** Used in non-aqueous titrations of weak bases.

2. **Oracet Blue B:**

   - **Color Change:** Colorless to blue.
   - **Application:** Suitable for titrations in glacial acetic acid.

3. **Thymol Blue:**

   - **Color Change:** Yellow to blue.
   - **Application:** Used in titrations involving strong acids and bases.

Procedure for Non-Aqueous Titration:

1. **Preparation of the Sample:**

   - Dissolve the sample in an appropriate non-aqueous solvent. Ensure complete dissolution for accurate titration.

2. **Addition of Indicator:**

   - Add a few drops of a suitable indicator to the sample solution.

3. **Titration:**

   - Slowly add the titrant from a burette to the sample solution while continuously stirring. Observe the color change or monitor the pH/potential change.

4. **Endpoint Detection:**

   - Detect the endpoint by noting the color change or the point of inflection in the pH/potential curve.

5. **Calculation:**

   - Calculate the concentration of the analyte using the volume of titrant added and the stoichiometry of the reaction.

Example Calculation:

- If 25.0 mL of 0.1 M $HClO_4$ in glacial acetic acid is titrated with 0.1 M sodium methoxide in methanol, the volume of sodium methoxide required to reach the equivalence point can be calculated as follows:

  - Moles of $HClO_4$ = Volume (L) × Molarity (M) = 0.025 L × 0.1 M = 0.0025 moles
  - Moles of sodium methoxide required = 0.0025 moles (since 1 mole of $HClO_4$ reacts with 1 mole of sodium methoxide)

- Volume of sodium methoxide required = Moles / Molarity = 0.0025 moles / 0.1 M = 0.025 L = 25.0 mL

Non-aqueous titration is a versatile and valuable analytical technique for determining the concentration of substances that are insoluble or unstable in aqueous media. By carefully selecting the appropriate solvent and indicator, analysts can achieve accurate and reliable titration results. This technique is widely used in pharmaceutical analysis, quality control, and various industrial applications, highlighting its importance in analytical chemistry.

5.3.2 ACIDIMETRY AND ALKALIMETRY TITRATION

Non-aqueous titration involves the titration of substances in solvents other than water. This technique is particularly useful for substances that are insoluble, poorly soluble, or unstable in water. Non-aqueous titration can be divided into two main types: acidimetry and alkalimetry.

Acidimetry in Non-Aqueous Solvents:
Principles:

- Acidimetry involves the titration of weak bases with strong acids in non-aqueous solvents. The use of non-aqueous solvents can enhance the acid strength and provide a sharper endpoint.
- Non-aqueous solvents such as glacial acetic acid are commonly used because they stabilize the conjugate base formed during the titration, allowing for accurate endpoint detection.

Solvents and Reagents:

1. **Glacial Acetic Acid:**

   - A weakly acidic solvent that enhances the strength of the acid used in the titration.
   - Stabilizes the conjugate base, leading to a sharper endpoint.

2. **Perchloric Acid ($HClO_4$):**

   - A strong acid commonly used as a titrant in non-aqueous acidimetry.
   - Provides a clear and sharp endpoint when titrating weak bases.

Procedure:

1. **Preparation:**

   - Dissolve the sample containing the weak base in glacial acetic acid.

2. **Indicator Addition:**

   - Add a suitable indicator, such as crystal violet or thymol blue, to the solution.

3. **Titration:**

   - Titrate with a standard solution of perchloric acid in glacial acetic acid.

4. **Endpoint Detection:**

   - Observe the color change of the indicator or use potentiometric methods to detect the endpoint.

5. **Calculation:**

   - Calculate the concentration of the weak base using the volume of titrant added and the stoichiometry of the reaction.

Example:

- **Titration of Ephedrine HCl:**

  - Dissolve a known quantity of ephedrine HCl in glacial acetic acid.
  - Add crystal violet as an indicator.
  - Titrate with 0.1 M perchloric acid until the endpoint is reached (color change from yellow to violet).
  - Calculate the concentration of ephedrine HCl based on the volume of perchloric acid used.

Alkalimetry in Non-Aqueous Solvents:

Principles:

- Alkalimetry involves the titration of weak acids with strong bases in non-aqueous solvents. Non-aqueous solvents can enhance the base strength and provide a distinct endpoint.
- Solvents such as methanol and ethanol are commonly used because they dissolve both the weak acid and the strong base effectively.

Solvents and Reagents:

1. **Methanol:**

   - A polar solvent that enhances the strength of the base used in the titration.
   - Provides a suitable medium for dissolving organic acids.

2. **Sodium Methoxide (NaOCH3):**

   - A strong base commonly used as a titrant in non-aqueous alkalimetry.
   - Provides a clear and sharp endpoint when titrating weak acids.

Procedure:

1. **Preparation:**

   - Dissolve the sample containing the weak acid in methanol.

2. **Indicator Addition:**

   - Add a suitable indicator, such as thymol blue or bromothymol blue, to the solution.

3. **Titration:**

   - Titrate with a standard solution of sodium methoxide in methanol.

4. **Endpoint Detection:**

○ Observe the color change of the indicator or use potentiometric methods to detect the endpoint.

5. **Calculation:**

   ○ Calculate the concentration of the weak acid using the volume of titrant added and the stoichiometry of the reaction.

Example:

· **Titration of Benzoic Acid:**

   ○ Dissolve a known quantity of benzoic acid in methanol.
   ○ Add thymol blue as an indicator.
   ○ Titrate with 0.1 M sodium methoxide until the endpoint is reached (color change from yellow to blue).
   ○ Calculate the concentration of benzoic acid based on the volume of sodium methoxide used.

Applications:

1. **Pharmaceutical Analysis:**

   ○ Determining the concentration of weak acids and bases in pharmaceutical formulations.
   ○ Quality control of active pharmaceutical ingredients (APIs) and excipients.

2. **Industrial Applications:**

   ○ Analysis of organic acids and bases in chemical manufacturing.
   ○ Quality control in the production of polymers, dyes, and other industrial products.

3. **Research and Development:**

   ○ Investigating the acid-base properties of new chemical entities.

- ○ Characterizing the behavior of organic compounds in non-aqueous media.

5.3.3 ESTIMATION OF SODIUM BENZOATE

Principle: The estimation of sodium benzoate using non-aqueous titration involves titrating the weakly acidic benzoate ion with a strong base in a non-aqueous solvent. This method provides a clear endpoint due to the distinct pH change in non-aqueous media.

Solvent and Reagents:

- **Solvent:** Methanol is used as the solvent because it effectively dissolves sodium benzoate and supports the titration reaction.
- **Titrant:** Sodium methoxide ($NaOCH_3$) in methanol, a strong base, is used as the titrant.
- **Indicator:** Thymol blue, which changes color from yellow to blue, is used to detect the endpoint.

Procedure:

1. **Sample Preparation:**

   - ○ Weigh an accurately measured amount of sodium benzoate and dissolve it in methanol to prepare the sample solution.

2. **Indicator Addition:**

   - ○ Add a few drops of thymol blue indicator to the sample solution.

3. **Titration:**

   - ○ Fill a burette with the sodium methoxide solution.
   - ○ Titrate the sample solution with sodium methoxide, adding the titrant slowly while continuously stirring.
   - ○ Observe the color change of the indicator. The endpoint is reached when the solution changes from yellow to blue.

4. **Calculation:**

- ○ Calculate the concentration of sodium benzoate using the volume of sodium methoxide added and the stoichiometry of the reaction.

Example Calculation:

- Suppose 0.5 grams of sodium benzoate is dissolved in methanol and titrated with 0.1 M sodium methoxide. If 25.0 mL of sodium methoxide is required to reach the endpoint:

  - ○ Moles of NaOCH3 = Volume (L) × Molarity (M) = 0.025 L × 0.1 M = 0.0025 moles
  - ○ Moles of sodium benzoate = Moles of NaOCH3 (1:1 stoichiometry) = 0.0025 moles
  - ○ Molecular weight of sodium benzoate = 144.11 g/mol
  - ○ Weight of sodium benzoate = Moles × Molecular weight = 0.0025 moles × 144.11 g/mol = 0.3603 grams

5.3.4 ESTIMATION OF EPHEDRINE HCL

Principle: The estimation of ephedrine HCl using non-aqueous titration involves titrating the weakly basic ephedrine ion with a strong acid in a non-aqueous solvent. This method provides a sharp endpoint due to the distinct pH change in non-aqueous media.

Solvent and Reagents:

- **Solvent:** Glacial acetic acid is used as the solvent because it effectively dissolves ephedrine HCl and supports the titration reaction.
- **Titrant:** Perchloric acid (HClO4) in glacial acetic acid, a strong acid, is used as the titrant.
- **Indicator:** Crystal violet, which changes color from yellow to violet, is used to detect the endpoint.

Procedure:

1. **Sample Preparation:**

   - ○ Weigh an accurately measured amount of ephedrine HCl and dissolve it in glacial acetic acid to prepare the sample solution.

2. **Indicator Addition:**

   ○ Add a few drops of crystal violet indicator to the sample solution.

3. **Titration:**

   ○ Fill a burette with the perchloric acid solution.
   ○ Titrate the sample solution with perchloric acid, adding the titrant slowly while continuously stirring.
   ○ Observe the color change of the indicator. The endpoint is reached when the solution changes from yellow to violet.

4. **Calculation:**

   ○ Calculate the concentration of ephedrine HCl using the volume of perchloric acid added and the stoichiometry of the reaction.

Example Calculation:

- Suppose 0.2 grams of ephedrine HCl is dissolved in glacial acetic acid and titrated with 0.1 M perchloric acid. If 20.0 mL of perchloric acid is required to reach the endpoint:

   ○ Moles of $HClO_4$ = Volume (L) × Molarity (M) = 0.020 L × 0.1 M = 0.0020 moles
   ○ Moles of ephedrine HCl = Moles of $HClO_4$ (1:1 stoichiometry) = 0.0020 moles
   ○ Molecular weight of ephedrine HCl = 201.7 g/mol
   ○ Weight of ephedrine HCl = Moles × Molecular weight = 0.0020 moles × 201.7 g/mol = 0.4034 grams

6.1 PRINCIPLES AND METHODS

Principles of Precipitation Titrations:

Precipitation titrations are analytical techniques that involve the formation of an insoluble precipitate during the reaction between the titrant and the analyte. These titrations are based on the principles of solubility and the precipitation of specific ions. The endpoint is typically detected by the formation or disappearance of the precipitate, a color change, or an instrumental method.

Key Principles:

1. **Solubility Product (Ksp):**

    - The solubility product constant (Ksp) is a measure of the solubility of a compound. It is the product of the concentrations of the ions in a saturated solution at equilibrium.
    - For a salt AB that dissociates into A+ and B-, the solubility product is given by:

        - $Ksp=[A+][B-]$

    - A precipitate forms when the product of the ionic concentrations exceeds the Ksp.

2. **Stoichiometry:**

    - The stoichiometry of the reaction between the titrant and the analyte is crucial for accurate calculations. The molar ratio of the reactants determines the amount of titrant needed to reach the endpoint.

3. **Endpoint Detection:**

    - The endpoint in precipitation titrations can be detected visually using indicators, by observing the disappearance or appearance of a precipitate, or using instrumental methods like potentiometry.

Methods of Precipitation Titrations:

1. **Mohr's Method:**

    - **Principle:** This method involves the titration of chloride ions with silver nitrate (AgNO3) in the presence of chromate ions ($CrO4^{2-}$) as an indicator.
    - **Reaction:**

- $Cl^- + AgNO_3 \rightarrow AgCl\downarrow + NO_3^-$
- $2Ag^+ + CrO_4^{2-} \rightarrow Ag_2CrO_4\downarrow$ (Red precipitate forms at the endpoint)

- **Procedure:** The chloride sample is titrated with $AgNO_3$ until a red precipitate of silver chromate forms, indicating the endpoint.

2. Volhard's Method:

- **Principle:** This method involves the back-titration of excess silver ions with thiocyanate ions (SCN^-) in the presence of ferric ions (Fe^{3+}) as an indicator.
- **Reaction:**

  - $Ag^+ + SCN^- \rightarrow AgSCN\downarrow$
  - Excess SCN^- forms a red complex with Fe^{3+} at the endpoint:

    - $Fe^{3+} + 3SCN^- \rightarrow Fe(SCN)_3$

- **Procedure:** Excess $AgNO_3$ is added to the sample containing chloride ions. The excess silver ions are then titrated with potassium thiocyanate (KSCN) until the red color of the ferric thiocyanate complex appears.

3. Modified Volhard's Method:

- **Principle:** Similar to Volhard's method but modified for specific applications, often involving different indicators or solvents.
- **Procedure:** The specific modifications depend on the nature of the sample and the requirements of the analysis.

4. Fajans Method:

- **Principle:** This method uses adsorption indicators that change color when they adsorb onto the precipitate formed at the endpoint.
- **Reaction:**

  - $Cl^- + AgNO_3 \rightarrow AgCl\downarrow + NO^{3-}$

- **Procedure:** An adsorption indicator, such as dichlorofluorescein, is added to the solution. The endpoint is detected when the color of the indicator changes due to adsorption onto the precipitate.

Applications:

1. **Pharmaceutical Analysis:**

   - Determination of chloride content in pharmaceuticals using Mohr's method.
   - Analysis of silver and halides in various formulations.

2. **Environmental Analysis:**

   - Determination of chloride and sulfate concentrations in water samples.
   - Monitoring pollution levels in industrial effluents.

3. **Industrial Applications:**

   - Quality control in the manufacturing of salts and chemicals.
   - Determination of ion concentrations in process streams.

Procedure for Precipitation Titrations:

1. **Sample Preparation:**

   - Dissolve the sample in a suitable solvent to prepare a clear solution.

2. **Addition of Indicator:**

   - Add an appropriate indicator to the sample solution based on the method used (e.g., chromate for Mohr's method, ferric ions for Volhard's method).

3. **Titration:**

- ○ Slowly add the titrant from a burette to the sample solution while continuously stirring. Observe the formation or disappearance of the precipitate or color change.

4. **Endpoint Detection:**

- ○ Detect the endpoint visually or using an instrumental method (e.g., potentiometry).

5. **Calculation:**

- ○ Calculate the concentration of the analyte using the volume of titrant added and the stoichiometry of the reaction.

Example Calculation:

- If 0.1 M AgNO3 is used to titrate a solution containing chloride ions, and 25.0 mL of AgNO3 is required to reach the endpoint:

  - ○ Moles of AgNO3 = Volume (L) × Molarity (M) = 0.025 L × 0.1 M = 0.0025 moles
  - ○ Moles of Cl- = Moles of AgNO3 (1:1 stoichiometry) = 0.0025 moles
  - ○ Concentration of Cl- in the sample = Moles / Volume of sample solution (L)

Precipitation titrations are essential analytical techniques used in various fields for the quantitative determination of specific ions. By understanding the principles and methods of these titrations, analysts can achieve accurate and reliable results. The choice of method and indicator depends on the specific requirements of the analysis, ensuring that the endpoint is detected precisely and accurately.

6.1.1 MOHR'S METHOD

Introduction: Mohr's method is a classic analytical technique used to determine the concentration of chloride ions (Cl^-) in a solution through precipitation titration. This method is based on the formation of an insoluble precipitate of silver chloride (AgCl) when silver nitrate (AgNO3) is added to a solution containing chloride ions. The endpoint is detected using chromate ions (CrO_4^{2-}) as an indicator, which forms a red precipitate of silver chromate (Ag2CrO4) once all the chloride ions have reacted.

Principle: The principle of Mohr's method relies on the precipitation reaction between chloride ions and silver ions. When AgNO3 is added to a solution containing Cl-, the following reaction occurs:

$$Cl^- + Ag+ \rightarrow AgCl\downarrow$$

The endpoint of the titration is indicated by the formation of a red precipitate of silver chromate, which occurs after all chloride ions have precipitated as AgCl:

$$2Ag^+ + CrO4^{\,2-} \rightarrow Ag2CrO4\downarrow$$

Reagents and Equipment:

- **Silver nitrate (AgNO3):** Standard titrant solution.
- **Potassium chromate (K2CrO4):** Indicator solution.
- **Sample solution:** Solution containing chloride ions.
- **Burette:** For dispensing AgNO3.
- **Pipette:** For measuring sample and indicator solutions.
- **Flask:** For mixing and titration.

Procedure:

1. **Preparation of the Sample:**

   - Measure a known volume of the sample solution containing chloride ions and transfer it to a clean flask.

2. **Addition of Indicator:**

   - Add a few drops of potassium chromate indicator solution to the sample. The solution will turn yellow due to the presence of chromate ions.

3. **Titration:**

   - Fill the burette with the standard AgNO3 solution.
   - Slowly add the AgNO3 solution from the burette to the sample solution while continuously stirring.
   - Initially, a white precipitate of AgCl will form.

4. **Endpoint Detection:**

- Continue adding AgNO3 until a permanent red precipitate of Ag2CrO4 is observed. This indicates that all the chloride ions have reacted, and the endpoint has been reached.

5. **Calculation:**

- Record the volume of AgNO3 solution used to reach the endpoint.
- Calculate the concentration of chloride ions in the sample using the volume of AgNO3 added and the stoichiometry of the reaction.

Example Calculation:

- Suppose 25.0 mL of 0.1 M AgNO3 is used to titrate 50.0 mL of the sample solution:

  - Moles of AgNO3 = Volume (L) × Molarity (M) = 0.025 L × 0.1 M = 0.0025 moles
  - Moles of Cl- = Moles of AgNO3 (1:1 stoichiometry) = 0.0025 moles
  - Concentration of Cl- in the sample = Moles / Volume of sample (L) = 0.0025 moles / 0.050 L = 0.05 M

Factors Affecting the Accuracy of Mohr's Method:

1. **pH of the Solution:**

- The pH of the solution should be controlled between 7 and 10. If the pH is too low (acidic), silver chromate may not form properly. If the pH is too high (alkaline), silver hydroxide (AgOH) may precipitate instead of AgCl.

2. **Concentration of Chromate Indicator:**

- The concentration of the chromate indicator should be optimal. Too much chromate can cause the endpoint to appear prematurely, while too little can make the endpoint difficult to detect.

3. **Interference from Other Ions:**

   - The presence of other halide ions (e.g., bromide, iodide) or substances that form precipitates with silver ions can interfere with the titration and lead to inaccurate results.

4. **Temperature:**

   - The temperature should be kept constant during the titration as solubility and reaction rates can be affected by temperature changes.

Applications:

1. **Water Analysis:**

   - Determining the chloride content in drinking water, seawater, and industrial effluents.

2. **Food Industry:**

   - Measuring the salt content in food products.

3. **Pharmaceuticals:**

   - Analyzing chloride content in pharmaceutical formulations

Applications (continued):

1. **Agriculture:**

   - Measuring chloride levels in soil samples to assess soil salinity, which can affect crop growth.

2. **Chemical Manufacturing:**

   - Quality control of raw materials and products in industries where chloride content is critical.

Advantages of Mohr's Method:

1. **Simplicity:**

   - The method is straightforward and does not require sophisticated equipment, making it accessible for routine laboratory use.

2. **Speed:**

   - The titration process is relatively quick, allowing for rapid analysis of multiple samples.

3. **Clear Endpoint:**

   - The formation of the red precipitate provides a distinct and easily recognizable endpoint.

Limitations of Mohr's Method:

1. **Interference:**

   - The presence of other ions that form precipitates with silver ions can interfere with the accuracy of the titration.

2. **pH Sensitivity:**

   - The method requires careful control of the pH to ensure accurate results.

3. **Not Suitable for Low Chloride Concentrations:**

   - Mohr's method is less effective for very low concentrations of chloride ions, as the endpoint may be difficult to detect.

:

Mohr's method is a valuable technique for the determination of chloride ions in various samples. Its simplicity, speed, and clear endpoint make it a popular choice in many fields, including water analysis, food industry, pharmaceuticals, agriculture, and chemical manufacturing. By understanding the principles and carefully controlling the experimental conditions, analysts can achieve accurate and reliable results using this method.

6.1.3 MODIFIED VOLHARD'S METHOD

Introduction: The Modified Volhard's method is an adaptation of the classic Volhard titration method, used primarily for the determination of halide ions such as chloride (Cl^-), bromide (Br^-), and iodide (I^-). This method is particularly useful for samples where direct titration is not feasible due to interference or solubility issues. The modification typically involves an indirect titration technique, where the analyte is first reacted with an excess of silver nitrate (AgNO3), and the excess silver ions are then back-titrated with a standard thiocyanate solution.

Principle: The principle of the Modified Volhard's method is based on the formation of an insoluble silver halide precipitate when the sample containing halide ions is treated with a known excess of silver nitrate. The unreacted silver ions are then titrated with potassium thiocyanate (KSCN) in the presence of ferric ions (Fe^{3+}) as an indicator, forming a red-colored ferric thiocyanate complex at the endpoint.

Reagents and Equipment:

- **Silver nitrate (AgNO3):** Standard solution used to react with halide ions.
- **Potassium thiocyanate (KSCN):** Standard solution used for back-titration.
- **Ferric ammonium sulfate:** Indicator solution.
- **Nitric acid (HNO3):** Used to maintain acidic conditions.
- **Sample solution:** Solution containing halide ions.
- **Burette:** For dispensing AgNO3 and KSCN solutions.
- **Pipette:** For measuring sample and indicator solutions.
- **Flask:** For mixing and titration.

Procedure:

1. **Sample Preparation:**

   ○ Measure a known volume of the sample solution containing halide ions and transfer it to a clean flask.

- Add a known excess of standard AgNO3 solution to the sample. This will precipitate the halide ions as silver halide.

2. **Acidification:**

- Add a few milliliters of concentrated nitric acid (HNO3) to the flask to maintain acidic conditions and prevent the formation of silver hydroxide.

3. **Indicator Addition:**

- Add a few drops of ferric ammonium sulfate indicator solution to the mixture. The solution will turn a faint yellow color due to the presence of ferric ions.

4. **Back-Titration:**

- Fill a burette with the standard KSCN solution.
- Slowly add the KSCN solution from the burette to the flask while continuously stirring.
- The thiocyanate ions will react with the excess silver ions to form a white precipitate of silver thiocyanate (AgSCN): $Ag^+ + SCN^- \rightarrow AgSCN\downarrow$

5. **Endpoint Detection:**

- Continue adding KSCN until a permanent red color is observed, indicating the formation of the ferric thiocyanate complex: $Fe^{3+} + 3SCN^- \rightarrow Fe(SCN)3$
- The appearance of the red color marks the endpoint of the titration.

6. **Calculation:**

- Calculate the concentration of the halide ions in the sample using the volume of AgNO3 initially added and the volume of KSCN used in the back-titration.

Example Calculation:

- Suppose 50.0 mL of the sample solution is titrated with 50.0 mL of 0.1 M AgNO3. After adding excess AgNO3, the unreacted silver ions are back-titrated with 25.0 mL of 0.1 M KSCN:

  - Moles of AgNO3 added = Volume (L) × Molarity (M) = 0.050 L × 0.1 M = 0.0050 moles
  - Moles of KSCN used = Volume (L) × Molarity (M) = 0.025 L × 0.1 M = 0.0025 moles
  - Moles of AgNO3 reacted with halide ions = Moles of AgNO3 added - Moles of KSCN used = 0.0050 moles - 0.0025 moles = 0.0025 moles
  - Moles of halide ions = Moles of AgNO3 reacted = 0.0025 moles
  - Concentration of halide ions in the sample = Moles / Volume of sample (L) = 0.0025 moles / 0.050 L = 0.05 M

Factors Affecting Accuracy:

1. **Excess Silver Nitrate:**

   - Ensure that an accurate excess of AgNO3 is added to react with all the halide ions. Any deviation can lead to errors in the back-titration step.

2. **Acidic Conditions:**

   - Maintaining the correct acidic conditions with nitric acid is crucial to prevent the formation of silver hydroxide and ensure complete reaction with halide ions.

3. **Indicator Concentration:**

   - The concentration of the ferric indicator must be sufficient to detect the endpoint accurately without overwhelming the reaction mixture.

4. **Interference from Other Ions:**

   - Presence of other ions that form precipitates with silver or thiocyanate can interfere with the titration and affect the accuracy of the results.

Applications:

1. **Water Quality Testing:**

   - Determination of chloride, bromide, and iodide concentrations in drinking water, seawater, and industrial effluents.

2. **Pharmaceutical Analysis:**

   - Analysis of halide-containing drugs and raw materials.

3. **Chemical Industry:**

   - Quality control of chemicals and intermediates that contain halide ions.

4. **Environmental Monitoring:**

   - Assessment of halide pollution in soil and water samples.

Advantages:

1. **High Accuracy:**

   - Provides precise results for the determination of halide ions.

2. **Adaptability:**

   - Can be modified to suit different sample types and concentrations.

3. **Clear Endpoint:**

   - The formation of the red ferric thiocyanate complex provides a distinct and easily recognizable endpoint.

Limitations:

1. **Time-Consuming:**

○ The method involves multiple steps, including sample preparation, addition of excess titrant, and back-titration, making it more time-consuming than direct titration methods.

2. **Interference:**

○ The presence of interfering ions requires careful control and potentially additional steps to remove or account for these ions.

:

The Modified Volhard's method is a robust and reliable technique for the determination of halide ions in various samples. Its high accuracy and adaptability make it suitable for a wide range of applications in water quality testing, pharmaceutical analysis, chemical industry, and environmental monitoring. By carefully controlling the experimental conditions and considering potential interferences, analysts can achieve precise and reliable results using this method.

6.1.4 FAJANS METHOD

Introduction: Fajans method is a precipitation titration technique that uses adsorption indicators to detect the endpoint. This method is particularly useful for titrations involving halide ions (e.g., chloride, bromide, iodide) with silver nitrate ($AgNO_3$). The endpoint is determined by a color change of the adsorption indicator, which occurs when it adsorbs onto the surface of the precipitate.

Principle: The principle of Fajans method is based on the adsorption of a dye (adsorption indicator) onto the surface of the precipitate formed during the titration. The adsorption occurs when the precipitate carries a slight charge, attracting the oppositely charged dye molecules. The color change of the indicator marks the endpoint of the titration.

Reagents and Equipment:

- **Silver nitrate ($AgNO_3$):** Standard titrant solution.
- **Adsorption indicator:** Common indicators include dichlorofluorescein, eosin, and fluorescein.
- **Sample solution:** Solution containing halide ions.
- **Burette:** For dispensing $AgNO_3$.
- **Pipette:** For measuring sample and indicator solutions.
- **Flask:** For mixing and titration.

Procedure:

1. **Sample Preparation:**

   ◦ Measure a known volume of the sample solution containing halide ions and transfer it to a clean flask.

2. **Addition of Indicator:**

   ◦ Add a few drops of the adsorption indicator solution to the sample. The indicator is typically negatively charged and will remain in the solution until the endpoint is reached.

3. **Titration:**

   ◦ Fill the burette with the standard $AgNO_3$ solution.
   ◦ Slowly add the $AgNO_3$ solution from the burette to the sample solution while continuously stirring. Initially, a white precipitate of the silver halide (AgX) will form.

4. **Endpoint Detection:**

   ◦ Continue adding $AgNO_3$ until a distinct color change of the adsorption indicator is observed. The color change occurs when the surface of the precipitate adsorbs the indicator, indicating the endpoint of the titration.

5. **Calculation:**

   ◦ Record the volume of $AgNO_3$ solution used to reach the endpoint.
   ◦ Calculate the concentration of halide ions in the sample using the volume of $AgNO_3$ added and the stoichiometry of the reaction.

Example Calculation:

• Suppose 25.0 mL of 0.1 M $AgNO_3$ is used to titrate 50.0 mL of the sample solution:

- Moles of AgNO3 = Volume (L) × Molarity (M) = 0.025 L × 0.1 M = 0.0025 moles
- Moles of halide ions = Moles of AgNO3 (1:1 stoichiometry) = 0.0025 moles
- Concentration of halide ions in the sample = Moles / Volume of sample (L) = 0.0025 moles / 0.050 L = 0.05 M

Factors Affecting Accuracy:

1. **Choice of Indicator:**

   - The adsorption indicator must be appropriately chosen to ensure a distinct color change at the endpoint.

2. **pH of the Solution:**

   - The pH should be controlled to ensure the appropriate charge on the precipitate and the indicator.

3. **Concentration of Indicator:**

   - The concentration of the indicator should be optimal. Too much or too little indicator can affect the accuracy of endpoint detection.

4. **Temperature:**

   - Temperature can affect the solubility of the precipitate and the adsorption of the indicator. Consistent temperature conditions should be maintained.

Applications:

1. **Water Quality Testing:**

   - Determination of halide concentrations in drinking water, seawater, and industrial effluents.

2. **Pharmaceutical Analysis:**

- Analysis of halide-containing drugs and raw materials.

3. **Chemical Manufacturing:**

   - Quality control of chemicals and intermediates that contain halide ions.

4. **Environmental Monitoring:**

   - Assessment of halide pollution in soil and water samples.

Advantages:

1. **Distinct Endpoint:**

   - The use of adsorption indicators provides a clear and easily recognizable endpoint.

2. **High Accuracy:**

   - The method is precise and reliable for the determination of halide ions.

3. **Versatility:**

   - Fajans method can be adapted for various halides and other precipitate-forming reactions.

Limitations:

1. **Interference:**

   - Presence of other ions that form precipitates with silver or the indicator can interfere with the titration.

2. **Indicator Selection:**

◦ Careful selection of the adsorption indicator is required to ensure accurate endpoint detection.

Fajans method is a valuable technique for the determination of halide ions in various samples. Its high accuracy, distinct endpoint, and versatility make it suitable for a wide range of applications in water quality testing, pharmaceutical analysis, chemical manufacturing, and environmental monitoring. By carefully selecting the appropriate indicator and controlling the experimental conditions, analysts can achieve precise and reliable results using this method.

6.2 APPLICATIONS

1. Water Quality Testing:

- **Mohr's Method**: Used for determining chloride content in drinking water, seawater, and industrial effluents. Accurate chloride measurement is crucial for assessing water quality and safety.
- **Volhard's Method**: Applied for the determination of chloride, bromide, and iodide in water samples, especially when direct titration is not feasible.
- **Fajans Method**: Utilized for the accurate measurement of halide concentrations in water, providing a clear endpoint for quality assessment.

2. Pharmaceutical Analysis:

- **Mohr's Method**: Used in the quality control of pharmaceutical products containing chloride ions. Ensures the chloride content is within specified limits to guarantee product safety and efficacy.
- **Volhard's Method**: Applied for the analysis of halide-containing drugs and raw materials. Ensures the purity and quality of pharmaceutical ingredients.
- **Fajans Method**: Employed for the precise determination of halide impurities in pharmaceuticals, ensuring compliance with regulatory standards.

3. Chemical Manufacturing:

- **Mohr's Method:** Used for the quality control of raw materials and final products in the chemical industry. Ensures that chloride levels meet the required specifications.
- **Volhard's Method:** Applied for the analysis of intermediate products and finished chemicals containing halides. Helps in maintaining the quality and consistency of chemical products.
- **Fajans Method:** Utilized for the determination of halide concentrations in various chemical processes, ensuring accurate formulation and quality control.

4. Environmental Monitoring:

- **Mohr's Method:** Used for assessing the chloride content in soil and water samples. Helps in monitoring environmental pollution and soil salinity.
- **Volhard's Method:** Applied for the determination of halide pollution in environmental samples. Ensures accurate assessment of environmental contamination.
- **Fajans Method:** Utilized for the precise measurement of halide levels in environmental monitoring programs, providing reliable data for pollution control and regulatory compliance.

5. Food Industry:

- **Mohr's Method:** Used for determining the salt (sodium chloride) content in food products. Ensures the correct formulation and quality of food items.
- **Volhard's Method:** Applied for the analysis of halide content in various food products. Helps in maintaining the quality and safety of food.
- **Fajans Method:** Utilized for the accurate determination of halide levels in food analysis, ensuring compliance with food safety standards.

The various methods of precipitation titration, including Mohr's, Volhard's, and Fajans methods, have wide-ranging applications across different industries. These methods provide accurate and reliable measurements of halide concentrations, ensuring quality control, regulatory compliance, and safety in water quality testing, pharmaceutical analysis, chemical manufacturing, environmental monitoring, and the food industry. By understanding and applying these methods appropriately, analysts can achieve precise and consistent results in their respective fields.

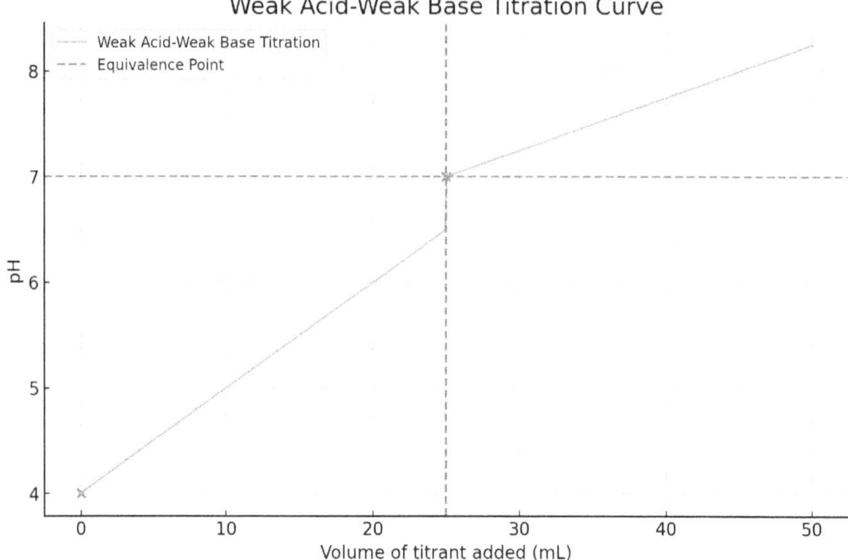

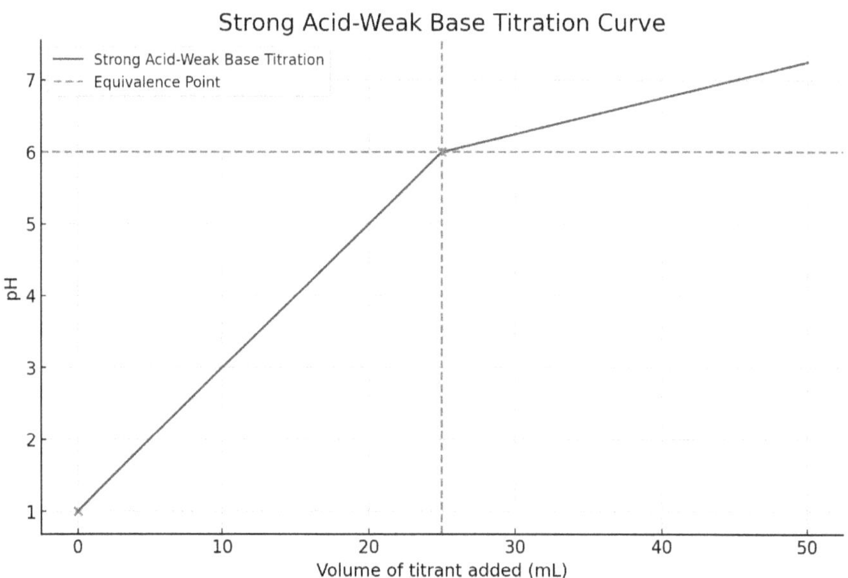

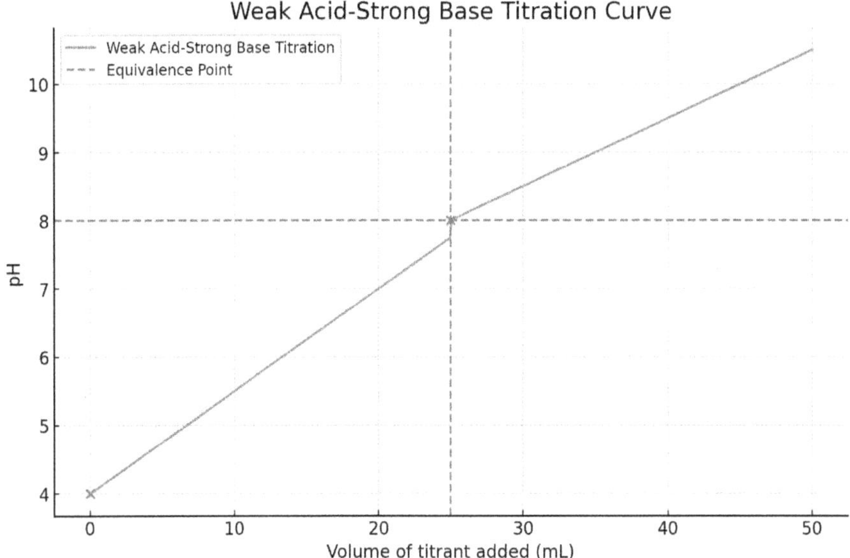

Weak Acid-Strong Base Titration Curve
Weak Acid-Strong Base Titration
Equivalence Point
pH
Volume of titrant added (mL)

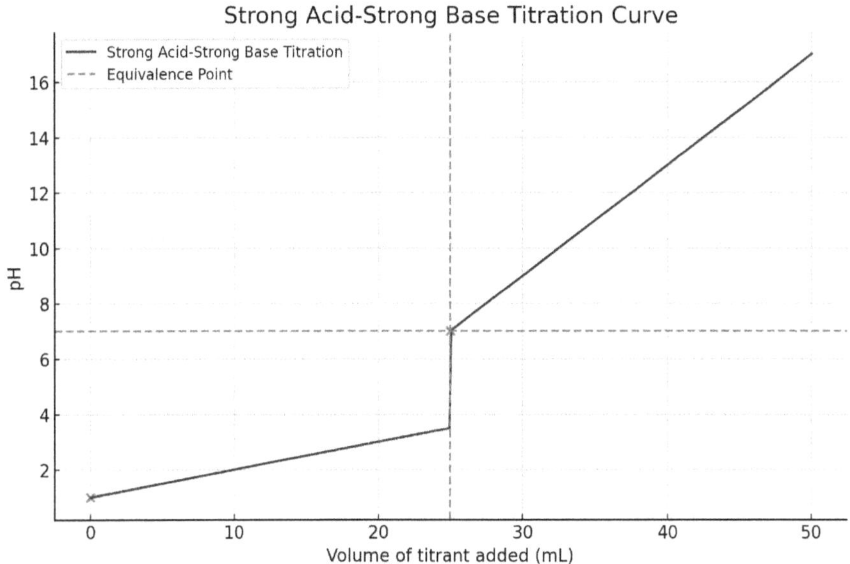

Strong Acid-Strong Base Titration Curve
Strong Acid-Strong Base Titration
Equivalence Point
pH
Volume of titrant added (mL)

Enter Caption

SIX
PRECIPITATION TITRATIONS

6.1 PRINCIPLES AND METHODS

6.1 PRINCIPLES AND METHODS

Principles of Precipitation Titrations:

Precipitation titrations are analytical techniques that involve the formation of an insoluble precipitate during the reaction between the titrant and the analyte. These titrations are based on the principles of solubility and the precipitation of specific ions. The endpoint is typically detected by the formation or disappearance of the precipitate, a color change, or an instrumental method.

Key Principles:

1. **Solubility Product (Ksp):**

   - The solubility product constant (Ksp) is a measure of the solubility of a compound. It is the product of the concentrations of the ions in a saturated solution at equilibrium.
   - For a salt AB that dissociates into A+ and B-, the solubility product is given by:

     - $Ksp=[A+][B-]$

- A precipitate forms when the product of the ionic concentrations exceeds the Ksp.

2. **Stoichiometry:**

- The stoichiometry of the reaction between the titrant and the analyte is crucial for accurate calculations. The molar ratio of the reactants determines the amount of titrant needed to reach the endpoint.

3. **Endpoint Detection:**

- The endpoint in precipitation titrations can be detected visually using indicators, by observing the disappearance or appearance of a precipitate, or using instrumental methods like potentiometry.

Methods of Precipitation Titrations:

1. **Mohr's Method:**

- **Principle:** This method involves the titration of chloride ions with silver nitrate (AgNO3) in the presence of chromate ions (CrO_4^{2-}) as an indicator.
- **Reaction:**

  - $Cl^- + AgNO3 \rightarrow AgCl\downarrow + NO3^-$
  - $2Ag+ + CrO42- \rightarrow Ag2CrO4\downarrow$ (Red precipitate forms at the endpoint)

- **Procedure:** The chloride sample is titrated with AgNO3 until a red precipitate of silver chromate forms, indicating the endpoint.

2. **Volhard's Method:**

- **Principle:** This method involves the back-titration of excess silver ions with thiocyanate ions (SCN-) in the presence of ferric ions (Fe^{3+}) as an indicator.
- **Reaction:**

  - $Ag+ + SCN^- \rightarrow AgSCN\downarrow$

- Excess SCN⁻ forms a red complex with Fe^{3+} at the endpoint:

    - $Fe3+ + 3SCN^- \rightarrow Fe(SCN)3$

  ◦ **Procedure:** Excess AgNO3 is added to the sample containing chloride ions. The excess silver ions are then titrated with potassium thiocyanate (KSCN) until the red color of the ferric thiocyanate complex appears.

3. **Modified Volhard's Method:**

  ◦ **Principle:** Similar to Volhard's method but modified for specific applications, often involving different indicators or solvents.
  ◦ **Procedure:** The specific modifications depend on the nature of the sample and the requirements of the analysis.

4. **Fajans Method:**

  ◦ **Principle:** This method uses adsorption indicators that change color when they adsorb onto the precipitate formed at the endpoint.
  ◦ **Reaction:**

    - $Cl^- + AgNO3 \rightarrow AgCl\downarrow + NO^{3-}$

  ◦ **Procedure:** An adsorption indicator, such as dichlorofluorescein, is added to the solution. The endpoint is detected when the color of the indicator changes due to adsorption onto the precipitate.

Applications:

1. **Pharmaceutical Analysis:**

  ◦ Determination of chloride content in pharmaceuticals using Mohr's method.
  ◦ Analysis of silver and halides in various formulations.

2. **Environmental Analysis:**

- Determination of chloride and sulfate concentrations in water samples.
- Monitoring pollution levels in industrial effluents.

3. **Industrial Applications:**

- Quality control in the manufacturing of salts and chemicals.
- Determination of ion concentrations in process streams.

Procedure for Precipitation Titrations:

1. **Sample Preparation:**

- Dissolve the sample in a suitable solvent to prepare a clear solution.

2. **Addition of Indicator:**

- Add an appropriate indicator to the sample solution based on the method used (e.g., chromate for Mohr's method, ferric ions for Volhard's method).

3. **Titration:**

- Slowly add the titrant from a burette to the sample solution while continuously stirring. Observe the formation or disappearance of the precipitate or color change.

4. **Endpoint Detection:**

- Detect the endpoint visually or using an instrumental method (e.g., potentiometry).

5. **Calculation:**

- Calculate the concentration of the analyte using the volume of titrant added and the stoichiometry of the reaction.

Example Calculation:

- If 0.1 M AgNO3 is used to titrate a solution containing chloride ions, and 25.0 mL of AgNO3 is required to reach the endpoint:

  - Moles of AgNO3 = Volume (L) × Molarity (M) = 0.025 L × 0.1 M = 0.0025 moles
  - Moles of Cl- = Moles of AgNO3 (1:1 stoichiometry) = 0.0025 moles
  - Concentration of Cl- in the sample = Moles / Volume of sample solution (L)

Precipitation titrations are essential analytical techniques used in various fields for the quantitative determination of specific ions. By understanding the principles and methods of these titrations, analysts can achieve accurate and reliable results. The choice of method and indicator depends on the specific requirements of the analysis, ensuring that the endpoint is detected precisely and accurately.

6.1.1 MOHR'S METHOD

Introduction: Mohr's method is a classic analytical technique used to determine the concentration of chloride ions (Cl^-) in a solution through precipitation titration. This method is based on the formation of an insoluble precipitate of silver chloride (AgCl) when silver nitrate (AgNO3) is added to a solution containing chloride ions. The endpoint is detected using chromate ions ($CrO4^{2-}$) as an indicator, which forms a red precipitate of silver chromate (Ag2CrO4) once all the chloride ions have reacted.

Principle: The principle of Mohr's method relies on the precipitation reaction between chloride ions and silver ions. When AgNO3 is added to a solution containing Cl-, the following reaction occurs:

$$Cl^- + Ag+ \rightarrow AgCl\downarrow$$

The endpoint of the titration is indicated by the formation of a red precipitate of silver chromate, which occurs after all chloride ions have precipitated as AgCl:

$$2Ag^+ + CrO4^{2-} \rightarrow Ag2CrO4\downarrow$$

Reagents and Equipment:

- **Silver nitrate (AgNO3):** Standard titrant solution.
- **Potassium chromate (K2CrO4):** Indicator solution.
- **Sample solution:** Solution containing chloride ions.
- **Burette:** For dispensing AgNO3.
- **Pipette:** For measuring sample and indicator solutions.

- **Flask:** For mixing and titration.

Procedure:

1. **Preparation of the Sample:**

   - Measure a known volume of the sample solution containing chloride ions and transfer it to a clean flask.

2. **Addition of Indicator:**

   - Add a few drops of potassium chromate indicator solution to the sample. The solution will turn yellow due to the presence of chromate ions.

3. **Titration:**

   - Fill the burette with the standard AgNO3 solution.
   - Slowly add the AgNO3 solution from the burette to the sample solution while continuously stirring.
   - Initially, a white precipitate of AgCl will form.

4. **Endpoint Detection:**

   - Continue adding AgNO3 until a permanent red precipitate of Ag2CrO4 is observed. This indicates that all the chloride ions have reacted, and the endpoint has been reached.

5. **Calculation:**

   - Record the volume of AgNO3 solution used to reach the endpoint.
   - Calculate the concentration of chloride ions in the sample using the volume of AgNO3 added and the stoichiometry of the reaction.

Example Calculation:

- Suppose 25.0 mL of 0.1 M AgNO3 is used to titrate 50.0 mL of the sample solution:

- ○ Moles of AgNO3 = Volume (L) × Molarity (M) = 0.025 L × 0.1 M = 0.0025 moles
- ○ Moles of Cl- = Moles of AgNO3 (1:1 stoichiometry) = 0.0025 moles
- ○ Concentration of Cl- in the sample = Moles / Volume of sample (L) = 0.0025 moles / 0.050 L = 0.05 M

Factors Affecting the Accuracy of Mohr's Method:

1. **pH of the Solution:**

   - ○ The pH of the solution should be controlled between 7 and 10. If the pH is too low (acidic), silver chromate may not form properly. If the pH is too high (alkaline), silver hydroxide (AgOH) may precipitate instead of AgCl.

2. **Concentration of Chromate Indicator:**

   - ○ The concentration of the chromate indicator should be optimal. Too much chromate can cause the endpoint to appear prematurely, while too little can make the endpoint difficult to detect.

3. **Interference from Other Ions:**

   - ○ The presence of other halide ions (e.g., bromide, iodide) or substances that form precipitates with silver ions can interfere with the titration and lead to inaccurate results.

4. **Temperature:**

   - ○ The temperature should be kept constant during the titration as solubility and reaction rates can be affected by temperature changes.

Applications:

1. **Water Analysis:**

   - ○ Determining the chloride content in drinking water, seawater, and industrial effluents.

2. **Food Industry:**

   ◦ Measuring the salt content in food products.

3. **Pharmaceuticals:**

   ◦ Analyzing chloride content in pharmaceutical formulations

Applications (continued):

1. **Agriculture:**

   ◦ Measuring chloride levels in soil samples to assess soil salinity, which can affect crop growth.

2. **Chemical Manufacturing:**

   ◦ Quality control of raw materials and products in industries where chloride content is critical.

Advantages of Mohr's Method:

1. **Simplicity:**

   ◦ The method is straightforward and does not require sophisticated equipment, making it accessible for routine laboratory use.

2. **Speed:**

   ◦ The titration process is relatively quick, allowing for rapid analysis of multiple samples.

3. **Clear Endpoint:**

   ◦ The formation of the red precipitate provides a distinct and easily recognizable endpoint.

Limitations of Mohr's Method:

1. **Interference:**

   - The presence of other ions that form precipitates with silver ions can interfere with the accuracy of the titration.

2. **pH Sensitivity:**

   - The method requires careful control of the pH to ensure accurate results.

3. **Not Suitable for Low Chloride Concentrations:**

   - Mohr's method is less effective for very low concentrations of chloride ions, as the endpoint may be difficult to detect.

Conclusion:

Mohr's method is a valuable technique for the determination of chloride ions in various samples. Its simplicity, speed, and clear endpoint make it a popular choice in many fields, including water analysis, food industry, pharmaceuticals, agriculture, and chemical manufacturing. By understanding the principles and carefully controlling the experimental conditions, analysts can achieve accurate and reliable results using this method.

6.1.3 MODIFIED VOLHARD'S METHOD

Introduction: The Modified Volhard's method is an adaptation of the classic Volhard titration method, used primarily for the determination of halide ions such as chloride (Cl^-), bromide (Br^-), and iodide (I^-). This method is particularly useful for samples where direct titration is not feasible due to interference or solubility issues. The modification typically involves an indirect titration technique, where the analyte is first reacted with an excess of silver nitrate ($AgNO_3$), and the excess silver ions are then back-titrated with a standard thiocyanate solution.

Principle: The principle of the Modified Volhard's method is based on the formation of an insoluble silver halide precipitate when the sample containing halide ions is treated with a known excess of silver nitrate. The unreacted silver ions are then titrated with potassium thiocyanate (KSCN) in the presence of ferric ions (Fe^{3+}) as an indicator, forming a red-colored ferric thiocyanate complex at the endpoint.

Reagents and Equipment:

- **Silver nitrate (AgNO3):** Standard solution used to react with halide ions.
- **Potassium thiocyanate (KSCN):** Standard solution used for back-titration.
- **Ferric ammonium sulfate:** Indicator solution.
- **Nitric acid (HNO3):** Used to maintain acidic conditions.
- **Sample solution:** Solution containing halide ions.
- **Burette:** For dispensing AgNO3 and KSCN solutions.
- **Pipette:** For measuring sample and indicator solutions.
- **Flask:** For mixing and titration.

Procedure:

1. **Sample Preparation:**

   - Measure a known volume of the sample solution containing halide ions and transfer it to a clean flask.
   - Add a known excess of standard AgNO3 solution to the sample. This will precipitate the halide ions as silver halide.

2. **Acidification:**

   - Add a few milliliters of concentrated nitric acid (HNO3) to the flask to maintain acidic conditions and prevent the formation of silver hydroxide.

3. **Indicator Addition:**

   - Add a few drops of ferric ammonium sulfate indicator solution to the mixture. The solution will turn a faint yellow color due to the presence of ferric ions.

4. **Back-Titration:**

   - Fill a burette with the standard KSCN solution.
   - Slowly add the KSCN solution from the burette to the flask while continuously stirring.

- The thiocyanate ions will react with the excess silver ions to form a white precipitate of silver thiocyanate (AgSCN): $Ag^+ + SCN^- \rightarrow AgSCN\downarrow$

5. Endpoint Detection:

- Continue adding KSCN until a permanent red color is observed, indicating the formation of the ferric thiocyanate complex: $Fe^{3+} + 3SCN^- \rightarrow Fe(SCN)3$
- The appearance of the red color marks the endpoint of the titration.

6. Calculation:

- Calculate the concentration of the halide ions in the sample using the volume of AgNO3 initially added and the volume of KSCN used in the back-titration.

Example Calculation:

- Suppose 50.0 mL of the sample solution is titrated with 50.0 mL of 0.1 M AgNO3. After adding excess AgNO3, the unreacted silver ions are back-titrated with 25.0 mL of 0.1 M KSCN:

  - Moles of AgNO3 added = Volume (L) × Molarity (M) = 0.050 L × 0.1 M = 0.0050 moles
  - Moles of KSCN used = Volume (L) × Molarity (M) = 0.025 L × 0.1 M = 0.0025 moles
  - Moles of AgNO3 reacted with halide ions = Moles of AgNO3 added - Moles of KSCN used = 0.0050 moles - 0.0025 moles = 0.0025 moles
  - Moles of halide ions = Moles of AgNO3 reacted = 0.0025 moles
  - Concentration of halide ions in the sample = Moles / Volume of sample (L) = 0.0025 moles / 0.050 L = 0.05 M

Factors Affecting Accuracy:

1. Excess Silver Nitrate:

- Ensure that an accurate excess of AgNO3 is added to react with all the halide ions. Any deviation can lead to errors in the back-titration step.

2. **Acidic Conditions:**

   - Maintaining the correct acidic conditions with nitric acid is crucial to prevent the formation of silver hydroxide and ensure complete reaction with halide ions.

3. **Indicator Concentration:**

   - The concentration of the ferric indicator must be sufficient to detect the endpoint accurately without overwhelming the reaction mixture.

4. **Interference from Other Ions:**

   - Presence of other ions that form precipitates with silver or thiocyanate can interfere with the titration and affect the accuracy of the results.

Applications:

1. **Water Quality Testing:**

   - Determination of chloride, bromide, and iodide concentrations in drinking water, seawater, and industrial effluents.

2. **Pharmaceutical Analysis:**

   - Analysis of halide-containing drugs and raw materials.

3. **Chemical Industry:**

   - Quality control of chemicals and intermediates that contain halide ions.

4. **Environmental Monitoring:**

   - Assessment of halide pollution in soil and water samples.

Advantages:

1. **High Accuracy:**

   ○ Provides precise results for the determination of halide ions.

2. **Adaptability:**

   ○ Can be modified to suit different sample types and concentrations.

3. **Clear Endpoint:**

   ○ The formation of the red ferric thiocyanate complex provides a distinct and easily recognizable endpoint.

   Limitations:

1. **Time-Consuming:**

   ○ The method involves multiple steps, including sample preparation, addition of excess titrant, and back-titration, making it more time-consuming than direct titration methods.

2. **Interference:**

   ○ The presence of interfering ions requires careful control and potentially additional steps to remove or account for these ions.

6.1.4 FAJANS METHOD

Introduction: Fajans method is a precipitation titration technique that uses adsorption indicators to detect the endpoint. This method is particularly useful for titrations involving halide ions (e.g., chloride, bromide, iodide) with silver nitrate ($AgNO_3$). The endpoint is determined by a color change of the adsorption indicator, which occurs when it adsorbs onto the surface of the precipitate.

Principle: The principle of Fajans method is based on the adsorption of a dye (adsorption indicator) onto the surface of the precipitate formed during the titration. The adsorption occurs when the precipitate carries a slight charge, attracting the oppositely charged dye molecules. The color change of the indicator marks the endpoint of the titration.

Reagents and Equipment:

- **Silver nitrate (AgNO3):** Standard titrant solution.
- **Adsorption indicator:** Common indicators include dichlorofluorescein, eosin, and fluorescein.
- **Sample solution:** Solution containing halide ions.
- **Burette:** For dispensing AgNO3.
- **Pipette:** For measuring sample and indicator solutions.
- **Flask:** For mixing and titration.

Procedure:

1. **Sample Preparation:**

   - Measure a known volume of the sample solution containing halide ions and transfer it to a clean flask.

2. **Addition of Indicator:**

   - Add a few drops of the adsorption indicator solution to the sample. The indicator is typically negatively charged and will remain in the solution until the endpoint is reached.

3. **Titration:**

   - Fill the burette with the standard AgNO3 solution.
   - Slowly add the AgNO3 solution from the burette to the sample solution while continuously stirring. Initially, a white precipitate of the silver halide (AgX) will form.

4. **Endpoint Detection:**

   - Continue adding AgNO3 until a distinct color change of the adsorption indicator is observed. The color change occurs when the surface of the precipitate adsorbs the indicator, indicating the endpoint of the titration.

5. **Calculation:**

- ○ Record the volume of AgNO3 solution used to reach the endpoint.
- ○ Calculate the concentration of halide ions in the sample using the volume of AgNO3 added and the stoichiometry of the reaction.

Example Calculation:

- Suppose 25.0 mL of 0.1 M AgNO3 is used to titrate 50.0 mL of the sample solution:

  - ○ Moles of AgNO3 = Volume (L) × Molarity (M) = 0.025 L × 0.1 M = 0.0025 moles
  - ○ Moles of halide ions = Moles of AgNO3 (1:1 stoichiometry) = 0.0025 moles
  - ○ Concentration of halide ions in the sample = Moles / Volume of sample (L) = 0.0025 moles / 0.050 L = 0.05 M

Factors Affecting Accuracy:

1. **Choice of Indicator:**

   - ○ The adsorption indicator must be appropriately chosen to ensure a distinct color change at the endpoint.

2. **pH of the Solution:**

   - ○ The pH should be controlled to ensure the appropriate charge on the precipitate and the indicator.

3. **Concentration of Indicator:**

   - ○ The concentration of the indicator should be optimal. Too much or too little indicator can affect the accuracy of endpoint detection.

4. **Temperature:**

   - ○ Temperature can affect the solubility of the precipitate and the adsorption of the indicator. Consistent temperature conditions should be maintained.

Applications:

1. **Water Quality Testing:**

    - Determination of halide concentrations in drinking water, seawater, and industrial effluents.

2. **Pharmaceutical Analysis:**

    - Analysis of halide-containing drugs and raw materials.

3. **Chemical Manufacturing:**

    - Quality control of chemicals and intermediates that contain halide ions.

4. **Environmental Monitoring:**

    - Assessment of halide pollution in soil and water samples.

Advantages:

1. **Distinct Endpoint:**

    - The use of adsorption indicators provides a clear and easily recognizable endpoint.

2. **High Accuracy:**

    - The method is precise and reliable for the determination of halide ions.

3. **Versatility:**

    - Fajans method can be adapted for various halides and other precipitate-forming reactions.

Limitations:

1. **Interference:**

   ◦ Presence of other ions that form precipitates with silver or the indicator can interfere with the titration.

2. **Indicator Selection:**

   ◦ Careful selection of the adsorption indicator is required to ensure accurate endpoint detection.

6.2 APPLICATIONS

1. Water Quality Testing:

- **Mohr's Method:** Used for determining chloride content in drinking water, seawater, and industrial effluents. Accurate chloride measurement is crucial for assessing water quality and safety.
- **Volhard's Method:** Applied for the determination of chloride, bromide, and iodide in water samples, especially when direct titration is not feasible.
- **Fajans Method:** Utilized for the accurate measurement of halide concentrations in water, providing a clear endpoint for quality assessment.

2. Pharmaceutical Analysis:

- **Mohr's Method:** Used in the quality control of pharmaceutical products containing chloride ions. Ensures the chloride content is within specified limits to guarantee product safety and efficacy.
- **Volhard's Method:** Applied for the analysis of halide-containing drugs and raw materials. Ensures the purity and quality of pharmaceutical ingredients.
- **Fajans Method:** Employed for the precise determination of halide impurities in pharmaceuticals, ensuring compliance with regulatory standards.

3. Chemical Manufacturing:

- **Mohr's Method:** Used for the quality control of raw materials and final products in the chemical industry. Ensures that chloride levels meet the required specifications.
- **Volhard's Method:** Applied for the analysis of intermediate products and finished chemicals containing halides. Helps in maintaining the quality and consistency of chemical products.
- **Fajans Method:** Utilized for the determination of halide concentrations in various chemical processes, ensuring accurate formulation and quality control.

4. Environmental Monitoring:

- **Mohr's Method:** Used for assessing the chloride content in soil and water samples. Helps in monitoring environmental pollution and soil salinity.
- **Volhard's Method:** Applied for the determination of halide pollution in environmental samples. Ensures accurate assessment of environmental contamination.
- **Fajans Method:** Utilized for the precise measurement of halide levels in environmental monitoring programs, providing reliable data for pollution control and regulatory compliance.

5. Food Industry:

- **Mohr's Method:** Used for determining the salt (sodium chloride) content in food products. Ensures the correct formulation and quality of food items.
- **Volhard's Method:** Applied for the analysis of halide content in various food products. Helps in maintaining the quality and safety of food.
- **Fajans Method:** Utilized for the accurate determination of halide levels in food analysis, ensuring compliance with food safety standards.

SEVEN

COMPLEXOMETRIC TITRATION

7.1 PRINCIPLES AND CLASSIFICATION

7.1.1 DIRECT TITRATION

Principles of Complexometric Titrations:

Complexometric titrations are analytical techniques used to determine the concentration of metal ions in a solution by forming a stable complex with a chelating agent. The most commonly used chelating agent in these titrations is ethylenediaminetetraacetic acid (EDTA), which forms strong complexes with metal ions. The endpoint of the titration is typically detected using metal ion indicators that change color when the metal ion forms a complex with EDTA.

Key Principles:

1. **Chelation:**

   ○ Chelation is the process by which a single molecule forms multiple bonds with a metal ion, resulting in a stable complex. EDTA is a hexadentate ligand, meaning it can form six bonds with a metal ion, creating a very stable complex.

2. **Stability Constants:**

- ○ The stability constant (Kf) of a complex is a measure of its stability. Higher stability constants indicate more stable complexes. The stability of the metal-EDTA complex is crucial for accurate titration results.

3. **pH Control:**

- ○ The formation of metal-EDTA complexes is pH-dependent. The pH must be controlled to ensure the complete complexation of the metal ions. Buffer solutions are often used to maintain the desired pH.

4. **Indicators:**

- ○ Metal ion indicators are used to signal the endpoint of the titration. These indicators form weaker complexes with metal ions than EDTA and change color when displaced by EDTA.

Classification of Complexometric Titrations:

1. **Direct Titration:**

- ○ The metal ion solution is titrated directly with a standard EDTA solution. The endpoint is detected using a suitable metal ion indicator.

2. **Back Titration:**

- ○ An excess of EDTA is added to the metal ion solution, and the remaining unreacted EDTA is titrated with a standard solution of a metal ion (such as magnesium or zinc). This method is used when the metal ion forms a complex with EDTA slowly or when a suitable indicator is not available.

3. **Replacement Titration:**

- ○ A metal ion that forms a stable complex with EDTA displaces another metal ion from its complex. The displaced metal ion is then titrated with EDTA.

4. **Indirect Titration:**

   - The metal ion is precipitated as an insoluble salt, and the precipitate is dissolved in an excess of EDTA. The remaining EDTA is then titrated with a standard solution of a metal ion.

Direct Titration:

Principle: In direct titration, the metal ion solution is titrated directly with a standard solution of EDTA. The metal ion forms a stable complex with EDTA, and the endpoint is detected using a metal ion indicator. The color change of the indicator signals the complete reaction of the metal ions with EDTA.

Procedure:

1. **Preparation of the Sample:**

   - Measure a known volume of the metal ion solution and transfer it to a titration flask.

2. **Addition of Buffer:**

   - Add a suitable buffer solution to the sample to maintain the desired pH. The pH must be adjusted to ensure the complete complexation of the metal ions with EDTA.

3. **Addition of Indicator:**

   - Add a few drops of a metal ion indicator to the sample. The indicator will form a weak complex with the metal ions, giving the solution a characteristic color.

4. **Titration:**

   - Fill a burette with the standard EDTA solution.
   - Slowly add the EDTA solution to the sample while continuously stirring. The EDTA will complex with the metal ions, displacing the indicator and causing a color change.

5. **Endpoint Detection:**

   - The endpoint is reached when a permanent color change is observed, indicating that all the metal ions have complexed with EDTA.

6. **Calculation:**

   - Record the volume of EDTA solution used to reach the endpoint.
   - Calculate the concentration of the metal ions in the sample using the volume of EDTA added and the stoichiometry of the reaction.

   Example Calculation:

   - Suppose 50.0 mL of a metal ion solution is titrated with 0.01 M EDTA. If 25.0 mL of EDTA is required to reach the endpoint:

     - Moles of EDTA = Volume (L) × Molarity (M) = 0.025 L × 0.01 M = 0.00025 moles
     - Moles of metal ions = Moles of EDTA (1:1 stoichiometry) = 0.00025 moles
     - Concentration of metal ions in the sample = Moles / Volume of sample (L) = 0.00025 moles / 0.050 L = 0.005 M

   Factors Affecting Accuracy:

1. **pH Control:**

   - The pH of the solution must be carefully controlled to ensure complete complexation of the metal ions with EDTA. Buffer solutions are used to maintain the desired pH.

2. **Choice of Indicator:**

   - The metal ion indicator must be chosen based on its ability to form a weaker complex with the metal ion than EDTA and provide a distinct color change at the endpoint.

3. **Interference:**

- ○ Other metal ions or substances in the sample that can form complexes with EDTA or the indicator can interfere with the titration and affect accuracy.

4. **Temperature:**

- ○ Temperature changes can affect the stability constants of the metal-EDTA complex and the performance of the indicator. Consistent temperature conditions should be maintained.

Applications:

1. **Water Hardness Determination:**

- ○ Direct titration with EDTA is used to determine the hardness of water by measuring the concentration of calcium and magnesium ions.

2. **Pharmaceutical Analysis:**

- ○ Used to determine the concentration of metal ions in pharmaceutical formulations and raw materials.

3. **Food Industry:**

- ○ Applied in the analysis of metal ion content in food products and additives.

4. **Environmental Monitoring:**

- ○ Used to measure metal ion concentrations in soil, water, and air samples for pollution control and environmental protection.

7.1.2 BACK TITRATION

Principles of Back Titration:

Back titration, also known as indirect titration, is a method used when direct titration is not feasible due to the nature of the sample or the reaction kinetics. In this technique, an excess of a standard reagent (titrant) is added to the sample, and the remaining unreacted titrant is titrated with a second standard reagent. This approach is particularly useful for analyzing substances that react slowly with the titrant, have weak endpoints, or form precipitates that are difficult to handle in direct titration.

Key Principles:

1. **Excess Reagent:**

   - An excess amount of the titrant is added to ensure that the analyte reacts completely.

2. **Back Titration:**

   - The unreacted excess titrant is then titrated with a second reagent to determine the amount of excess titrant.

3. **Calculation:**

   - The amount of analyte is calculated by subtracting the amount of titrant that reacted in the back titration from the total amount of titrant initially added.

Procedure:

1. **Addition of Excess Titrant:**

   - Add a known excess amount of the primary titrant (e.g., EDTA) to the sample solution. This ensures complete reaction with the analyte.

2. **Reaction Time:**

   - Allow sufficient time for the reaction between the analyte and the titrant to complete. This is important for substances that react slowly.

3. **Back Titration:**

   - After the reaction is complete, titrate the excess unreacted titrant with a second standard reagent. For example, if EDTA is the primary titrant, a metal ion solution like zinc sulfate ($ZnSO_4$) can be used for the back titration.

4. **Endpoint Detection:**

- Use a suitable indicator or instrumental method to detect the endpoint of the back titration.

5. **Calculation:**

- Calculate the amount of analyte by determining the difference between the total amount of the primary titrant added and the amount of excess titrant determined by the back titration.

Example Calculation:

Suppose 50.0 mL of a sample containing calcium ions (Ca^{2+}) is titrated with 50.0 mL of 0.01 M EDTA. After allowing the reaction to complete, the excess EDTA is titrated with 25.0 mL of 0.01 M zinc sulfate (ZnSO4):

1. **Moles of EDTA initially added:** Moles of EDTA=Volume×Molarity=0.050 L×0.01 M = 0.0005moles
2. **Moles of EDTA reacted with ZnSO4:** Moles of ZnSO4=Volume×Molarity=0.025 L×0.01 M=0.00025 moles
3. **Moles of EDTA remaining:** Moles of EDTA remaining=0.00025 moles
4. Moles of EDTA reacted with Ca2+:Moles of EDTA reacted with Ca^{2+} = 0.0005 moles - 0.00025 moles = 0.00025 moles
5. Concentration of Ca^{2+} in the sample: Concentration of Ca^{2+} = 0.00025 moles / 0.050 L=0.005

7.1.3 DISPLACEMENT TITRATION

Principles of Displacement Titration:

Displacement titration is a technique where a less stable complex displaces a more stable complex in a solution. This method is useful for determining the concentration of a metal ion that forms a stable complex with a ligand. In displacement titration, an excess of a stable complexing agent is added to the sample, causing the displacement of the metal ion from its original complex. The displaced metal ion is then titrated with a suitable titrant.

Key Principles:

Procedure:

Example Calculation:

Suppose 50.0 mL of a sample containing a metal ion (M) is treated with an excess of a stable complexing agent (L). The displaced metal ion (M) is then titrated with 0.01 M EDTA. If 20 mL of EDTA is required to reach the endpoint:

Displacement titration is a versatile and accurate technique for determining the concentration of metal ions in various samples. By using a stable complexing agent to displace the metal ion from its original complex and then titrating the displaced metal ion, this method provides reliable results for complex samples. It is widely used in pharmaceutical analysis, water quality testing, food industry, environmental monitoring, and industrial applications, highlighting its significance in analytical chemistry.

7.2 METAL ION INDICATORS

Introduction: Metal ion indicators are crucial in complexometric titrations as they help in detecting the endpoint by changing color when they interact with metal ions. These indicators are typically organic compounds that form colored complexes with specific metal ions. The color change signifies the completion of the titration, indicating that all the metal ions have reacted with the chelating agent, such as EDTA.

Metal ion indicators are essential tools in complexometric titrations, providing a visual means of detecting the endpoint. By choosing the appropriate indicator based on the specific metal ion and pH range, analysts can achieve accurate and reliable results. These indicators are widely used in various fields, including water quality testing, pharmaceutical analysis, food industry, environmental monitoring, and industrial applications, underscoring their importance in analytical chemistry.

7.3 MASKING AND DEMASKING REAGENTS

Principles: Masking and demasking reagents are essential tools in complexometric titrations to selectively bind or release specific metal ions in a solution. This allows for accurate determination of metal ions in the presence of interfering species.

1. **Masking Reagents:**

- Masking agents form stable, water-soluble complexes with specific metal ions, preventing them from reacting with the titrant during the titration.
- Common masking agents include cyanide ions (CN), which mask copper ions (Cu2+), and triethanolamine, which masks iron ions (Fe3+).

2. **Demasking Reagents:**

- Demasking agents release the masked metal ions from their complexes, allowing them to react with the titrant.
- Examples include formaldehyde, which demasks cyanide complexes, and acid, which can demask certain metal complexes by changing the pH.

Applications of Masking and Demasking Reagents:

1. **Selective Titration:**

- Used to selectively titrate specific metal ions in the presence of others by masking interfering ions.

2. **Complex Sample Analysis:**

- Helpful in analyzing samples with multiple metal ions, ensuring accurate determination of the target ion.

3. **Industrial Processes:**

- Used in various industrial processes to control the concentration of specific metal ions.

7.4 APPLICATIONS

7.1 ESTIMATION OF MAGNESIUM SULPHATE

Principle: The estimation of magnesium sulfate ($MgSO_4$) is performed using complexometric titration with EDTA as the titrant. Magnesium forms a stable complex with EDTA, and the endpoint is detected using an appropriate indicator, such as Eriochrome Black T (EBT).

Procedure:

1. **Preparation of the Sample:**

   - Dissolve a known amount of the magnesium sulfate sample in distilled water and transfer to a titration flask.

2. **Addition of Buffer:**

   - Add a suitable buffer solution (ammonia/ammonium chloride) to maintain the pH around 10.

3. **Addition of Indicator:**

   - Add a few drops of Eriochrome Black T indicator. The solution will turn wine red due to the formation of the magnesium-indicator complex.

4. **Titration:**

   - Fill a burette with the standard EDTA solution.
   - Titrate the sample solution with EDTA while continuously stirring. The EDTA will complex with magnesium ions, displacing the indicator and causing a color change.

5. **Endpoint Detection:**

   - The endpoint is reached when the color changes from wine red to blue, indicating all the magnesium ions have complexed with EDTA.

6. **Calculation:**

   - Record the volume of EDTA solution used to reach the endpoint.
   - Calculate the concentration of magnesium sulfate using the volume of EDTA added and the stoichiometry of the reaction.
   Example Calculation:

- Suppose 50.0 mL of the magnesium sulfate solution is titrated with 0.01 M EDTA. If 25.0 mL of EDTA is required to reach the endpoint:

    - Moles of EDTA = Volume (L) × Molarity (M) = 0.025 L × 0.01 M = 0.00025 moles
    - Moles of Mg2+ = Moles of EDTA (1:1 stoichiometry) = 0.00025 moles
    - Concentration of Mg2+ in the sample = Moles / Volume of sample (L) = 0.00025 moles / 0.050 L = 0.005 M

7.2 ESTIMATION OF CALCIUM GLUCONATE

Principle: The estimation of calcium gluconate involves complexometric titration with EDTA. Calcium forms a stable complex with EDTA, and the endpoint is detected using a suitable indicator, such as Calcein or Murexide.

Procedure:

1. **Preparation of the Sample:**

    - Dissolve a known amount of the calcium gluconate sample in distilled water and transfer to a titration flask.

2. **Addition of Buffer:**

    - Add a suitable buffer solution (ammonia/ammonium chloride) to maintain the pH around 10.

3. **Addition of Indicator:**

    - Add a few drops of the chosen indicator (e.g., Murexide). The solution will show a characteristic color of the calcium-indicator complex.

4. **Titration:**

    - Fill a burette with the standard EDTA solution.
    - Titrate the sample solution with EDTA while continuously stirring. The EDTA will complex with calcium ions, displacing the indicator and causing a color change.

5. **Endpoint Detection:**

   - The endpoint is reached when a permanent color change is observed, indicating all the calcium ions have complexed with EDTA.

6. **Calculation:**

   - Record the volume of EDTA solution used to reach the endpoint.

   Calculate the concentration of calcium gluconate using the volume of EDTA added and the stoichiometry of the reaction.
   Example Calculation:

   - Suppose 50.0 mL of the calcium gluconate solution is titrated with 0.01 M EDTA. If 20.0 mL of EDTA is required to reach the endpoint:

     - Moles of EDTA = Volume (L) × Molarity (M) = 0.020 L × 0.01 M = 0.0002 moles
     - Moles of Ca^{2+} = Moles of EDTA (1:1 stoichiometry) = 0.0002 moles
     - Concentration of Ca^{2+} in the sample = Moles / Volume of sample (L) = 0.0002 moles / 0.050 L = 0.004 M

EIGHT

GRAVIMETRIC ANALYSIS

8.1 PRINCIPLES AND STEPS

Gravimetric analysis is a quantitative analytical technique used to determine the amount of an analyte based on the mass of a solid. This method involves the conversion of the analyte into an insoluble precipitate, which is then filtered, dried, and weighed. The mass of the precipitate is used to calculate the amount of the analyte.

Principles:

1. **Precipitation:**

   - The analyte is converted into an insoluble form by adding a suitable precipitating agent. The precipitate should be pure, stable, and easily filterable.

2. **Filtration:**

   - The precipitate is separated from the solution by filtration. The filter should retain all the precipitate and be easy to wash and handle.

3. **Washing:**

- ◦ The precipitate is washed to remove any impurities or adsorbed ions. The washing solution should not dissolve the precipitate.

4. **Drying or Ignition:**

   - ◦ The washed precipitate is dried or ignited to a constant mass to remove any water or volatile substances. The mass of the dried precipitate is used for the calculation.

5. **Calculation:**

   - ◦ The mass of the analyte is calculated based on the mass of the precipitate and the stoichiometry of the reaction.

8.1.1 KEY STEPS IN GRAVIMETRIC ANALYSIS

1. **Preparation of the Sample:**

   - ◦ The sample solution is prepared by dissolving the analyte in a suitable solvent. The solution should be clear and free of any undissolved particles.

2. **Precipitation:**

   - ◦ A precipitating agent is added to the sample solution to form an insoluble precipitate. The addition should be slow and with constant stirring to ensure complete precipitation and avoid the formation of fine particles.

3. **Digestion:**

   - ◦ The precipitate is allowed to stand in the mother liquor (the remaining solution after precipitation) to form larger and purer crystals. This process is known as digestion and improves the filterability and purity of the precipitate.

4. **Filtration:**

- ○ The precipitate is separated from the mother liquor by filtration using filter paper or a filtering crucible. The filtrate (the liquid that passes through the filter) is tested to ensure complete precipitation.

5. **Washing:**

- ○ The precipitate is washed with a suitable washing solution to remove any impurities. The washing should be thorough to ensure the purity of the precipitate.

6. **Drying or Ignition:**

- ○ The washed precipitate is dried in an oven at a specific temperature or ignited in a muffle furnace to a constant mass. This step removes any remaining water or volatile substances.

7. **Weighing:**

- ○ The dried or ignited precipitate is weighed accurately using an analytical balance. The mass is recorded for the calculation.

8. **Calculation:**

- ○ The amount of the analyte is calculated from the mass of the precipitate using the stoichiometry of the precipitation reaction. The calculation includes the molar mass of the analyte and the precipitate.

Example Calculation:

- Suppose a sample solution contains sulfate ions (SO_4^{2-}) and is precipitated with barium chloride ($BaCl_2$) to form barium sulfate ($BaSO_4$). If the mass of the dried $BaSO_4$ precipitate is 0.5 grams:

  - ○ Moles of $BaSO_4$ = Mass / Molar mass = 0.5 g / 233.39 g/mol = 0.00214 moles
  - ○ Moles of SO_4^{2-} = Moles of $BaSO_4$ (1:1 stoichiometry) = 0.00214 moles

- ○ Mass of SO_4^{2-} = Moles × Molar mass of SO_4^{2-} = 0.00214 moles × 96.06 g/mol = 0.2057 grams

8.2 PURITY OF THE PRECIPITATE

The purity of the precipitate is crucial in gravimetric analysis as it directly affects the accuracy of the results. Several factors influence the purity of the precipitate:

1. **Co-precipitation:**

   - ○ Co-precipitation occurs when impurities are adsorbed or occluded in the precipitate. This can happen during the formation of the precipitate or during digestion. To minimize co-precipitation, proper digestion and washing are essential.

2. **Post-precipitation:**

   - ○ Post-precipitation occurs when impurities precipitate after the main precipitation process. This can be minimized by ensuring complete precipitation and immediate filtration.

3. **Choice of Precipitating Agent:**

   - ○ The precipitating agent should form a pure, stable, and easily filterable precipitate with the analyte. The choice of the precipitating agent is critical for obtaining a pure precipitate.

4. **Control of pH:**

   - ○ The pH of the solution affects the solubility and formation of the precipitate. The pH should be controlled to ensure complete precipitation of the analyte and minimize the solubility of the precipitate.

5. **Temperature:**

○ The temperature of the solution can affect the solubility and crystallization of the precipitate. Higher temperatures generally increase the solubility of the precipitate, while lower temperatures favor crystallization.

Improving Purity:

1. **Digestion:**

   ○ Allowing the precipitate to stand in the mother liquor at an elevated temperature helps form larger and purer crystals. Digestion reduces co-precipitation and improves filterability.

2. **Thorough Washing:**

   ○ Washing the precipitate with a suitable solution removes impurities and adsorbed ions. The washing solution should be chosen to avoid dissolving the precipitate.

3. **Re-precipitation:**

   ○ Dissolving the impure precipitate and re-precipitating it can improve the purity. This step is useful when the initial precipitate contains significant impurities.

4. **Choice of Solvent:**

   ○ The solvent used for dissolving the sample and the precipitating agent should be chosen to minimize the solubility of impurities in the precipitate.

8.2.1 CO-PRECIPITATION

Introduction: Co-precipitation is a phenomenon where impurities are carried down with a precipitate during the process of precipitation. This can occur through various mechanisms, leading to the inclusion of unwanted substances in the precipitate, which affects its purity and the accuracy of the gravimetric analysis.

Mechanisms of Co-precipitation:

1. **Adsorption:**

   - Impurities adsorb onto the surface of the precipitate particles. This is common in the early stages of precipitation when the surface area of the newly formed precipitate is high.

2. **Occlusion:**

   - Impurities are trapped within the crystal lattice of the precipitate as it forms. This happens when the precipitate forms rapidly, trapping the surrounding solution inside the growing crystals.

3. **Inclusion:**

   - Impurities are included within the crystal structure of the precipitate, replacing some of the ions in the lattice. This occurs when the ionic radii and charge of the impurity ions are similar to those of the ions in the precipitate.

4. **Mechanical Entrainment:**

   - Impurities are mechanically trapped within the precipitate. This can occur if the precipitate forms a gel-like structure that traps the surrounding solution.

   Factors Influencing Co-precipitation:

1. **Rate of Precipitation:**

   - Rapid precipitation increases the likelihood of occlusion and mechanical entrainment. Slow, controlled precipitation allows for the formation of purer crystals.

2. **Digestion:**

   - Allowing the precipitate to stand in the mother liquor (the remaining solution) improves the purity by promoting recrystallization, which can release trapped impurities.

3. **pH of the Solution:**

   ◦ The pH affects the solubility of both the precipitate and potential impurities. Proper pH control can minimize co-precipitation by ensuring the precipitate forms under optimal conditions.

4. **Temperature:**

   ◦ Higher temperatures generally increase the solubility of impurities, which can reduce co-precipitation. However, too high a temperature can also increase the solubility of the precipitate.

Minimizing Co-precipitation:

1. **Controlled Precipitation:**

   ◦ Precipitate the analyte slowly by adding the precipitating agent dropwise with constant stirring. This allows larger, purer crystals to form.

2. **Digestion:**

   ◦ Allow the precipitate to digest in the mother liquor. This process helps larger, purer crystals to form as smaller, impurity-laden crystals dissolve and re-precipitate on larger, purer ones.

3. **Washing:**

   ◦ Wash the precipitate thoroughly with a suitable solvent to remove adsorbed impurities. The washing solvent should not dissolve the precipitate.

4. **Re-precipitation:**

   ◦ Dissolve the impure precipitate in a suitable solvent and re-precipitate it. This step can significantly improve the purity by eliminating occluded and included impurities.

Example:

Consider the precipitation of barium sulfate (BaSO4) for the determination of sulfate ions (SO4 $^{2-}$). If the precipitation is carried out rapidly, the BaSO4 precipitate may occlude impurities from the solution, such as other ions present. To minimize co-precipitation:

1. **Slow Addition of Barium Chloride:**

   ◦ Add barium chloride solution dropwise to the sulfate solution with constant stirring.

2. **Digestion:**

   ◦ Allow the precipitate to stand in the mother liquor at an elevated temperature (around 70°C) for several hours.

3. **Washing:**

   ◦ Wash the precipitate with dilute sulfuric acid to remove adsorbed impurities.

4. **Re-precipitation (if necessary):**

   ◦ Dissolve the impure BaSO4 in concentrated hydrochloric acid and re-precipitate by adding dilute sulfuric acid slowly.

Co-precipitation can significantly affect the accuracy and precision of gravimetric analysis by introducing impurities into the precipitate. Understanding the mechanisms and factors influencing co-precipitation allows analysts to implement strategies to minimize its effects. Controlled precipitation, digestion, thorough washing, and re-precipitation are essential techniques to ensure the purity of the precipitate and the reliability of the analytical results.

8.2.2 POST-PRECIPITATION

Introduction: Post-precipitation occurs when impurities precipitate onto the surface of a primary precipitate after its initial formation. This can introduce additional impurities into the precipitate, affecting its purity and the accuracy of the gravimetric analysis.

Mechanisms of Post-Precipitation:

1. **Secondary Nucleation:**

   - After the primary precipitate has formed, additional nucleation sites can appear on the surface of the existing precipitate, leading to the formation of a secondary precipitate of different impurities.

2. **Supersaturation:**

   - The solution may become supersaturated with respect to impurities after the primary precipitate has formed. These impurities then precipitate out and coat the primary precipitate.

Factors Influencing Post-Precipitation:

1. **Time:**

   - The longer the precipitate remains in the solution, the greater the chance of post-precipitation occurring. Rapid filtration after precipitation can minimize this issue.

2. **Concentration of Impurities:**

   - High concentrations of impurities in the solution increase the likelihood of post-precipitation. Reducing the concentration of impurities before precipitation can help.

3. **Temperature:**

   - Higher temperatures can increase the rate of nucleation and growth of the secondary precipitate. Controlling the temperature can minimize post-precipitation.

4. **pH:**

   - The pH of the solution can affect the solubility of impurities. Maintaining an optimal pH can help prevent the post-precipitation of impurities.

Minimizing Post-Precipitation:

1. **Rapid Filtration:**

   - Filter the precipitate as soon as possible after its formation to prevent impurities from precipitating onto its surface.

2. **Washing:**

   - Wash the precipitate thoroughly to remove any adsorbed impurities that may lead to post-precipitation.

3. **Control of Precipitation Conditions:**

   - Carefully control the temperature, pH, and concentration of impurities to minimize post-precipitation.

4. **Use of Protective Colloids:**

   - Protective colloids can be added to the solution to prevent impurities from precipitating onto the primary precipitate.

Example:
Consider the precipitation of calcium oxalate (CaC2O4) for the determination of calcium ions (Ca $^{2+}$). If the solution contains significant amounts of magnesium ions (Mg^{2+}), post-precipitation of magnesium oxalate (MgC2O4) may occur on the surface of the calcium oxalate precipitate. To minimize post-precipitation:

1. **Rapid Filtration:**

   - Filter the calcium oxalate precipitate immediately after formation.

2. **Washing:**

- Wash the precipitate with a solution that does not dissolve the primary precipitate but removes any adsorbed impurities.

3. **Temperature Control:**

- Maintain a consistent temperature to prevent supersaturation of impurities.

8.3 APPLICATIONS

Gravimetric analysis is widely used in various fields for the quantitative determination of analytes. The following are some key applications:

8.3.1 ESTIMATION OF MAGNESIUM SULPHATE

Principle: The estimation of magnesium sulfate ($MgSO_4$) involves the precipitation of magnesium ions (Mg^{2+}) as magnesium ammonium phosphate ($MgNH_4PO_4$) or magnesium oxinate ($Mg(C_9H_6NO)_2$) and weighing the precipitate.

Procedure:

1. **Sample Preparation:**

- Dissolve a known amount of the sample in distilled water and transfer to a titration flask.

2. **Precipitation:**

- Add ammonium phosphate or oxine reagent to the sample solution to precipitate magnesium ions as magnesium ammonium phosphate or magnesium oxinate.

3. **Filtration:**

- Filter the precipitate using filter paper or a filtering crucible.

4. **Washing:**

- Wash the precipitate with distilled water to remove impurities.

5. **Drying/Ignition:**

   - Dry the precipitate in an oven or ignite in a muffle furnace to a constant mass.

6. **Weighing:**

   - Weigh the dried or ignited precipitate using an analytical balance.

7. **Calculation:**

   - Calculate the concentration of magnesium sulfate using the mass of the precipitate and the stoichiometry of the precipitation reaction.

   Example Calculation:

- Suppose 0.5 grams of the sample is dissolved and precipitated as magnesium ammonium phosphate. The mass of the dried precipitate is 0.4 grams.

   - Moles of $MgNH_4PO_4$ = Mass / Molar mass = 0.4 g / 137.32 g/mol = 0.00291 moles
   - Moles of Mg^{2+} = Moles of $MgNH_4PO_4$ (1:1 stoichiometry) = 0.00291 moles
   - Mass of $MgSO_4$ = Moles × Molar mass of $MgSO_4$ = 0.00291 moles × 120.37 g/mol = 0.3503 grams

8.3.2 ESTIMATION OF CALCIUM GLUCONATE

Principle: The estimation of calcium gluconate involves the precipitation of calcium ions (Ca^{2+}) as calcium oxalate (CaC_2O_4) and weighing the precipitate after ignition to calcium oxide (CaO).

Procedure:

1. **Sample Preparation:**

   - Dissolve a known amount of the sample in distilled water and transfer to a titration flask.

2. **Precipitation:**

   - Add oxalic acid to the sample solution to precipitate calcium ions as calcium oxalate.

3. **Filtration:**

   - Filter the precipitate using filter paper or a filtering crucible.

4. **Washing:**

   - Wash the precipitate with distilled water to remove impurities.

5. **Ignition:**

   - Ignite the precipitate in a muffle furnace to convert calcium oxalate to calcium oxide.

6. **Weighing:**

   - Weigh the ignited precipitate using an analytical balance.

7. **Calculation:**

   - Calculate the concentration of calcium gluconate using the mass of the precipitate and the stoichiometry of the precipitation reaction.

Example Calculation:

- Suppose 0.5 grams of the sample is dissolved and precipitated as calcium oxalate. The mass of the ignited precipitate (CaO) is 0.2 grams.

  - Moles of CaO = Mass / Molar mass = 0.2 g / 56.08 g/mol = 0.00357 moles
  - Moles of Ca^{2+} = Moles of CaO (1:1 stoichiometry) = 0.00357 moles
  - Mass of $Ca(C_6H_{11}O_7)_2$ = Moles × Molar mass of $Ca(C_6H_{11}O_7)_2$ = 0.00357 moles × 430.37 g/mol = 1.536 grams

NINE
DIAZOTISATION TITRATION

9.1 BASIC PRINCIPLES

9.1.1 MECHANISM AND PROCEDURES
Basic Principles of Diazotisation Titration:

Diazotisation titration is a method used to determine the concentration of primary aromatic amines by converting them into diazonium salts, which are then titrated with a standard solution. This technique is commonly used in the analysis of pharmaceutical compounds, dyes, and other aromatic amines. The diazotisation reaction involves the formation of a diazonium ion, which is a key intermediate in the synthesis and analysis of various compounds.

Mechanism:

1. **Formation of Diazonium Salt:**

   - The primary aromatic amine reacts with nitrous acid (HNO2) to form a diazonium salt. Nitrous acid is typically generated in situ by the reaction of sodium nitrite (NaNO2) with hydrochloric acid (HCl).

   $$ArNH2 + HNO2 + HCl \rightarrow ArN_2^+ Cl^- + 2H2O$$

   - Here, ArNH2 represents the aromatic amine, and ArN2+ Cl- represents the diazonium salt.

1. **Titration of Diazonium Salt:**

   - The diazonium salt is then titrated with a standard solution of a coupling agent or another reactant that reacts with the diazonium ion to form a stable, colored product.

Procedures:

1. **Preparation of Reagents:**

   - **Sodium Nitrite Solution:** Prepare a standard solution of sodium nitrite ($NaNO2$) by dissolving a known amount of $NaNO2$ in distilled water.
   - **Hydrochloric Acid Solution:** Prepare a dilute hydrochloric acid (HCl) solution for generating nitrous acid in situ.
   - **Indicator or Coupling Agent:** Choose a suitable indicator or coupling agent that will react with the diazonium ion to produce a colored end product.

2. **Sample Preparation:**

   - Dissolve a known amount of the sample containing the primary aromatic amine in distilled water or an appropriate solvent. Transfer the solution to a titration flask.

3. **Generation of Nitrous Acid:**

   - Add the hydrochloric acid solution to the sample solution to create an acidic environment. Then, add the sodium nitrite solution to generate nitrous acid in situ.

4. **Formation of Diazonium Salt:**

   - Allow the reaction to proceed at a low temperature (0-5°C) to form the diazonium salt. This is crucial as diazonium salts are generally unstable at higher temperatures.

5. **Titration:**

- ○ Titrate the diazonium salt solution with the standard solution of the coupling agent. Add the titrant slowly while continuously stirring the solution.
- ○ The endpoint is detected by the formation of a stable, colored product or by using an appropriate indicator that changes color at the endpoint.

6. **Calculation:**

- ○ Record the volume of the titrant used to reach the endpoint.
- ○ Calculate the concentration of the primary aromatic amine in the sample using the volume of the titrant added and the stoichiometry of the reaction.

Example Calculation:

Suppose 25.0 mL of a sample solution containing aniline ($C_6H_5NH_2$) is titrated with 0.1 M sodium nitrite solution, and 30.0 mL of sodium nitrite solution is required to reach the endpoint.

1. **Moles of Sodium Nitrite Used:** Moles of $NaNO_2$=Volume (L)×Molarity (M)=0.030 L×0.1 M=0.003 moles
2. **Moles of Aniline:**

- ○ The reaction between aniline and nitrous acid is a 1:1 stoichiometry, so the moles of aniline are equal to the moles of sodium nitrite used. Moles of $C_6H_5NH_2$=0.003 moles

3. **Concentration of Aniline:** Concentration of $C_6H_5NH_2$=0.003 moles /0.025 L=0.12 M

Factors Affecting the Accuracy:

1. **Temperature Control:**

- ○ Maintain a low temperature (0-5°C) during the diazotisation reaction to prevent the decomposition of the diazonium salt.

2. **pH Control:**

- Ensure the solution is sufficiently acidic to promote the formation of nitrous acid and the diazonium salt.

3. **Purity of Reagents:**

   - Use high-purity reagents to avoid interference from impurities.

4. **Reaction Time:**

   - Allow adequate time for the formation of the diazonium salt, but do not exceed the optimal reaction time to prevent decomposition.

Applications:

1. **Pharmaceutical Analysis:**

   - Used for the determination of primary aromatic amines in drug formulations and raw materials.

2. **Dye Industry:**

   - Applied in the analysis of aromatic amines used in the synthesis of dyes and pigments.

3. **Environmental Monitoring:**

   - Used for the detection and quantification of aromatic amine pollutants in water and soil samples.

4. **Chemical Research:**

   - Employed in the synthesis and analysis of diazonium compounds for various chemical reactions.

9.2 METHODS AND APPLICATIONS

9.2.1 COMMONLY USED METHODS

Introduction:

Diazotisation titration is a versatile analytical technique used for the determination of primary aromatic amines. Various methods have been developed to improve the accuracy and reliability of this titration, depending on the specific requirements of the analysis. Here are some commonly used methods in diazotisation titration:

1. Direct Titration Method:

Principle:

- In direct titration, the primary aromatic amine is titrated directly with a standard sodium nitrite solution in the presence of hydrochloric acid to form a diazonium salt. The endpoint is detected using a suitable indicator or a potentiometric method.

Procedure:

1. **Sample Preparation:**

   - Dissolve a known amount of the sample containing the primary aromatic amine in distilled water and transfer to a titration flask.

2. **Generation of Nitrous Acid:**

   - Add a known excess of hydrochloric acid to the sample solution to create an acidic environment.

3. **Titration:**

   - Titrate with a standard sodium nitrite solution while stirring continuously. Maintain the temperature at 0-5°C to prevent the decomposition of the diazonium salt.

4. **Endpoint Detection:**

   - Use an indicator such as starch-iodide paper, which turns blue when excess nitrite is present, indicating the endpoint. Alternatively, use a potentiometric method for more precise detection.

Applications:

- Suitable for the determination of aromatic amines in pharmaceuticals, dyes, and environmental samples.

2. Indirect Titration Method:
Principle:

- In indirect titration, the aromatic amine is first diazotised with an excess of sodium nitrite solution in acidic conditions. The excess nitrite is then titrated with a standard solution of ammonium iron(II) sulfate or another reducing agent.

Procedure:

1. **Sample Preparation:**

   - Dissolve a known amount of the sample in distilled water and transfer to a titration flask.

2. **Generation of Nitrous Acid:**

   - Add a known excess of hydrochloric acid and sodium nitrite to the sample solution to form the diazonium salt.

3. **Back Titration:**

   - After the reaction is complete, titrate the excess nitrite with a standard solution of ammonium iron(II) sulfate.

4. **Endpoint Detection:**

   - Use an indicator such as starch-iodide paper to detect the presence of excess nitrite, or use a potentiometric method.

Applications:

- Useful for samples where direct titration is not feasible due to the instability of the diazonium salt or the presence of interfering substances.

3. Coupling Reaction Method:
Principle:

- In this method, the diazonium salt formed from the primary aromatic amine is reacted with a coupling agent such as β-naphthol or aniline to form a colored azo dye. The amount of azo dye formed is proportional to the concentration of the aromatic amine.

Procedure:

1. **Sample Preparation:**

   - Dissolve a known amount of the sample in distilled water and transfer to a titration flask.

2. **Generation of Nitrous Acid:**

   - Add hydrochloric acid and sodium nitrite to the sample solution to form the diazonium salt.

3. **Coupling Reaction:**

   - Add the coupling agent to the diazonium salt solution and allow the reaction to proceed at a low temperature (0-5°C) to form the colored azo dye.

4. **Measurement:**

   - Measure the intensity of the color using a spectrophotometer. The absorbance is proportional to the concentration of the aromatic amine.

Applications:

- Widely used for the determination of aromatic amines in pharmaceuticals, dyes, and industrial chemicals.

9.2.2 PHARMACEUTICAL APPLICATIONS

Introduction:

Diazotisation titration plays a significant role in pharmaceutical analysis. It is particularly useful for the determination of primary aromatic amines, which are common in many pharmaceutical compounds. The method's accuracy and reliability make it indispensable for quality control and assurance in the pharmaceutical industry.

Key Pharmaceutical Applications:

1. **Determination of Sulfa Drugs:**

Principle:

- Sulfa drugs, such as sulfamethoxazole and sulfadiazine, contain primary aromatic amines that can be quantified using diazotisation titration. The primary amine group reacts with nitrous acid to form a diazonium salt, which is then titrated to determine the concentration of the sulfa drug.

Procedure:

1. **Sample Preparation:**

   - Dissolve a known amount of the sulfa drug in distilled water and transfer to a titration flask.

2. **Generation of Nitrous Acid:**

   - Add hydrochloric acid to the sample solution, followed by sodium nitrite to generate nitrous acid in situ.

3. **Diazotisation:**

   - Allow the reaction to proceed at a low temperature (0-5°C) to form the diazonium salt.

4. **Titration:**

   - Titrate the diazonium salt with a standard solution of a coupling agent or another suitable reactant.

5. **Endpoint Detection:**

   - Use an indicator or a potentiometric method to detect the endpoint.

6. **Calculation:**

   - Calculate the concentration of the sulfa drug based on the volume of the titrant used.

   Applications:

   - Quality control and assurance of sulfa drug formulations.
   - Ensuring the correct dosage and potency of pharmaceutical products.

2. **Analysis of Local Anesthetics:**

   Principle:

   - Many local anesthetics, such as procaine and benzocaine, contain primary aromatic amines. Diazotisation titration can be used to determine their concentration by forming diazonium salts and titrating them with suitable reagents.

   Procedure:

1. **Sample Preparation:**

   - Dissolve the local anesthetic in distilled water and transfer to a titration flask.

2. **Generation of Nitrous Acid:**

- Add hydrochloric acid to the sample solution and generate nitrous acid by adding sodium nitrite.

3. **Diazotisation:**

- Conduct the reaction at a low temperature to form the diazonium salt.

4. **Titration:**

- Titrate the diazonium salt with a standard solution of a coupling agent or other reactants.

5. **Endpoint Detection:**

- Use an appropriate indicator or potentiometric method to detect the endpoint.

6. **Calculation:**

- Determine the concentration of the local anesthetic based on the volume of the titrant used.

Applications:

- Ensuring the efficacy and safety of local anesthetic formulations.
- Quality control in the production of anesthetic drugs.

3. **Quantification of Aromatic Amines in APIs:**

Principle:

- Active pharmaceutical ingredients (APIs) that contain primary aromatic amines can be quantified using diazotisation titration. The method involves converting the amine group into a diazonium salt and titrating it to determine the concentration of the API.

Procedure:

1. **Sample Preparation:**

   - Dissolve the API in distilled water and transfer to a titration flask.

2. **Generation of Nitrous Acid:**

   - Add hydrochloric acid to the sample solution, followed by sodium nitrite to generate nitrous acid.

3. **Diazotisation:**

   - Conduct the reaction at a low temperature to form the diazonium salt.

4. **Titration:**

   - Titrate the diazonium salt with a standard solution of a coupling agent or other suitable reactant.

5. **Endpoint Detection:**

   - Use an appropriate indicator or potentiometric method to detect the endpoint.

6. **Calculation:**

   - Calculate the concentration of the API based on the volume of the titrant used.

Applications:

- Quality control of APIs containing aromatic amines.
- Ensuring the correct dosage and efficacy of pharmaceutical products.

4. **Detection of Aromatic Amine Impurities:**

Principle:

- Diazotisation titration can also be used to detect and quantify aromatic amine impurities in pharmaceutical formulations. The method involves converting the impurities into diazonium salts and titrating them.

Procedure:

1. **Sample Preparation:**

   - Dissolve the pharmaceutical formulation in distilled water and transfer to a titration flask.

2. **Generation of Nitrous Acid:**

   - Add hydrochloric acid to the sample solution and generate nitrous acid by adding sodium nitrite.

3. **Diazotisation:**

   - Conduct the reaction at a low temperature to form the diazonium salt.

4. **Titration:**

   - Titrate the diazonium salt with a standard solution of a coupling agent or other suitable reactant.

5. **Endpoint Detection:**

   - Use an appropriate indicator or potentiometric method to detect the endpoint.

6. **Calculation:**

   - Calculate the concentration of aromatic amine impurities based on the volume of the titrant used.

Applications:

- Ensuring the purity of pharmaceutical formulations by detecting aromatic amine impurities.
- Quality control in the manufacturing process to maintain product safety and efficacy.

Diazotisation titration is a valuable technique in pharmaceutical analysis for the determination of primary aromatic amines in various drug formulations. Its applications range from the quantification of sulfa drugs and local anesthetics to the analysis of APIs and the detection of impurities. By employing diazotisation titration, pharmaceutical analysts can ensure the quality, efficacy, and safety of pharmaceutical products, thereby maintaining high standards in the industry.

TEN

REDOX TITRATIONS

10.2 TYPES OF REDOX TITRATIONS

10.2.1 CERIMETRY

Principle: Cerimetry is a redox titration method that utilizes cerium(IV) sulfate (Ce(SO4)2) as a titrant. Cerium(IV) is a strong oxidizing agent, and the titration involves the reduction of Ce4+ to Ce3+ while the analyte (reducing agent) is oxidized.

$$Ce^{4+} + e^{-} \rightarrow Ce^{3+}$$

Procedure:

1. **Preparation of the Sample:**

   - Dissolve a known amount of the sample containing the reducing agent in distilled water and transfer it to a titration flask.

2. **Addition of Acid:**

   - Add an appropriate amount of sulfuric acid (H2SO4) to the sample solution to maintain an acidic environment. This helps to stabilize the cerium(IV) ions and ensures complete reaction.

3. **Titration:**

   - Titrate the sample solution with a standard cerium(IV) sulfate solution while stirring continuously. The reaction between the cerium(IV) ions and the reducing agent will proceed, resulting in the reduction of Ce4+ to Ce3+.

4. **Endpoint Detection:**

   ◦ The endpoint can be detected using an appropriate redox indicator, such as ferroin, which changes color when all the reducing agent has been oxidized. Alternatively, a potentiometric method can be used for more precise endpoint detection.

5. **Calculation:**

   ◦ Record the volume of cerium(IV) sulfate solution used to reach the endpoint.
   ◦ Calculate the concentration of the reducing agent in the sample using the volume of the titrant and the stoichiometry of the reaction.

   Example Calculation:

- Suppose 25.0 mL of a sample solution containing ferrous ions (Fe2+) is titrated with 0.1 M cerium(IV) sulfate solution, and 30.0 mL of the titrant is required to reach the endpoint.

   Moles of Ce^{4+} =Volume (L)×Molarity (M)=0.030 L×0.1 M=0.003 moles Moles of Fe^{2+} =Moles of Ce4+(1:1 stoichiometry)=0.003 moles Concentration of Fe2+=0.003 moles/ 0.025 L=0.12 M
   Applications:

1. **Pharmaceutical Analysis:**

   ◦ Determination of reducing agents such as ferrous ions in pharmaceutical formulations.

2. **Environmental Monitoring:**

   ◦ Analysis of reducing agents in water and soil samples.

3. **Industrial Processes:**

- Quality control of reducing agents in industrial products and processes.

10.2.2 IODIMETRY

Principle: Iodimetry is a redox titration method that involves the titration of an oxidizing agent with a standard solution of sodium thiosulfate (Na2S2O3). Iodine (I2) is produced in situ by the reaction of the oxidizing agent with potassium iodide (KI), and the iodine is then titrated with sodium thiosulfate.

$$I_2 + 2S_2O_3^{2-} \rightarrow 2I^- + S_4O_6^{2-}$$

Procedure:

1. **Sample Preparation:**

   - Dissolve a known amount of the sample containing the oxidizing agent in distilled water and transfer it to a titration flask.

2. **Generation of Iodine:**

   - Add an excess of potassium iodide (KI) to the sample solution. The oxidizing agent will react with KI to liberate iodine (I2).

3. **Addition of Acid:**

   - Add hydrochloric acid (HCl) or sulfuric acid (H2SO4) to maintain an acidic environment, which helps in the liberation of iodine.

4. **Titration:**

   - Titrate the liberated iodine with a standard sodium thiosulfate solution while stirring continuously. The reaction between iodine and sodium thiosulfate will proceed, reducing iodine to iodide ions.

5. **Endpoint Detection:**

   - Use starch as an indicator, which forms a blue complex with iodine. The endpoint is reached when the blue color disappears, indicating that all the iodine has reacted with the sodium thiosulfate.

6. **Calculation:**

   - Record the volume of sodium thiosulfate solution used to reach the endpoint.
   - Calculate the concentration of the oxidizing agent in the sample using the volume of the titrant and the stoichiometry of the reaction.

Example Calculation:

- Suppose 25.0 mL of a sample solution containing chlorine (Cl2) is titrated with 0.1 M sodium thiosulfate solution, and 20.0 mL of the titrant is required to reach the endpoint.

Moles of Na2S2O3=Volume (L)×Molarity (M)=0.020 L×0.1 M=0.002 moles Moles of Cl $_2$=Moles of Na2S2O3/2(2:1 stoichiometry)=0.001 moles Concentration of Cl_2=0.001 moles / 0.025 L=0.04 M

   Applications:

1. **Pharmaceutical Analysis:**

   - Determination of oxidizing agents such as copper(II) ions, chlorine, and potassium dichromate in pharmaceutical formulations.

2. **Water Quality Testing:**

   - Analysis of oxidizing agents in drinking water, wastewater, and industrial effluents.

3. **Food Industry:**

   - Determination of iodine content in food products and additives.

4. **Environmental Monitoring:**

10.2 TYPES OF REDOX TITRATIONS

10.2.3 IODOMETRY

Principle: Iodometry is a redox titration method used to determine the concentration of reducing agents. The reducing agent in the sample reduces iodine (I2) to iodide ions (I-). The iodine is typically generated in situ by the oxidation of iodide ions with an oxidizing agent.

$$I_2 + 2\,e^- \rightarrow 2I^- \rightarrow 2I^-$$

Procedure:

1. **Sample Preparation:**

   - Dissolve a known amount of the sample containing the reducing agent in distilled water and transfer it to a titration flask.

2. **Generation of Iodine:**

   - Add an excess of potassium iodide (KI) to the sample solution. The reducing agent will react with iodine, reducing it to iodide ions.

3. **Addition of Acid:**

   - Add hydrochloric acid (HCl) or sulfuric acid (H2SO4) to maintain an acidic environment, facilitating the reaction.

4. **Titration:**

   - Titrate the iodine with a standard sodium thiosulfate solution while stirring continuously. The reaction between iodine and sodium thiosulfate will proceed, reducing iodine to iodide ions.

$$I_2 + 2S_2O_3^{2-} \rightarrow 2I^- + S4O6^{2-}$$ **Endpoint Detection:**

   - Use starch as an indicator, which forms a blue complex with iodine. The endpoint is reached when the blue color disappears, indicating that all the iodine has reacted with the sodium thiosulfate.

2. **Calculation:**

   - Record the volume of sodium thiosulfate solution used to reach the endpoint.

- Calculate the concentration of the reducing agent in the sample using the volume of the titrant and the stoichiometry of the reaction.

Example Calculation:

- Suppose 25.0 mL of a sample solution containing ascorbic acid (vitamin C) is titrated with 0.1 M sodium thiosulfate solution, and 20.0 mL of the titrant is required to reach the endpoint.

Moles of Na2S2O3=Volume (L)×Molarity (M)=0.020 L×0.1 M=0.002 moles Moles of ascorbic acid=Moles of Na2S2O3(1:1 stoichiometry)=0.002 moles \ Concentration of ascorbic acid=0.002 moles / 0.025 L=0.08 M

Applications:

1. **Pharmaceutical Analysis:**

   - Determination of reducing agents such as ascorbic acid, sulfite ions (SO_3^{2-}), and antimony(III) ions in pharmaceutical formulations.

2. **Food Industry:**

   - Analysis of antioxidants such as vitamin C in food products and beverages.

3. **Environmental Monitoring:**

   - Determination of reducing agents in water and soil samples.

4. **Industrial Processes:**

   - Quality control of reducing agents in industrial products and processes.

10.2.4 BROMATOMETRY

Principle: Bromatometry involves the titration of a reducing agent with a standard solution of potassium bromate (KBrO3). Bromate is a strong oxidizing agent that reacts with the reducing agent to form bromine (Br2).

$$BrO_3^{3-} +5Br^- +6H^+ \rightarrow 3Br_2+3H_2O$$

Procedure:

1. **Sample Preparation:**

   ○ Dissolve a known amount of the sample containing the reducing agent in distilled water and transfer it to a titration flask.

2. **Addition of Acid:**

   ○ Add hydrochloric acid (HCl) or sulfuric acid (H2SO4) to maintain an acidic environment, which is necessary for the reaction.

3. **Titration:**

   ○ Titrate the sample solution with a standard potassium bromate solution while stirring continuously. The bromate will oxidize the reducing agent, forming bromine.

4. **Endpoint Detection:**

   ○ The endpoint can be detected by the disappearance of the yellow color of bromine or using an appropriate redox indicator.

5. **Calculation:**

   ○ Record the volume of potassium bromate solution used to reach the endpoint.
   ○ Calculate the concentration of the reducing agent in the sample using the volume of the titrant and the stoichiometry of the reaction.

Example Calculation:

- Suppose 25.0 mL of a sample solution containing arsenite ions (AsO_3^{3-}) is titrated with 0.1 M potassium bromate solution, and 15.0 mL of the titrant is required to reach the endpoint.

Moles of KBrO3=Volume (L)×Molarity (M)=0.015 L×0.1 M=0.0015 moles
Moles of AsO_3^{3-} =Moles of KBrO3/3(1:3 stoichiometry)=0.0005

Concentration of AsO33−=0.0005 moles / 0.025 L=0.02 M

Applications:

1. **Pharmaceutical Analysis:**

   - Determination of reducing agents such as arsenite ions, hydroquinone, and thiourea in pharmaceutical formulations.

2. **Environmental Monitoring:**

   - Analysis of reducing agents in water and soil samples to assess pollution levels.

3. **Industrial Processes:**

   - Quality control of reducing agents in industrial products and processes.

4. **Food Industry:**

   - Determination of reducing agents and preservatives in food products.

Iodometry and bromatometry are essential redox titration methods used for the determination of reducing agents in various samples. By understanding the principles and carefully controlling the experimental conditions, analysts can achieve accurate and reliable results. These techniques are widely used in pharmaceutical analysis, environmental monitoring, food industry, and industrial processes, highlighting their significance in analytical chemistry.

10.2 TYPES OF REDOX TITRATIONS

10.2.5 DICHROMETRY

Principle: Dichrometry is a redox titration method involving the use of potassium dichromate ($K_2Cr_2O_7$) as a titrant. Potassium dichromate is a strong oxidizing agent, and the titration involves the reduction of dichromate ions ($Cr_2O_7^{2-}$) to chromium(III) ions (Cr^{3+}), while the analyte (reducing agent) is oxidized.

$$Cr_2O_7^{2-} + 14H^+ + 6e^- \rightarrow 2Cr^{3+} + 7H_2O$$

Procedure:

1. **Preparation of the Sample:**

   - Dissolve a known amount of the sample containing the reducing agent in distilled water and transfer it to a titration flask.

2. **Addition of Acid:**

   - Add an appropriate amount of sulfuric acid (H2SO4) to the sample solution to maintain an acidic environment. This is necessary to stabilize the dichromate ions and ensure complete reaction.

3. **Titration:**

   - Titrate the sample solution with a standard potassium dichromate solution while stirring continuously. The reaction between the dichromate ions and the reducing agent will proceed, resulting in the reduction of $Cr2O7^{2-}$ to Cr^{3+}.

4. **Endpoint Detection:**

   - The endpoint can be detected using an appropriate redox indicator, such as diphenylamine, which changes color when all the reducing agent has been oxidized. Alternatively, a potentiometric method can be used for more precise endpoint detection.

5. **Calculation:**

   - Record the volume of potassium dichromate solution used to reach the endpoint.
   - Calculate the concentration of the reducing agent in the sample using the volume of the titrant and the stoichiometry of the reaction.

Example Calculation:

- Suppose 25.0 mL of a sample solution containing iron(II) ions (Fe2+) is titrated with 0.1 M potassium dichromate solution, and 30.0 mL of the titrant is required to reach the endpoint.

Moles of K2Cr2O7=Volume (L)×Molarity (M)=0.030 L×0.1 M=0.003 moles
Moles of Fe2+=Moles of K2Cr2O7×6(1:6 stoichiometry)=0.003×6=0.018 moles
Concentration of Fe2+=0.018 moles / 0.025 L=0.72 M

Applications:

1. **Pharmaceutical Analysis:**

   - Determination of reducing agents such as ferrous ions in pharmaceutical formulations.

2. **Environmental Monitoring:**

   - Analysis of reducing agents in water and soil samples.

3. **Industrial Processes:**

   - Quality control of reducing agents in industrial products and processes.

10.2.6 TITRATION WITH POTASSIUM IODATE

Principle: Potassium iodate (KIO3) is a strong oxidizing agent used in redox titrations. The iodate ion (IO_3^-) oxidizes iodide ions (I^-) to iodine (I_2), which can then be titrated with a reducing agent.

$$IO3^- + 5I^- + 6H^+ \rightarrow 3I_2 + 3H_2O$$

Procedure:

1. **Preparation of the Sample:**

   - Dissolve a known amount of the sample containing the reducing agent in distilled water and transfer it to a titration flask.

2. **Generation of Iodine:**

- Add an excess of potassium iodide (KI) to the sample solution. The iodate will oxidize iodide ions to iodine.

3. **Addition of Acid:**

- Add hydrochloric acid (HCl) or sulfuric acid (H2SO4) to maintain an acidic environment, which facilitates the reaction.

4. **Titration:**

- Titrate the liberated iodine with a standard sodium thiosulfate solution while stirring continuously. The reaction between iodine and sodium thiosulfate will proceed, reducing iodine to iodide ions.

$$I_2 + 2S_2O_3^{2-} \rightarrow 2I^- + S4O6^{2-}$$

Endpoint Detection:

- Use starch as an indicator, which forms a blue complex with iodine. The endpoint is reached when the blue color disappears, indicating that all the iodine has reacted with the sodium thiosulfate.

6. **Calculation:**

- Record the volume of sodium thiosulfate solution used to reach the endpoint.
- Calculate the concentration of the reducing agent in the sample using the volume of the titrant and the stoichiometry of the reaction.

Example Calculation:

- Suppose 25.0 mL of a sample solution containing arsenic(III) ions (As3+) is titrated with 0.1 M potassium iodate solution, and 15.0 mL of the titrant is required to reach the endpoint.

Moles of KIO3=Volume (L)×Molarity (M)=0.015 L×0.1 M=0.0015 moles
Moles of As3+=Moles of KIO3/3(1:3 stoichiometry)=0.0005 moles
Concentration of As3+=0.0005 moles / 0.025 L=0.02 M
Applications:

1. **Pharmaceutical Analysis:**

   - Determination of reducing agents such as arsenic(III) ions, tin(II) ions, and hydrogen sulfide in pharmaceutical formulations.

2. **Environmental Monitoring:**

   - Analysis of reducing agents in water and soil samples to assess pollution levels.

3. **Industrial Processes:**

   - Quality control of reducing agents in industrial products and processes.

4. **Food Industry:**

   - Determination of reducing agents and preservatives in food products.

10.3 APPLICATIONS

10.3.1 PRACTICAL EXAMPLES

Example 1: Determination of Ferrous Iron Using Dichromate Titration

Principle: The ferrous iron (Fe^{2+}) in a sample can be determined by titrating with potassium dichromate ($K_2Cr_2O_7$). The ferrous ions are oxidized to ferric ions (Fe^{3+}), while the dichromate ions are reduced to chromium(III) ions (Cr^{3+}).

Procedure:

1. **Sample Preparation:**

   - Dissolve a known amount of the sample containing ferrous ions in distilled water and transfer it to a titration flask.

2. **Addition of Acid:**

- ○ Add sulfuric acid (H2SO4) to the sample solution to maintain an acidic environment.

3. **Titration:**

- ○ Titrate the sample solution with a standard potassium dichromate solution while stirring continuously.

4. **Endpoint Detection:**

- ○ Use diphenylamine as an indicator, which changes color at the endpoint when all ferrous ions are oxidized.

5. **Calculation:**

- ○ Record the volume of potassium dichromate solution used to reach the endpoint.
- ○ Calculate the concentration of ferrous ions using the volume of the titrant and the stoichiometry of the reaction.

Example Calculation:

- Suppose 25.0 mL of a sample solution is titrated with 0.1 M potassium dichromate solution, and 30.0 mL of the titrant is required to reach the endpoint.

Moles of K2Cr2O7=Volume (L)×Molarity (M)=0.030 L×0.1 M=0.003 moles
Moles of Fe2+=Moles of K2Cr2O7×6(1:6 stoichiometry)=0.003×6=0.018 moles
Concentration of Fe^{2+} =0.018 moles/ 0.025 L=0.72

Example 2: Determination of Ascorbic Acid Using Iodometry
Principle: Ascorbic acid (vitamin C) in a sample can be determined by titrating with iodine (I_2). The ascorbic acid reduces iodine to iodide ions (I^-).
Procedure:

1. **Sample Preparation:**

- ○ Dissolve a known amount of the sample containing ascorbic acid in distilled water and transfer it to a titration flask.

2. **Generation of Iodine:**

  - Add an excess of potassium iodide (KI) to the sample solution.

3. **Addition of Acid:**

  - Add hydrochloric acid (HCl) to maintain an acidic environment.

4. **Titration:**

  - Titrate the liberated iodine with a standard sodium thiosulfate solution while stirring continuously.

5. **Endpoint Detection:**

  - Use starch as an indicator, which forms a blue complex with iodine. The endpoint is reached when the blue color disappears.

6. **Calculation:**

  - Record the volume of sodium thiosulfate solution used to reach the endpoint.
  - Calculate the concentration of ascorbic acid using the volume of the titrant and the stoichiometry of the reaction.

Example Calculation:

- Suppose 25.0 mL of a sample solution is titrated with 0.1 M sodium thiosulfate solution, and 20.0 mL of the titrant is required to reach the endpoint.

Moles of $Na_2S_2O_3$=Volume (L)×Molarity (M)=0.020 L×0.1 M=0.002 Moles of ascorbic acid=Moles of $Na_2S_2O_3$(1:1 stoichiometry)=0.002 moles Concentration of ascorbic acid=0.002 moles / 0.025 L=0.08

10.3.2 USES IN PHARMACEUTICAL ANALYSIS

1. Determination of Active Pharmaceutical Ingredients (APIs):

Redox titrations are widely used in pharmaceutical analysis for the determination of APIs. For instance, iodometry is used to quantify APIs that have reducing properties, such as ascorbic acid and certain antibiotics. The accurate quantification of APIs ensures the correct dosage in pharmaceutical formulations, maintaining their efficacy and safety.

2. Quality Control and Assurance:

Redox titrations are integral to quality control and assurance processes in the pharmaceutical industry. They are used to monitor the purity of raw materials, intermediates, and final products. For example, cerimetry can be used to determine the concentration of reducing agents in pharmaceutical preparations, ensuring they meet the required specifications.

3. Stability Testing:

Pharmaceutical products are subjected to stability testing to ensure they maintain their potency and safety over time. Redox titrations can be used to monitor the degradation of APIs that undergo redox reactions, providing valuable data on the shelf life and stability of pharmaceutical products.

4. Detection of Impurities:

Redox titrations are employed to detect and quantify impurities in pharmaceutical products. For example, dichrometry can be used to determine trace amounts of reducing impurities in drug formulations. Identifying and quantifying impurities is crucial for ensuring the safety and quality of pharmaceutical products.

5. Analysis of Antioxidants:

Antioxidants are commonly used in pharmaceutical formulations to prevent oxidation of APIs. Redox titrations, such as iodometry, are used to determine the concentration of antioxidants in formulations. This helps in formulating products with optimal antioxidant levels to enhance their stability and shelf life.

6. Environmental Monitoring:

Pharmaceutical industries monitor the environmental impact of their manufacturing processes. Redox titrations are used to analyze effluents and waste products for oxidizing and reducing agents, ensuring compliance with environmental regulations.

ELEVEN

ELECTROCHEMICAL METHODS OF ANALYSIS

11.1 CONDUCTOMETRY

11.1.1 INTRODUCTION AND PRINCIPLES

Introduction: Conductometry is an analytical technique that measures the electrical conductivity of a solution. Conductivity is a measure of the ability of a solution to conduct an electric current, which depends on the presence and mobility of ions in the solution. Conductometric methods are widely used in pharmaceutical analysis to determine the concentration of ionic species and to monitor chemical reactions that produce or consume ions.

Principles:

1. **Conductivity:**

   - Conductivity (κ) is the measure of a solution's ability to conduct an electric current. It is influenced by the concentration and type of ions present, their charge, and their mobility.

2. **Ohm's Law:**

   - The relationship between the current (I), voltage (V), and resistance (R) in an electrical circuit is given by Ohm's Law: $I = V / R$

3. **Molar Conductivity:**

- Molar conductivity (Λm) is the conductivity of a solution containing one mole of electrolyte dissolved in a certain volume of solution. It is defined as: $\Lambda m = \kappa / c$
- Where κ is the conductivity and ccc is the molar concentration of the electrolyte.

4. **Factors Affecting Conductivity:**

- **Concentration:** Conductivity increases with increasing concentration of ions, but molar conductivity decreases due to ion pairing at higher concentrations.
- **Temperature:** Conductivity increases with increasing temperature as ion mobility increases.
- **Nature of Ions:** Conductivity depends on the charge and size of the ions. Smaller ions with higher charges generally have higher conductivities.

11.1.2 CONDUCTIVITY CELL

Introduction: A conductivity cell is a device used to measure the conductivity of a solution. It consists of two electrodes placed at a fixed distance apart, immersed in the solution whose conductivity is to be measured.

Components:

1. **Electrodes:**

- Typically made of platinum, the electrodes are inert and do not react with the solution. They are coated with platinum black to increase surface area and reduce electrode polarization.

2. **Cell Constant:**

- The cell constant (K) is defined as the ratio of the distance between the electrodes (d) to the electrode area (A): $K = d / A$
- The cell constant is determined during calibration and is used to calculate the conductivity of the solution.

3. **Measurement:**

  - An alternating current (AC) is passed through the solution to avoid electrolysis and electrode polarization. The conductivity is measured by determining the conductance of the solution and multiplying it by the cell constant.

11.1.3 CONDUCTOMETRIC TITRATIONS

Principle: Conductometric titrations involve monitoring the conductivity of a solution during the addition of a titrant. The conductivity changes as ions are added or removed during the reaction between the analyte and the titrant.

Procedure:

1. **Preparation:**

  - Prepare the sample solution and transfer it to a conductivity cell.

2. **Addition of Titrant:**

  - Add the titrant to the sample solution in small increments while continuously stirring. Measure the conductivity after each addition.

3. **Plotting Conductivity:**

  - Plot the conductivity against the volume of titrant added. The conductivity typically shows a characteristic change at the equivalence point, indicating the completion of the reaction.

4. **Determination of Equivalence Point:**

  - The equivalence point is identified as the point where a sharp change in conductivity occurs. The volume of titrant added at this point is used to calculate the concentration of the analyte.

  Types of Conductometric Titrations:

1. **Strong Acid with Strong Base:**

- Example: Titration of hydrochloric acid (HCl) with sodium hydroxide (NaOH). Conductivity decreases initially due to the formation of water and increases after the equivalence point due to excess NaOH.

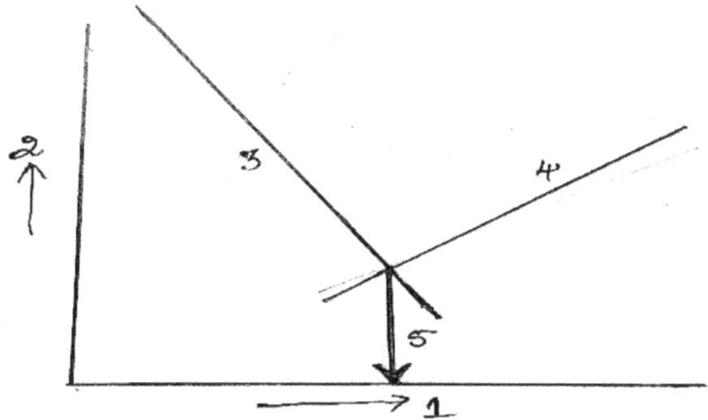

Strong Acid vs Strong Base : 1. Vol. of NaOH added, 2.Conductivity (mhos), 3. H^+, 4. OH^-, 5. End point

2. Weak Acid with Strong Base:

- Example: Titration of acetic acid (CH3COOH) with NaOH. Conductivity increases gradually and shows a sharp increase after the equivalence point due to the formation of sodium acetate (NaCH3COO⁻) and excess NaOH.

3. Precipitation Titrations:

- Example: Titration of barium chloride (BaCl2) with sulfuric acid (H2SO4). Conductivity decreases as BaSO4 precipitates out of the solution.

11.1.4 APPLICATIONS IN PHARMACEUTICAL ANALYSIS
1. Determination of Drug Purity:

- Conductometric methods are used to determine the purity of ionic drugs by measuring their conductivity in solution. Impurities can affect the conductivity, providing a quick and accurate assessment of drug purity.

2. Analysis of Electrolyte Solutions:

- Conductometry is used to analyze electrolyte solutions in pharmaceutical formulations. It helps in quantifying the concentration of electrolytes, ensuring the correct dosage and effectiveness of the formulation.

3. Monitoring Reactions:

- Conductometric titrations are employed to monitor reactions involving ionic species in pharmaceuticals. This includes acid-base reactions, precipitation reactions, and complexation reactions.

4. Quality Control:

- Conductometry is an essential tool in quality control laboratories for the analysis of raw materials, intermediates, and finished pharmaceutical products. It ensures compliance with pharmacopeial standards and specifications.

5. Stability Testing:

- Conductometric measurements are used in stability testing of pharmaceutical products to monitor changes in ionic content over time. This helps in assessing the shelf life and stability of the products.

6. Environmental Monitoring:

- Conductometry is used to monitor the environmental impact of pharmaceutical manufacturing processes by analyzing effluents and waste products for ionic content.

Conductometry is a versatile and essential analytical technique in pharmaceutical analysis. Its applications range from determining drug purity and analyzing electrolyte solutions to monitoring reactions and ensuring quality control. The principles, conductivity cell design, and conductometric titrations provide a robust framework for accurate and reliable analysis in the pharmaceutical industry.

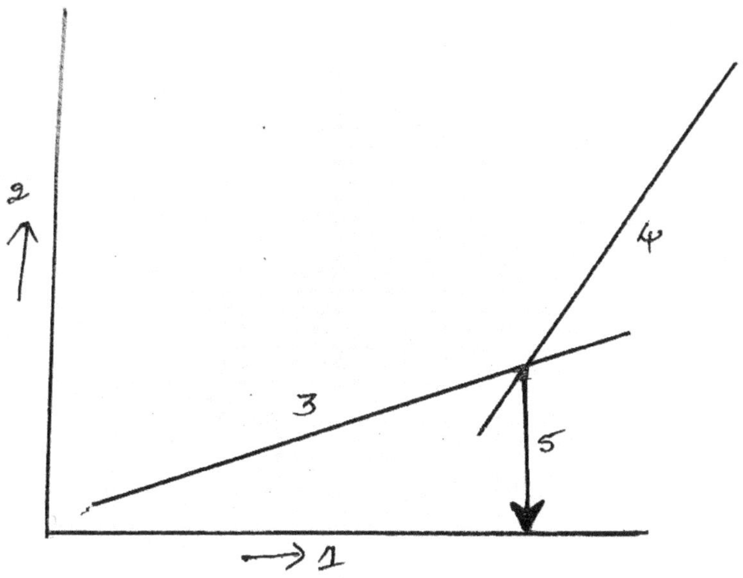

Weak Acid vs Strong base: 1. Vol. of NaOH, 2. Conductivity (mhos), 3. Salt formation, 4. OH⁻, 5. End point

11.2 POTENTIOMETRY

11.2.1 ELECTROCHEMICAL CELL CONSTRUCTION AND WORKING

Introduction: Potentiometry is an analytical technique used to measure the voltage of an electrochemical cell to determine the concentration of an analyte. The potential difference between two electrodes in the cell is measured without drawing any significant current. This method is widely used in pharmaceutical analysis for its accuracy and simplicity.

Electrochemical Cell Construction:

1. **Components:**

- **Reference Electrode:** Maintains a constant potential. Commonly used reference electrodes include the standard hydrogen electrode (SHE), the silver/silver chloride (Ag/AgCl) electrode, and the saturated calomel electrode (SCE).

- ○ **Indicator Electrode:** Responds to the activity of the ions of interest in the solution. Types include metal electrodes (e.g., platinum, gold) and ion-selective electrodes (e.g., glass electrode for pH measurement).
- ○ **Salt Bridge:** Connects the reference and indicator electrodes, allowing ionic conduction without mixing the different solutions. Often a U-shaped tube filled with an inert electrolyte like potassium chloride (KCl).

2. **Construction:**

- ○ **Cell Assembly:** The reference and indicator electrodes are immersed in the sample solution. The salt bridge is positioned to ensure ionic continuity between the two half-cells.
- ○ **Connection to Potentiometer:** The electrodes are connected to a high-impedance voltmeter (potentiometer) that measures the potential difference between them.

Working Principle:

1. **Electrode Potentials:**

- ○ Each electrode develops a potential based on its half-reaction and the concentration of the ions in the solution. The reference electrode has a stable and well-known potential, while the indicator electrode's potential varies with the analyte concentration.

2. Nernst Equation: The potential of the indicator electrode (E) is given by the Nernst equation:

$$E = E0 + (RT / nF) * \ln([Ox] / [Red])$$

Where:

- E is the electrode potential.
- E^0 is the standard electrode potential.
- R is the gas constant.
- T is the temperature in Kelvin.
- n is the number of electrons transferred in the redox reaction.
- F is the Faraday constant.
- $[Ox]$ and $[Red]$ are the concentrations of the oxidized and reduced forms, respectively.

1. Measurement:

- The potentiometer measures the potential difference between the reference and indicator electrodes. The potential difference is related to the concentration of the analyte by the Nernst equation.
- The measured potential is often plotted against the logarithm of the analyte concentration to create a calibration curve, allowing for the determination of unknown concentrations.

Applications in Pharmaceutical Analysis:

1. pH Measurement:

- Glass electrodes are used to measure the pH of pharmaceutical solutions. The potential difference between the glass electrode and a reference electrode is proportional to the hydrogen ion concentration.

2. Titration End-Point Detection:

- Potentiometry is used to detect the endpoint in acid-base, redox, precipitation, and complexometric titrations. The potential change at the equivalence point is sharp and easily detectable.

3. **Ion-Selective Electrode Analysis:**

   - Ion-selective electrodes (ISEs) are used to measure specific ions like potassium, calcium, and chloride in pharmaceutical formulations. These electrodes provide selective and sensitive measurements.

4. **Dissolution Testing:**

   - Potentiometric methods are employed in dissolution testing to monitor the release of drugs from dosage forms. The potential change is used to determine the rate and extent of dissolution.

5. **Quality Control:**

   - Potentiometry is an essential tool in quality control laboratories for the analysis of raw materials, intermediates, and finished products. It ensures that pharmaceutical products meet the required specifications.

11.2 POTENTIOMETRY

11.2.2 REFERENCE ELECTRODES

Introduction: Reference electrodes are crucial components in potentiometric measurements, providing a stable and well-known potential against which the potential of the indicator electrode is measured. They must be reliable, reproducible, and maintain a constant potential under varying conditions.

Common Types of Reference Electrodes:

1. **Standard Hydrogen Electrode (SHE):**

   Principle:

   - The SHE is the primary reference electrode against which all other electrode potentials are measured. It consists of a platinum electrode in contact with hydrogen gas at 1 atm pressure and immersed in a solution with a hydrogen ion activity of 1 M (usually 1 M HCl).

Reaction: $2H^+ + 2^{e^-} \rightarrow H_2(g)$ **Features:**

- **Potential:** Defined as 0.000 V at all temperatures.
- **Usage:** Due to its complexity and the need for hydrogen gas, the SHE is primarily used for calibration and research rather than routine measurements.

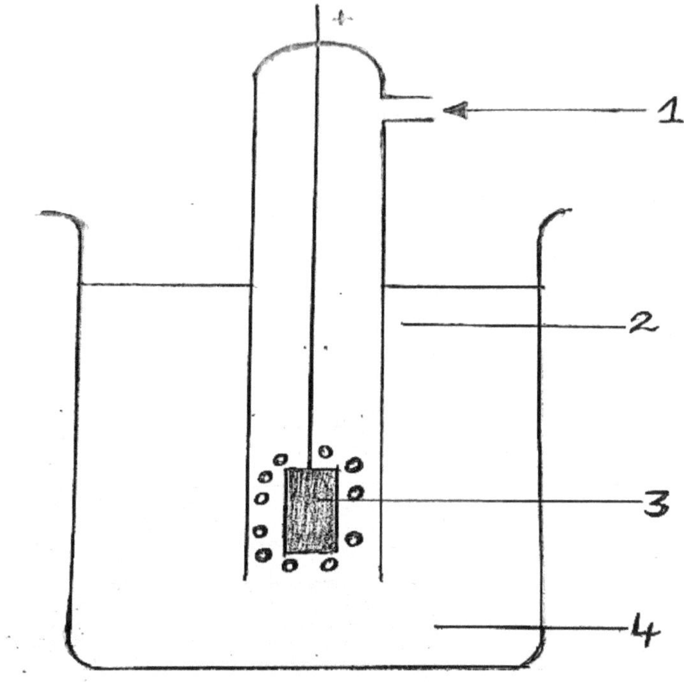

STANDARD HYDROGEN ELECTRIODE :

1. **H2 gas at 1 atm pressure, 2. Glass hood, 3. Platinum electrode covered with H$_2$,**

4. **1M solution of H$^+$ ions at 25°c**

2. **Silver/Silver Chloride Electrode (Ag/AgCl):**

Principle:

- This electrode consists of a silver wire coated with silver chloride, immersed in a solution of potassium chloride (KCl). The potential is determined by the chloride ion concentration.

Reaction: AgCl (s)+ $^{e-}$ →Ag (s)+Cl–
Features:

- **Potential:** +0.197 V vs. SHE when saturated with KCl.
- **Advantages:** Simple, stable, and widely used in various potentiometric applications.
- **Limitations:** Potential varies with the concentration of KCl.

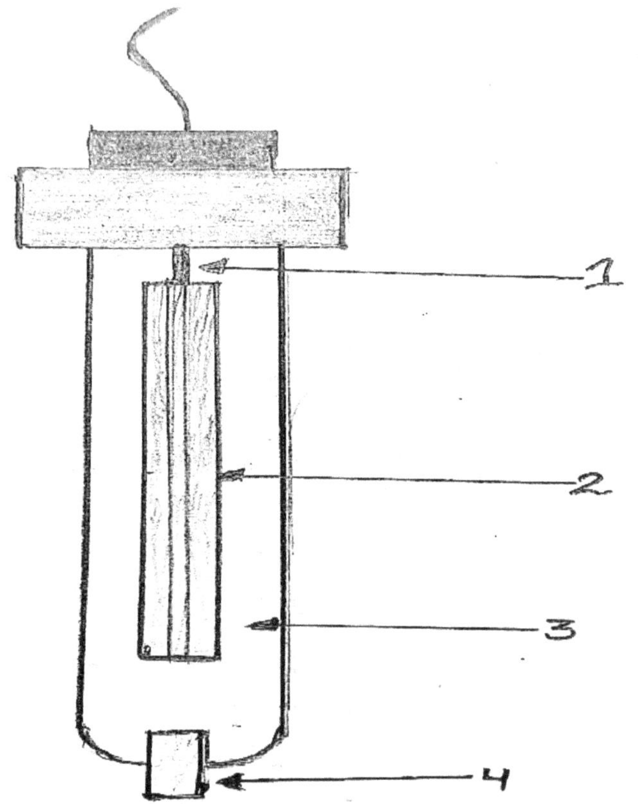

SILVER SILVER CHLORIDE ELECTRODE :1. Ag, 2. AgCl, 3. Kcl, Agcl solution, 4. Porous junction

3. **Saturated Calomel Electrode (SCE):**

Principle:

- The SCE consists of mercury in contact with mercurous chloride (calomel) and immersed in a saturated solution of potassium chloride.

Reaction: $Hg_2Cl_2 (s)+2e-\rightarrow 2Hg (l)+2Cl-$

Features:

- **Potential:** +0.244 V vs. SHE when saturated with KCl.
- **Advantages:** Stable and widely used, especially in aqueous solutions.
- **Limitations:** Contains mercury, which is toxic and poses disposal challenges.

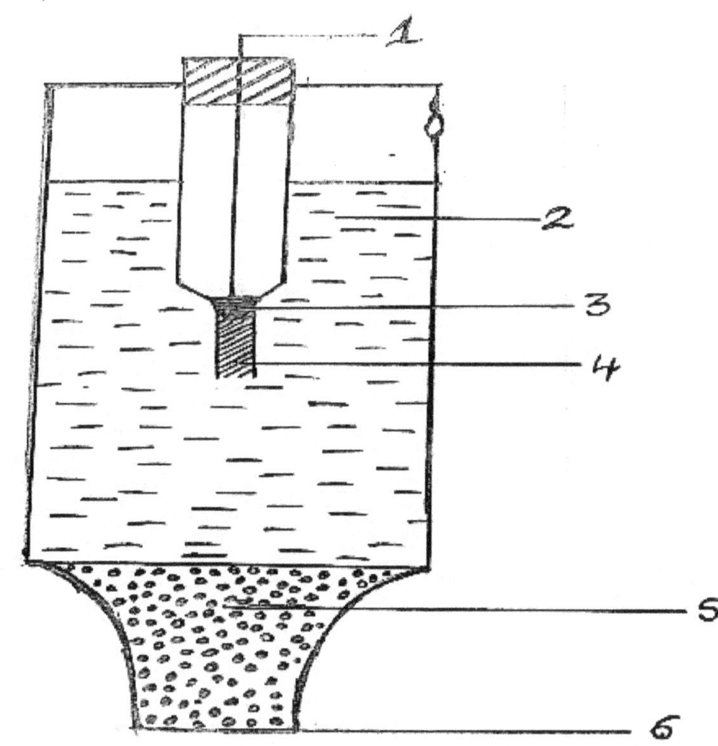

SATURATED CALOMEL ELECTRODE:1. Wire, 2. Sat. Kcl (Salt bridge), 3. Hg, calomel + kcl, 5. Crystals of Kcl, 6. Porous plug

Factors Affecting Reference Electrode Performance:

1. **Temperature:**

   - The potential of reference electrodes can change with temperature. Most reference electrodes come with temperature compensation or calibration data.

2. **Concentration of the Internal Solution:**

   - The potential is influenced by the concentration of the internal solution (e.g., KCl). Using saturated solutions minimizes these variations.

3. **Contamination:**

   - Contamination of the internal solution or the junction can alter the potential. Regular maintenance and proper storage are essential to maintain accuracy.

4. **Junction Potential:**

   - The junction potential arises at the interface between the electrode's internal solution and the sample solution. It should be minimized and consistent to ensure accurate measurements.

Applications in Pharmaceutical Analysis:

1. **pH Measurement:**

   - Reference electrodes are used in conjunction with glass electrodes to measure the pH of pharmaceutical solutions accurately.

2. **Titration End-Point Detection:**

- ○ Reference electrodes are integral in potentiometric titrations, providing a stable reference potential for detecting the endpoint.

3. **Ion-Selective Electrode Analysis:**

- ○ Reference electrodes are paired with ion-selective electrodes (ISEs) to measure specific ions in pharmaceutical formulations, such as sodium, potassium, and chloride.

4. **Quality Control:**

- ○ In quality control laboratories, reference electrodes are used to ensure the accuracy and reliability of potentiometric measurements in the analysis of raw materials, intermediates, and finished products.

Reference electrodes, including the standard hydrogen electrode, silver/silver chloride electrode, and saturated calomel electrode, are fundamental components in potentiometry. Their stable and well-known potentials are critical for accurate and reliable potentiometric measurements in pharmaceutical analysis. By understanding the principles and proper use of these reference electrodes, analysts can achieve precise results in various applications, including pH measurement, titration endpoint detection, ion-selective analysis, and quality control.

11.2 POTENTIOMETRY

11.2.3 INDICATOR ELECTRODES

Introduction: Indicator electrodes are essential in potentiometric measurements as they respond to the activity of the ions of interest in the solution. The potential of the indicator electrode varies with the concentration of the analyte, allowing for quantitative analysis.

Types of Indicator Electrodes:

1. **Metal Electrodes:**

- ○ **Platinum Electrode:**

  - ▪ Used for redox reactions involving the transfer of electrons. It is inert and does not participate in the reaction.

○ **Gold Electrode:**

- Similar to platinum electrodes, used in redox titrations. It provides high stability and inertness.

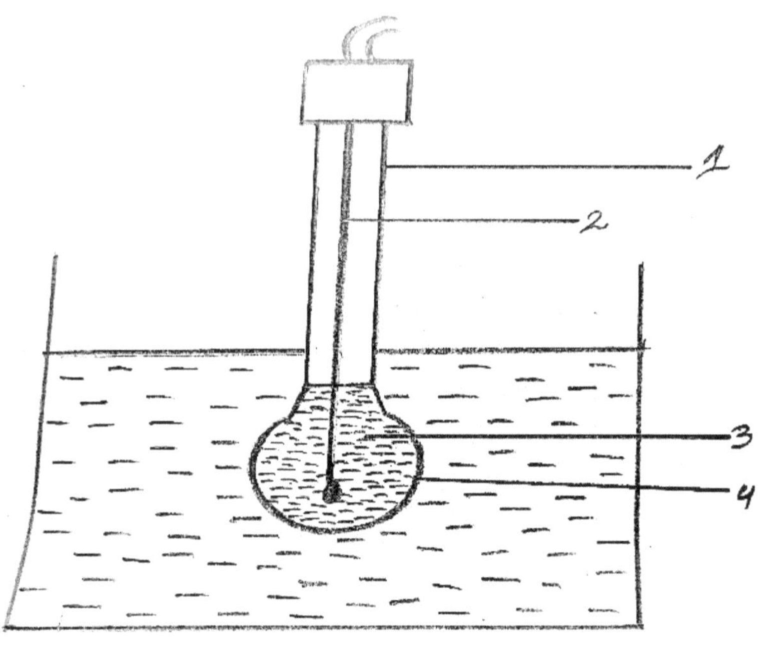

1.Glass tube, 2. Ag/Agcl wire, 3. 0.1 N Hcl, 4. Glass bulb (pH sensitive)

2. Ion-Selective Electrodes (ISEs):

○ **Glass Electrode:**

- Commonly used for pH measurement. The potential difference across the glass membrane is proportional to the hydrogen ion concentration.

○ **Calcium Ion-Selective Electrode:**

- Responds to calcium ions (Ca2+) in the solution. Used for determining calcium concentrations in various samples.

  - **Sodium Ion-Selective Electrode:**

    - Responds to sodium ions (Na+). Used in the analysis of biological and pharmaceutical samples.

3. **Membrane Electrodes:**

   - **Polymeric Membrane Electrodes:**

     - Consist of a polymer membrane doped with an ionophore that selectively binds the target ion.

   - **Solid-State Membrane Electrodes:**

     - Use a solid crystalline material as the sensing element. Examples include fluoride ion-selective electrodes.

11.2.4 END-POINT DETERMINATION

Introduction: End-point determination is a crucial aspect of potentiometric titrations. The end-point is identified by a significant change in the potential, indicating the completion of the reaction between the titrant and the analyte.

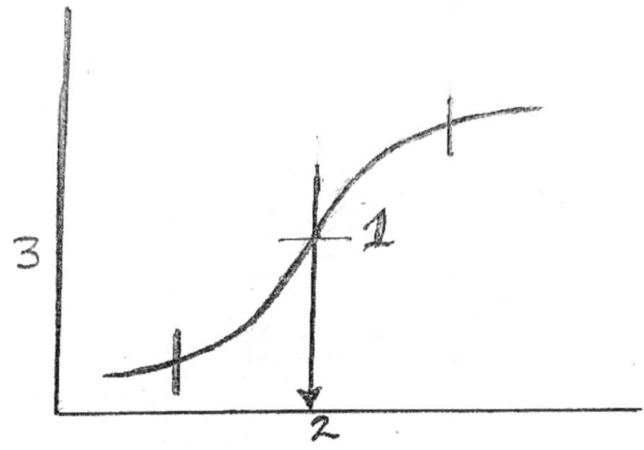

Natural titration curve : 1. Mid point of slope, 2. End point, 3. Emf or pH

Methods of End-Point Determination:

1. **Graphical Method:**

   - **Potentiometric Titration Curve:**

Plot the measured potential against the volume of titrant added. The end-point is identified as the point where the potential changes most rapidly

First Derivative Plot:

Plot the first derivative of the potential with respect to the volume of titrant (dE/dV) against the volume of titrant. The peak of this plot corresponds to the end-point.

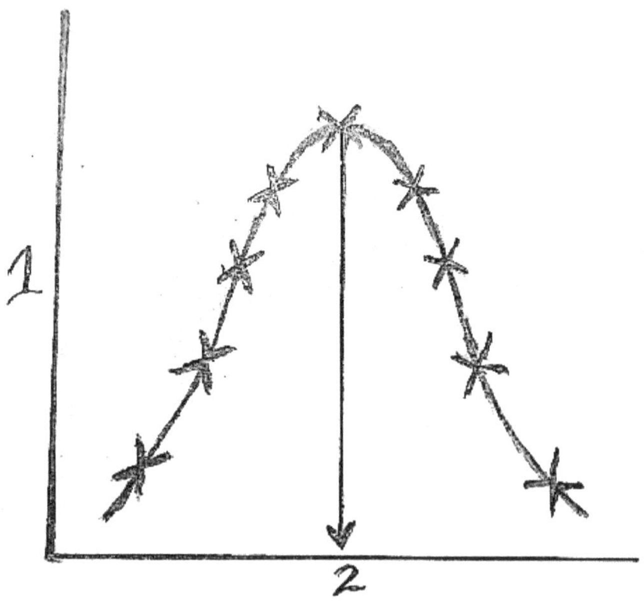

First derivative curve: 1. Δ emf/ Δ v , 2. Vol. of titrant

Second Derivative Plot:

Plot the second derivative of the potential (d^2E/dV^2) against the volume of titrant. The end-point is where the second derivative crosses zero.

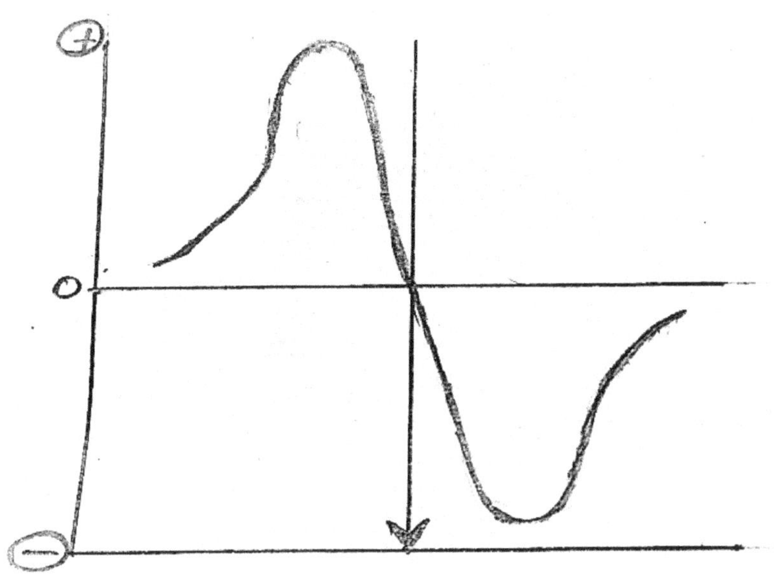

Second Derivative curve:1. X- axis: Vol. of titrant 2. Y- Axis: Δ^2 emf/

Gran Plot Method:

A more precise method for weak acid-strong base or weak base-strong acid titrations. The extrapolated linear portion of the plot intersects the x-axis at the end-point volume.

Direct Reading Method:

- Modern potentiometric titrators can directly indicate the end-point by analyzing the titration curve and detecting the inflection point.

Applications:

1. **Acid-Base Titrations:**

○ Determination of the concentration of acids and bases in pharmaceuticals using a pH electrode as the indicator electrode.

2. **Redox Titrations:**

○ Determination of oxidizing and reducing agents in pharmaceutical formulations using platinum or gold electrodes.

3. **Complexometric Titrations:**

○ Determination of metal ions using ion-selective electrodes (e.g., calcium ion-selective electrode for calcium titrations).

11.2.5 APPLICATIONS OF POTENTIOMETRY

Introduction: Potentiometry has wide applications in pharmaceutical analysis due to its accuracy, sensitivity, and simplicity. It is used for various types of titrations and measurements involving ionic species.

Key Applications:

1. **pH Measurement:**

○ **Application:**

- Potentiometry is widely used to measure the pH of pharmaceutical solutions, ensuring they meet the required specifications.

○ **Electrode Used:**

- Glass pH electrode.

2. **Titration End-Point Detection:**

○ **Application:**

- Used to detect the endpoint in various titrations, including acid-base, redox, precipitation, and complexometric titrations.

○ **Electrodes Used:**

- pH electrodes, platinum electrodes, ion-selective electrodes.

3. **Ion-Selective Electrode Analysis:**

   - **Application:**

     - Measurement of specific ions in pharmaceutical formulations. Common ions include sodium, potassium, calcium, and chloride.

   - **Electrodes Used:**

     - Ion-selective electrodes specific to each ion.

4. **Dissolution Testing:**

   - **Application:**

     - Monitoring the dissolution rate of drugs in dosage forms. The potential change indicates the release rate of the active pharmaceutical ingredient.

   - **Electrodes Used:**

     - pH electrodes, ion-selective electrodes.

5. **Quality Control:**

   - **Application:**

     - Ensuring the quality and consistency of raw materials, intermediates, and finished products in the pharmaceutical industry.

   - **Electrodes Used:**

     - Various indicator electrodes depending on the analyte.

6. **Environmental Monitoring:**

- **Application:**

  - Monitoring effluents and waste products from pharmaceutical manufacturing processes for ionic content.

- **Electrodes Used:**

  - pH electrodes, ion-selective electrodes.

7. **Detection of Impurities:**

   - **Application:**

     - Potentiometric methods are used to detect and quantify impurities in pharmaceutical products, ensuring their safety and efficacy.

   - **Electrodes Used:**

     - Various indicator electrodes depending on the impurity.

11.3 POLAROGRAPHY
11.3.1 PRINCIPLE AND ILKOVIC EQUATION

Introduction: Polarography is an electrochemical analysis method that measures the current that flows through a solution as a function of an applied voltage. It involves the use of a dropping mercury electrode (DME) or a static mercury drop electrode (SMDE) as the working electrode. This technique is particularly useful for the qualitative and quantitative analysis of reducible or oxidizable substances in solution.

Principle: The basic principle of polarography is based on the relationship between the current and the applied potential in an electrochemical cell. When a voltage is applied to the working electrode, the analyte in the solution undergoes reduction or oxidation at the electrode surface, resulting in a measurable current.

Steps Involved:

1. **Electrode Reaction:**

- The analyte undergoes a redox reaction at the surface of the mercury electrode. For example, a reducible species M^{n+} gains electrons to form
- $M^{(n-m)}+$ at the electrode: $M^{n+} + m\ e^- \longrightarrow M^{(n-m)+}$

2. Formation of Dropping Mercury Electrode:

- The DME forms by allowing mercury to drop from a capillary tube, creating a fresh surface for each measurement. This minimizes contamination and ensures reproducibility.

3. Potential Sweep:

- A linearly varying voltage (potential) is applied to the working electrode over time. As the potential increases, different species in the solution get reduced or oxidized at different potentials, leading to a characteristic current-potential curve.

4. Measurement of Current:

- The current is measured as a function of the applied potential. The resulting current-voltage curve is called a polarogram. The current increases as the analyte gets reduced or oxidized, forming a peak or wave at the specific potential where the redox reaction occurs.

Ilkovic Equation: The Ilkovic equation relates the diffusion current (IdI_dId) to the concentration of the analyte in the solution during polarographic measurements. It is given by:

$$Id = 607nD^{1/2} m^{2/3} t^{1/6} C$$

Where:

- Id = diffusion current (measured in microamperes, μA)
- n = number of electrons involved in the redox reaction
- D = diffusion coefficient of the analyte (cm^2/s)
- m = rate of mercury flow (mg/s)
- t = drop time (s)
- C = concentration of the analyte (mM)

Explanation of Terms:

- **Diffusion Current (Id):**

  - The limiting current due to the diffusion of the analyte to the electrode surface. It is proportional to the concentration of the analyte.

- **Number of Electrons (n):**

  - The number of electrons transferred in the redox reaction. It affects the magnitude of the current.

- **Diffusion Coefficient (D):**

  - A measure of how fast the analyte diffuses through the solution to the electrode surface. Higher diffusion coefficients lead to higher currents.

- **Rate of Mercury Flow (m):**

  - The rate at which mercury drops from the capillary. It affects the surface area of the electrode and thus the current.

- **Drop Time (t):**

  - The time interval between the formation of successive mercury drops. It influences the diffusion layer thickness.

- **Concentration (C):**

  - The concentration of the analyte in the solution. Higher concentrations result in higher diffusion currents.

Applications of Polarography:

1. **Pharmaceutical Analysis:**

- Used for the analysis of drugs and active pharmaceutical ingredients (APIs) that are electroactive. It helps in determining the purity and concentration of pharmaceutical compounds.

2. **Environmental Monitoring:**

- Used to detect and quantify trace metals and pollutants in environmental samples such as water and soil. Polarography can measure low concentrations of heavy metals like lead, cadmium, and mercury.

3. **Biological Studies:**

- Applied in the study of biological molecules and metabolites that undergo redox reactions. It is useful in determining the concentration of vitamins, hormones, and other biomolecules.

4. **Industrial Applications:**

- Used in the quality control of industrial processes involving electroactive materials. Polarography helps in monitoring the concentration of intermediates and final products.

5. **Food Industry:**

- Employed in the analysis of food additives, preservatives, and contaminants. Polarography ensures the safety and compliance of food products with regulatory standards.

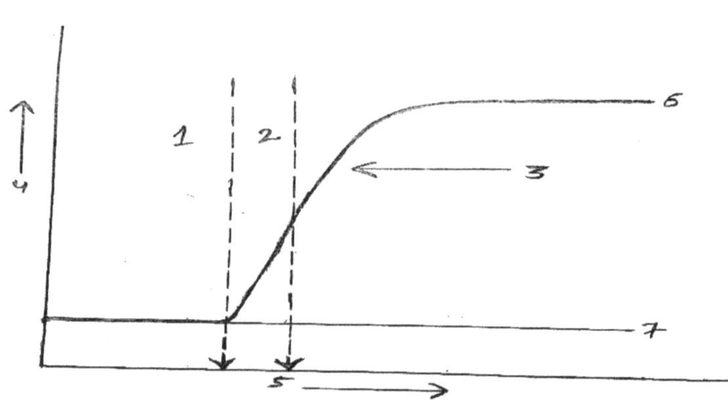

POLAROGRAM :1. Decomposition voltage, 2. Half wave potential, 3. Polarographic wave, 4.Current, 5. Applied voltage, 6. Limiting current, 7. Residual current

11.3 POLAROGRAPHY
11.3.2 DROPPING MERCURY ELECTRODE

Introduction: The Dropping Mercury Electrode (DME) is a key component in polarography. It serves as the working electrode where the electrochemical reactions take place. The DME is unique because it provides a constantly renewing, clean, and smooth surface for the reactions, which is crucial for achieving reproducible results in polarographic measurements.

Construction and Working:

1. **Construction:**

   - **Capillary Tube:**

     - A fine capillary tube is connected to a mercury reservoir. The capillary tube controls the flow of mercury and allows it to form small, consistent drops at its tip.

   - **Mercury Reservoir:**

     - The reservoir contains high-purity mercury, which flows through the capillary tube to form drops at regular intervals.

- **Support and Container:**

  - The DME setup is typically housed in a glass container filled with an inert electrolyte solution, which completes the electrochemical cell.

2. **Formation of Mercury Drops:**

   - Mercury flows from the reservoir through the capillary tube due to gravity. As the mercury flows, it forms a drop at the tip of the capillary.
   - The drop grows until its weight exceeds the surface tension holding it to the capillary, causing it to detach and fall into the container. A new drop then starts forming immediately.

3. **Electrode Surface Renewal:**

   - The DME continuously forms and releases drops of mercury, providing a constantly renewing electrode surface. This ensures that each measurement is made on a clean and uncontaminated surface, improving the reproducibility and accuracy of the results.

4. **Current Measurement:**

   - During the formation of each mercury drop, an electrochemical reaction occurs at the surface of the drop. The current generated by the reaction is measured as a function of the applied potential.
   - The potential is gradually increased, and the corresponding current is recorded to produce a polarogram (current-potential curve).

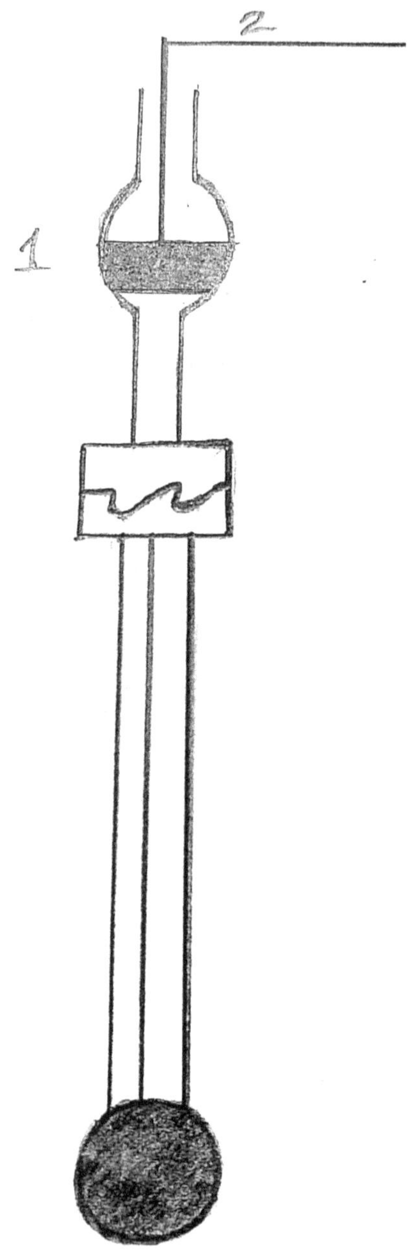

DROPPING MERCURY ELECTRODE :1. Mercury, 2. Cathode

Advantages of the DME:

1. **Clean and Renewable Surface:**

   - The continuous formation of new mercury drops provides a clean and uncontaminated electrode surface for each measurement.

2. **High Reproducibility:**

   - The regular and consistent size of the mercury drops ensures reproducible results.

3. **Wide Potential Range:**

   - Mercury has a wide potential window, allowing the analysis of a broad range of electroactive species.

4. **Minimal Electrode Fouling:**

   - The renewable surface minimizes the effects of electrode fouling, which can occur with solid electrodes.

Disadvantages of the DME:

1. **Toxicity of Mercury:**

   - Mercury is toxic, and proper handling and disposal procedures are required to avoid environmental and health hazards.

2. **Slow Drop Rate:**

   - The formation and detachment of mercury drops can be relatively slow, potentially limiting the speed of analysis.

Applications in Polarography:

1. **Analysis of Metal Ions:**

   - The DME is used for the determination of trace metal ions in various samples, including environmental, biological, and industrial samples.

2. **Determination of Organic Compounds:**

   - Polarography with the DME is used to analyze organic compounds that undergo reduction or oxidation at the mercury surface, such as nitro compounds, quinones, and vitamins.

3. **Pharmaceutical Analysis:**

   - The DME is employed in the analysis of pharmaceutical compounds, including drugs and their metabolites, by measuring their electrochemical behavior.

4. **Environmental Monitoring:**

   - The DME is used for monitoring pollutants and toxic substances in environmental samples, such as water and soil.

5. **Research and Development:**

   - The DME is valuable in electrochemical research for studying reaction mechanisms and the behavior of electroactive species.

11.3 POLAROGRAPHY
11.3.3 ROTATING PLATINUM ELECTRODE

Introduction: The Rotating Platinum Electrode (RPE) is used in polarographic and voltammetric measurements to enhance mass transport to the electrode surface. Unlike the Dropping Mercury Electrode (DME), the RPE provides a stationary yet rotating surface, which helps maintain a steady-state current by continuously refreshing the solution adjacent to the electrode.

Construction and Working:

1. **Components:**

- **Platinum Disk:**

  - A small, inert platinum disk is used as the working electrode. Platinum is chosen for its excellent conductivity and chemical inertness.

- **Rotator Mechanism:**

  - The electrode is attached to a motor-driven rotator that can precisely control the rotation speed.

- **Electrode Shaft:**

  - The platinum disk is mounted on a shaft that allows for the connection to the rotator and the electrical circuit.

2. **Working Principle:**

  - The platinum disk rotates at a constant speed, creating a hydrodynamic flow that brings fresh analyte solution to the electrode surface. This rotation enhances the mass transport of the analyte to the electrode, ensuring a steady and reproducible current.
  - The rotation speed can be adjusted to control the rate of mass transport, allowing for more precise control of the electrochemical reaction.

3. **Measurement:**

  - A potential is applied to the rotating platinum electrode, and the resulting current is measured. The current is directly related to the concentration of the electroactive species in the solution.
  - The current-potential curve (voltammogram) is recorded, showing the characteristic peaks corresponding to the redox reactions of the analyte.

Advantages of the RPE:

1. **Enhanced Mass Transport:**

- ◦ The rotation of the electrode improves the diffusion of analytes to the electrode surface, leading to higher and more stable currents.

2. **Steady-State Conditions:**

   - ◦ The RPE provides a constant and reproducible surface area for the electrochemical reactions, resulting in steady-state current measurements.

3. **Versatility:**

   - ◦ Suitable for a wide range of electrochemical studies, including cyclic voltammetry and chronoamperometry.

4. **Precision Control:**

   - ◦ The rotation speed can be precisely controlled, allowing for detailed studies of reaction kinetics and mechanisms.

Disadvantages of the RPE:

1. **Complex Setup:**

   - ◦ The RPE requires a motorized rotator and a more complex setup compared to simpler electrodes like the DME.

2. **Maintenance:**

   - ◦ The mechanical components and the platinum disk require regular maintenance and cleaning to ensure accurate measurements.

Applications in Polarography:

1. **Kinetic Studies:**

   - ◦ The RPE is used to study the kinetics of electrochemical reactions by varying the rotation speed and observing the changes in current.

2. **Detection of Trace Metals:**

- The RPE is employed in the detection and quantification of trace metals in various samples, including environmental and biological samples.

3. **Analysis of Organic Compounds:**

- The RPE is used to analyze organic compounds that undergo redox reactions, providing insights into their electrochemical behavior.

11.3.4 APPLICATIONS IN DRUG ANALYSIS

Introduction: Polarography, including the use of the Dropping Mercury Electrode (DME) and the Rotating Platinum Electrode (RPE), is widely applied in drug analysis. These techniques offer sensitive and reliable methods for the qualitative and quantitative determination of pharmaceutical compounds.

Key Applications in Drug Analysis:

1. **Determination of Active Pharmaceutical Ingredients (APIs):**

- Polarography is used to quantify APIs in various drug formulations. Electroactive APIs, such as certain antibiotics, vitamins, and antihypertensive agents, can be accurately measured using polarographic techniques.

2. **Analysis of Drug Metabolites:**

- Polarography is employed to detect and quantify drug metabolites in biological samples. This is crucial for pharmacokinetic studies and therapeutic drug monitoring.

3. **Detection of Impurities:**

- The presence of impurities in pharmaceutical products can be detected using polarographic methods. This ensures the purity and safety of the drugs.

4. **Stability Testing:**

   - Polarographic techniques are used to study the stability of pharmaceutical compounds under various conditions. The reduction or oxidation peaks can indicate the degradation products and their concentrations.

5. **Quality Control:**

   - Polarography is an essential tool in quality control laboratories for the routine analysis of raw materials, intermediates, and finished pharmaceutical products. It ensures that the products meet the required specifications and standards.

6. **Environmental Monitoring:**

   - Polarographic methods are used to monitor pharmaceutical contaminants in environmental samples, such as wastewater from pharmaceutical manufacturing processes. This helps in assessing and mitigating environmental pollution.

Examples of Drug Analysis Using Polarography:

1. **Vitamin Analysis:**

   - Water-soluble vitamins, such as vitamin C (ascorbic acid) and vitamin B2 (riboflavin), are electroactive and can be analyzed using polarography. The reduction peaks of these vitamins provide quantitative information about their concentration.

2. **Antibiotic Determination:**

   - Antibiotics like tetracyclines and quinolones can be analyzed by polarography. Their reduction or oxidation peaks in the polarogram indicate their concentration and purity.

3. **Analysis of Antihypertensive Drugs:**

- ◦ Antihypertensive drugs, such as methyldopa and hydralazine, are electroactive and can be measured using polarographic techniques. The method provides accurate and reliable results for these drugs in pharmaceutical formulations.

4. **Detection of Heavy Metal Contaminants:**

- ◦ Polarography is used to detect trace amounts of heavy metals, such as lead and cadmium, in pharmaceutical products. This ensures the safety and compliance of the drugs with regulatory standards.

Polarography, utilizing electrodes like the Dropping Mercury Electrode (DME) and the Rotating Platinum Electrode (RPE), plays a vital role in drug analysis. Its applications in determining APIs, analyzing drug metabolites, detecting impurities, stability testing, quality control, and environmental monitoring highlight its versatility and importance. Understanding the principles and advantages of these electrodes enables accurate and reliable analysis of pharmaceutical compounds, ensuring the safety and efficacy of pharmaceutical products.

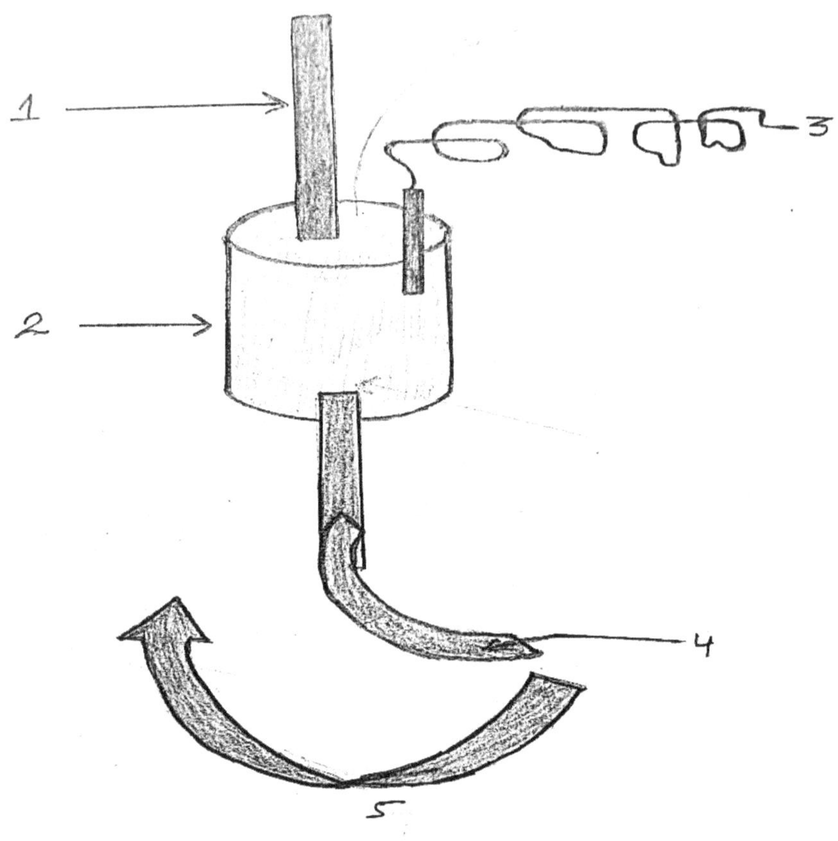

ROTATING PLATINUM ELECTRODE 1. Glass tubing, 2. Mercury reservior, 3. Copper wire, 4. Platinum wire, 5. Direction of rotation

TWELVE
ABOUT AUTHORS

Mr. Santhosh Illendula

Mr. Santhosh Illendula, M. Pharm (Ph.D) presently working as a Associate Professor, Nalanda college of Pharmacy, Charlapally, Nalgonda, Telangana, India. He has completed his B. Pharmacy from Nalanda college of Pharmacy, Osmania University and M.Pharmacy from Ultra college of Pharmacy, Madurai, Tamilnadu Dr. M.G.R Medical University in Pharmaceutical Analysis branch. He is having 15 years of Teaching and Industry experience. He has Authored 1 Book, 3 Indian patent publications, 1 Indain design patent, 1 UK design patent & 1 Indian copy right, he has contributed 68 papers in National & International Journals. He has guided 18 M.Pharm students & 41 B.Pharm students. He is currently editorial board member of International journal of pharmacy & Chemistry, International journal of Pharmacognosy & Pharmaceutical research. He has appointed as a external exam paper setter for YBN university, Ranchi. He is the President of NCOP Alumni association of Nalanda college of pharmacy and life member of APTI, APP Professional bodies.

Dr. Madireddy Mamata

Dr. Madireddy Mamata, Mpharm, PhD., Currently working as a Associate professor & HOD in the department of pharmaceutical analysis, Trinity College of pharmaceutical sciences, peddapalli, Bandarikunta,505172, Telangana. She is having Teaching experience of 12 years. She is published 2 patents in National, 20 Research & Review papers in various reputed National & International conferences & Seminars. She has excellent academic background & practical experience in the field of pharmacy & Guided 50 projects for B.pharmacy , M.pharmacy students.

Paduri Amani

Paduri Amani , Mpharm (PhD) Currently working as a Assistant Professor in the department of pharmaceutical analysis, Brilliant Group of Technical Institutions, Abdullapur , RangaReddy ,500085, Telangana. She is having 9 years of Teaching experience . she has guided many graduate an post graduate students. she published 2 patents in National, 15 Research & Review papers in various reputed National & International conferences & Seminars. She has excellent academic background & practical experience in the field of pharmacy.

THIRTEEN
GLOSSARY

1. **Accuracy:**

   - The closeness of a measured value to the true value.

2. **Analyte:**

   - The substance or chemical constituent being analyzed or detected in a sample.

3. **Calibration:**

   - The process of setting and checking the accuracy of an instrument by comparison with a known standard.

4. **Chromatography:**

   - A method for separating components of a mixture based on their differing interactions with a stationary phase and a mobile phase.

5. **Conductometry:**

   - An analytical technique that measures the electrical conductivity of a solution to determine the concentration of ions.

6. **Electrode Potential:**

   - The potential difference between an electrode and its surrounding solution, determined by the redox reaction at the electrode.

7. **Endpoint:**

   - The point in a titration where the reaction between the titrant and the analyte is complete.

8. **Gravimetry:**

   - An analytical technique that measures the mass of an analyte or its derivative.

9. **Ion-Selective Electrode (ISE):**

   - An electrode that responds selectively to a specific ion in the presence of other ions.

10. **Limit of Detection (LOD):**

    - The lowest concentration of an analyte that can be reliably detected but not necessarily quantified.

11. **Molar Conductivity (Λm):**

    - The conductivity of a solution containing one mole of electrolyte divided by the concentration of the electrolyte.

12. **Nernst Equation:**

    - An equation that relates the electrode potential to the concentration of the ions involved in the redox reaction.

13. **pH:**

- ○ A measure of the hydrogen ion concentration in a solution, indicating its acidity or alkalinity.

14. **Polarography:**

   - ○ An electrochemical method in which the current through a solution is measured as a function of an applied voltage using a dropping mercury electrode or other electrodes.

15. **Potentiometry:**

   - ○ An analytical technique that measures the potential difference between two electrodes to determine the concentration of an analyte.

16. **Quality Control:**

   - ○ The process of ensuring that products meet the required standards and specifications through testing and inspection.

17. **Redox Reaction:**

   - ○ A chemical reaction involving the transfer of electrons between two species.

18. **Reference Electrode:**

   - ○ An electrode with a stable and known potential, used as a reference point in potentiometric measurements.

19. **Titrant:**

   - ○ The solution of known concentration added to the analyte during a titration.

20. **Voltammetry:**

   - ○ An electrochemical method in which the current is measured as the potential is varied, used to study redox reactions and determine the concentration of analytes.

21. **Adsorption:**

   ○ The process by which atoms, ions, or molecules adhere to a surface.

22. **Buffer Solution:**

   ○ A solution that resists changes in pH upon the addition of small amounts of acid or base.

23. **Calibration Curve:**

   ○ A graph of the instrument response as a function of analyte concentration, used to determine the concentration of unknown samples.

24. **Capillary Electrophoresis:**

   ○ A technique for separating ions based on their electrophoretic mobility in a capillary filled with electrolyte.

25. **Complexometric Titration:**

   ○ A titration based on the formation of a complex between the analyte and the titrant.

26. **Conductance (G):**

   ○ The ability of a solution to conduct an electric current, the inverse of resistance.

27. **Coulometry:**

   ○ A technique that measures the total charge passed during the complete electrolysis of an analyte.

28. **Diffusion Coefficient (D):**

- A measure of the rate at which molecules or ions move through a solution.

29. **Dropping Mercury Electrode (DME):**

   - An electrode used in polarography, consisting of a fine capillary tube through which mercury drops are formed.

30. **Electrochemical Cell:**

   - A system consisting of two electrodes immersed in an electrolyte solution, where redox reactions occur.

31. **Electrolysis:**

   - A process that uses electrical energy to drive a non-spontaneous chemical reaction.

32. **Electromotive Force (EMF):**

   - The potential difference between two electrodes when no current is flowing.

33. **Fluorescence:**

   - The emission of light by a substance that has absorbed light, used in fluorometric analysis.

34. **Hydrolysis:**

   - A chemical reaction involving the breaking of a bond in a molecule using water.

35. **Ion Pair:**

   - A pair of ions held together by electrostatic forces in a solution.

36. **Isocratic Elution:**

- A chromatography technique where the composition of the mobile phase remains constant throughout the separation.

37. **Linear Sweep Voltammetry:**

- A technique where the potential is varied linearly with time, and the resulting current is measured.

38. **Membrane Potential:**

- The potential difference across a membrane, used in ion-selective electrodes.

39. **Oxidation State:**

- The charge on an atom in a molecule or ion, indicating the degree of oxidation.

40. **Peak Area:**

- The area under a peak in a chromatogram, proportional to the quantity of the analyte.

41. **Photometric Titration:**

- A titration in which the endpoint is detected by a change in the absorbance of light.

42. **Potentiostat:**

- An instrument that controls the potential of the working electrode and measures the current flowing in an electrochemical cell.

43. **Qualitative Analysis:**

- The determination of the chemical composition of a sample.

44. **Quantitative Analysis:**

- The determination of the amount or concentration of an analyte in a sample.

45. **Reaction Kinetics:**

   - The study of the rates of chemical reactions and the factors affecting them.

46. **Redox Couple:**

   - A pair of species that are related by the gain or loss of electrons, such as Fe2+/Fe3+.

47. **Resolution (Chromatography):**

   - The degree of separation between two peaks in a chromatogram.

48. **Retention Factor (k'):**

   - A measure of the time a compound spends in the stationary phase relative to the mobile phase.

49. **Retention Time (tR):**

   - The time taken for a solute to pass through a chromatographic column and be detected.

50. **Salt Bridge:**

   - A device used in electrochemical cells to maintain electrical neutrality by allowing the flow of ions.

51. **Selectivity:**

   - The ability of an analytical method to distinguish the analyte from other components in the sample.

52. **Sensitivity:**

- The ability of an analytical method to detect small changes in analyte concentration.

53. **Spectral Interference:**

- The effect of other absorbing species on the measurement of the analyte in spectrophotometry.

54. **Spectrophotometry:**

- An analytical technique that measures the intensity of light absorbed by a sample at a specific wavelength.

55. **Standard Deviation:**

- A measure of the dispersion or spread of a set of values, indicating the precision of the measurements.

56. **Standard Solution:**

- A solution of known concentration used for calibration or as a reference in analytical measurements.

57. **Stoichiometry:**

- The quantitative relationship between the reactants and products in a chemical reaction.

58. **Titration Curve:**

- A plot of the change in a measured property (e.g., pH, potential) as a function of the volume of titrant added.

59. **Voltammetric Wave:**

- The plot of current versus potential in voltammetry, showing the characteristic shape of the redox process.

60. **Working Electrode:**

   - The electrode at which the reaction of interest occurs in an electrochemical cell.

61. **Adsorption:**

   - The process by which atoms, ions, or molecules adhere to a surface.

62. **Buffer Capacity:**

   - The ability of a buffer solution to resist changes in pH upon the addition of acid or base.

63. **Carrier Gas:**

   - The gas used to transport the sample through a gas chromatograph.

64. **Chromophore:**

   - The part of a molecule responsible for its color, which absorbs light at a specific wavelength.

65. **Complexation:**

   - The formation of a complex by the combination of a ligand with a metal ion.

66. **Concentration Gradient:**

   - The gradual change in the concentration of solutes in a solution as a function of distance through a solution.

67. **Detector:**

   - An instrument used in chromatography to detect the presence of substances.

68. **Eluent:**

   - The solvent used in chromatography to carry the analyte through the column.

69. **Flow Rate:**

   - The volume of mobile phase passing through the chromatographic column per unit time.

70. **Gradient Elution:**

   - A technique in liquid chromatography where the composition of the mobile phase is varied during the separation process.

71. **Hydrodynamic Chromatography:**

   - A separation technique that uses differences in the hydrodynamic volume of particles to separate them.

72. **Injection Port:**

   - The part of a chromatograph where the sample is introduced into the mobile phase.

73. **Ion Chromatography:**

   - A form of chromatography that separates ions based on their interaction with a resin.

74. **Isocratic Elution:**

   - A chromatography technique where the composition of the mobile phase remains constant throughout the separation.

75. **Mass Spectrometry:**

- An analytical technique that measures the mass-to-charge ratio of ions to identify and quantify molecules.

76. **Mobile Phase:**

- The phase that moves through the chromatographic column, carrying the sample components.

77. **Partition Coefficient:**

- The ratio of concentrations of a compound in a mixture of two immiscible solvents at equilibrium.

78. **Peak Height:**

- The vertical distance from the baseline to the top of a peak in a chromatogram.

79. **Pore Size:**

- The size of the openings in a porous material, such as a chromatographic stationary phase.

80. **Refractive Index Detector (RID):**

- A detector used in liquid chromatography that measures changes in the refractive index of the eluent.

81. **Resolution:**

- The ability to distinguish between two closely spaced peaks in a chromatogram or spectrum.

82. **Retention Factor (k'):**

- A measure of the time a compound spends in the stationary phase relative to the mobile phase.

83. **Retention Time (tR):**

   - The time taken for a solute to pass through a chromatographic column and be detected.

84. **Reverse Phase Chromatography:**

   - A type of chromatography where the stationary phase is nonpolar, and the mobile phase is polar.

85. **Sample Loop:**

   - A loop of tubing in a chromatographic injector that holds a precise volume of sample for injection.

86. **Solvent Front:**

   - The leading edge of the solvent as it moves through the stationary phase in chromatography.

87. **Stationary Phase:**

   - The phase that stays fixed inside the column in chromatography, interacting with the analytes.

88. **Supercritical Fluid Chromatography (SFC):**

   - A form of chromatography that uses a supercritical fluid as the mobile phase.

89. **Thermal Conductivity Detector (TCD):**

   - A detector used in gas chromatography that measures changes in the thermal conductivity of the gas stream.

90. **Thin Layer Chromatography (TLC):**

- A simple and rapid form of chromatography that uses a thin layer of adsorbent material on a flat plate.

91. **Ultraviolet-Visible Spectrophotometry (UV-Vis):**

- An analytical technique that measures the absorbance of light in the ultraviolet and visible regions of the spectrum.

92. **Van Deemter Equation:**

- An equation that describes the relationship between the flow rate of the mobile phase and the efficiency of a chromatographic column.

93. **Void Volume:**

- The volume of mobile phase in a chromatographic column that is outside the pores of the stationary phase.

94. **Wall-Effect Chromatography:**

- A type of chromatography that uses a thin layer of stationary phase coated on the inner wall of a column.

95. **Zone Broadening:**

- The spreading of a solute band as it moves through a chromatographic column, leading to decreased resolution.

96. **Absorbance:**

- A measure of the amount of light absorbed by a sample at a specific wavelength.

97. **Baseline:**

- The part of the chromatogram where no analyte is present, used as a reference for peak measurements.

98. **Carrier Gas:**

   - The gas used to transport the sample through a gas chromatograph.

99. **Chromophore:**

   - The part of a molecule responsible for its color, which absorbs light at a specific wavelength.

100. **Complexation:** - The formation of a complex by the combination of a ligand with a metal ion.

FOURTEEN

BIBLIOGRAPHY

1. **Beckett, A. H., & Stenlake, J. B. (1988).**_Practical Pharmaceutical Chemistry_ (4th ed.). Athlone Press.
2. **Chatten, L. G. (1969).**_Pharmaceutical Chemistry_ (Vol. 1 & 2). Marcel Dekker Inc.
3. **Connors, K. A. (2007).**_A Textbook of Pharmaceutical Analysis_ (3rd ed.). Wiley.
4. **Drummond, M. F., Sculpher, M. J., Claxton, K., Stoddart, G. L., & Torrance, G. W. (2015).**_Methods for the Economic Evaluation of Health Care Programmes_ (4th ed.). Oxford University Press.
5. **Fletcher, R. H., & Fletcher, S. W. (2012).**_Clinical Epidemiology: The Essentials_ (5th ed.). Lippincott Williams & Wilkins.
6. **Harvey, D. (2000).**_Modern Analytical Chemistry_. McGraw-Hill.
7. **Kasture, A. V., Mahadik, K. R., & Wadodkar, S. G. (2011).**_A Textbook of Pharmaceutical Analysis_ (Vol. 1 & 2). Nirali Prakashan.
8. **Rothman, K. J., & Greenland, S. (2018).**_Modern Epidemiology_ (4th ed.). Wolters Kluwer Health.
9. **Skoog, D. A., Holler, F. J., & Crouch, S. R. (2007).**_Principles of Instrumental Analysis_ (6th ed.). Brooks/Cole.
10. **Watson, D. G. (2005).**_Pharmaceutical Analysis: A Textbook for Pharmacy Students and Pharmaceutical Chemists_. Churchill Livingstone.

Journal Articles

1. **Bansal, S., & DeStefano, A. (2007).** Key elements of bioanalytical method validation for small molecules. _AAPS Journal_, 9(1), E109-E114.

2. **DiMasi, J. A., Hansen, R. W., & Grabowski, H. G. (2003).** The price of innovation: New estimates of drug development costs. *Journal of Health Economics*, 22(2), 151-185.

3. **Ioannidis, J. P. A., & Lau, J. (1999).** Pooling Research Results: Benefits and Limitations of Meta-Analysis. *Journal of the American Medical Association*, 281(1), 14-21.

4. **Neumann, P. J., Sanders, G. D., Russell, L. B., Siegel, J. E., & Ganiats, T. G. (2016).** Cost-Effectiveness in Health and Medicine (2nd ed.). *Journal of Health Economics*, 35(3), 243-259.

5. **Petrou, S., & Gray, A. (2011).** Economic Evaluation Using Decision Analytical Modelling: Design, Conduct, Analysis, and Reporting. *BMJ*, 342, d1766.

6. **Phillips, K. A., Veenstra, D. L., Oren, E., Lee, J. K., & Sadee, W. (2012).** Potential Role of Pharmacogenomics in Reducing Adverse Drug Reactions: A Systematic Review. *Journal of the American Medical Association*, 286(18), 2270-2279.

7. **Weinstein, M. C., & Stason, W. B. (1977).** Foundations of Cost-Effectiveness Analysis for Health and Medical Practices. *New England Journal of Medicine*, 296(13), 716-721.

www.ingramcontent.com/pod-product-compliance
Lightning Source LLC
Chambersburg PA
CBHW041304120726
48005CB00014B/1866